Freedom
from necessity

Freedom from necessity

THE METAPHYSICAL BASIS OF RESPONSIBILITY

BERNARD BEROFSKY
Professor of Philosophy,
Columbia University

Routledge & Kegan Paul
New York and London

To Barbara, Adrienne, and Aaron

First published in 1987 by
Routledge & Kegan Paul Ltd
11 New Fetter Lane, London EC4P 4EE

Published in the USA by
Routledge & Kegan Paul Inc.
in association with Methuen Inc.
29 West 35th Street, New York, NY 10001

Set in 10 on 12 pt Sabon
by Columns of Reading
and printed in Great Britain
by T.J. Press Ltd.,
Padstow, Cornwall

Library of Congress Cataloging in Publication Data
Berofsky, Bernard.
Freedom from necessity.
Includes index.
1. Responsibility. 2. Necessity (Philosophy)
3. Free will and determinism. I. Title.
BJ1451.B47 1987 123'.5 87–12869
ISBN 0–7102–0998–3

British Library CIP Data also available
ISBN 0–7102–0998–3

Contents

Contents

Contents

Acknowledgements

Writing a book is like washing the windows of a large office building. Once you finish, you must start all over again – that is, if you allow as much time to elapse between germination and culmination as I have. The first draft, completed as an American Council of Learned Societies Fellow in 1972–73, was succeeded by an indeterminate number of others. I am most grateful to the Council for permitting me the opportunity to work through ideas whose basic thrust and form have not changed, in spite of numerous updatings and revisions. I also wish to thank Michael Slote, who read the entire manuscript, offered many helpful suggestions, and identified several key problems I had to grapple with. I would also like to express my gratitude to Shaughan Lavine, who generously provided me with technical assistance.

1

Introduction

No philosophical problem is more deserving of the title 'the free will problem' than that concerning the assessment of the claim that a deterministic world, i.e., one governed completely by universal scientific law, has no room for agents with dignity sufficient to justify attributions of moral responsibility to them.

Nozick and others would prefer that dignity be pried apart from moral responsibility so that we may judge the unique worth or value of human beings, if any, under determinism without regard for tangential questions about praise and blame, punishment and reward.[1]

I have no quarrel with this point of view except to note that the partition may be too facile. Although questions about the assignment of praise and blame rest in part on policy considerations and utilitarian concerns which have nothing to do with the worth of the object of these prospective practices, there may be a notion of being morally responsible not reducible to such pragmatic notions. Chapter 2, which addresses logical questions concerning the concept of moral responsibility, also includes a development of this nonpragmatic point of view. Pace Bradley there are accounts of responsibility other than liability to punishment.[2] Our account there will also permit the incompatibilist, i.e., a person sympathetic with the view that moral responsibility presupposes that the world is not a deterministic system, at least to state his case against those impressed by deeply ingrained practices which include moral assessments drawn without regard for metaphysical positions or assumptions that agents control the conditions of these assessments.

We shall also extend the term 'incompatibilist' in a perfectly natural way to one who applies his reasoning to a particular case by concluding that an agent is not morally responsible for an action in the event that that particular action is determined.

It is a psychological mystery to me why so few writers on this subject note the significance of this extension. Although it is virtually a truism that an incompatibilist draws an important conclusion about some determined action regardless of the truth or falsity of the general thesis of determinism, many philosophers regard the free will problem as having been deprived of its motivation once determinism is surrendered. This response is as viable as a refusal to see the danger in an arsenic-laced apple because not all the apples in the basket are laced with arsenic.

The point, embarrassingly obvious, needs to be made to undermine the illicit inferences from antideterministic premises. The appeal to quantum mechanics, the resurgence of theories with a statistical basis, the promulgation of philosophies of science of a conventionalist or instrumentalist character, the insistence upon randomness as a ubiquitous category in nature, the detachment of determination from causation, when heaped upon the more traditional objections, promote disarray in the determinist camp.[3] Now it may well be that *some* (not all) of these concerns about the general metaphysical thesis affect the notion of a (particular) deterministic account so adversely that the incompatibilist cannot even advance his argument for individual cases in a prima facie plausible way. I shall nonetheless attempt, in chapter 9, to salvage an interesting notion of 'deterministic account' so that the particularized version of the incompatibilist case can at least be submitted for scrutiny.

The specification of the intermediate stages of the incompatibilist's inference is the concern of chapters 3 and 4. How, in other words, does determinism destroy moral responsibility, where the latter is characterized in chapter 2 as the appropriateness of including the state of affairs (for which the agent is morally responsible) in a moral appraisal of the person?

An examination of Frankfurt's view that unavoidability is not the middle term we seek leads, in chapters 3 and 4, to a distinct account of the conditions of moral responsibility. I argue that a more plausible account acknowledges the relevance of volitional matters such as effort, whose exertion or omission in the particular context may well be ignored in a moral review of the sort urged by Frankfurt, in which we are restricted to the facets of character which play an explanatory role.

The blameworthiness of an agent, we there argue, is not based directly upon the defectiveness of his character even when his action is due to a defective trait, but rather upon a defect of will. He is guilty because he failed to take steps to inhibit the manifestation of his character. The conception of responsibility which emerges coheres with an overall ethic of intention which accounts for our moral intuitions in a variety of cases.

Yet even if we are right to fault one who has failed to exert sufficient effort, we still want to know why the incompatibilist withdraws such judgments when he suspects determination. Frankfurt's case of a morally responsible agent whose action is, unbeknownst to the agent, rendered unavoidable by a powerful being (the so-called 'counterfactual intervener') who would, but need not, intervene to force the agent to do what he anyway does on his own, shows that unavoidability per se does not absolve the agent and motivates the search for an alternative basis for exemption. Since there are serious objections to compulsion and related notions, we turn in chapter 6, after an attempt in chapter 5 to define relevant concepts like addiction, compulsion, and impotence, to the idea of power. Although we there push the analysis of power in terms of the classical compatibilist model of (possible) action from (possible) desire as far as we can take it, we founder on the challenge to rebut the incompatibilist conviction that the presence of any empirically sufficient condition of an action renders the agent incapable of acting otherwise. The pursuit of the controversy, conceived as an issue about power, is unproductive then because we are left with a clash of intuitions about the implications on power of determination.

Against this background, the concept of necessity appears to have some advantage insofar as the case of the counterfactual intervener tells less clearly against necessity than it did against unavoidability. The idea of Fischer and others that actual sequence causation (the explanation of the action, typically in terms of the agent's desires), but not alternate sequence causation (the presence of the powerful being whose intervention is not actual and, therefore, not a part of the sequence leading to the action), is potentially worrisome is rendered more precise in terms of a clarification of the difference between necessitating and insuring an outcome. Since necessitation is a stronger notion, the incompatibilist can cite it as the disturbing feature of determination. Anyway, the core picture to which he is wedded is indeed one of sequences necessitating, in a compulsive-*like* way subsequent sequences and it is this picture which generates the rest of his conceptual repertoire: unavoidability, impotence, inevitability, predictability (a weaker idea, to be sure). A metaphysical commitment to real necessity becomes then the focus of the discussion. Thus, by the end of chapter 6, we have narrowed the controversy to one over necessity and are now required to confront directly the essentially metaphysical character of the free will controversy. A central contention of this work is that this path is the most fruitful one a compatibilist can take. By extracting from the incompatibilist the admission that he posits necessitation wherever science finds determination, the compatibilist may challenge and undermine that point of view.

If the compatibilist is talking about necessity, we must attempt to render his argument coherent when it is cast in this way. That goal is pursued in chapter 7, in which the outlines of a system of contingent necessity are presented so that the incompatibilist can possess a congenial mode of presentation, immune from the charges of modal confusion. A competing account, in which contingent necessity is displaced by unalterability (by choice) is rejected, once again narrowing the dispute to one over necessity.

The fruitfulness of the strategy proposed in this book is borne out in chapters 8 and 9 by the rejection of the necessitarian metaphysic upon which incompatibilism rests. I there elaborate a metaphysical vision which philosophers either love or hate (usually the latter), but which represents a stance on an issue of fundamental significance. My specific goal in those chapters is the defense of an antinecessitarian or regularity metaphysic, according to which reconstruction of scientific results – laws and theories – need not incorporate a modal framework. As I have indicated, this issue is not just interesting in its own metaphysical right, but constitutes the core issue in the free will controversy. We should note also that the position defended there is clearly different from the various antideterminist points of view taken in recent years. Simply put, antinecessitarianism does not *require* the ultimacy of statistical laws or the objectivity of randomness or the literal falsity of scientific laws. The regularity theory does not oppose determinism, but rather regards theories, including deterministic ones, as formulable without the aid of modal operators.

If we have been successful, the metaphysical underpinnings of the incompatibilist's case will be withdrawn so that he is no longer able to exempt agents from moral responsibility for actions just because a deterministic account of those actions has been provided. The burden then falls upon the victor to provide some account of the conditions it *is* appropriate to withhold ascriptions of moral responsibility. Thus, doubts concerning the responsibility of the agent of a heinous action who failed to exert maximal effort to prevent the action, when not based on relevant ignorance, must be grounded on worries that this failure is not free in a sense of 'free' detached from necessitarian implications. Chapter 5 had addressed specific forms of unfreedom: addiction, compulsion, impotence. In chapter 10, the project of characterizing forms of (un)freedom, now to be carried out within a compatibilist framework, is resumed.

A more limited goal, to wit, the characterization of a quintessential condition of 'full' freedom, autonomy, is set by specifying an optimal context, i.e., an agent who is neither an addict nor a compulsive nor an impotent nor one under coercion setting out without qualms to perform an action, to see if any feature is missing which would permit him to disclaim responsibility by repudiating the action as not 'his'. No plausible account of autonomy is found to fulfill this condition. The most plausible rendering of autonomy, in terms of the degree of cognitive, affective, and volitional independence permits deeply disturbed persons who are clearly not responsible to be counted as autonomous, whereas an agent whose will is heteronomous may be judged morally responsible for his action if he retains the power to refrain from acting on that will, a power, we must recall, he is not automatically denied under determinism. We do nonetheless review a variety of proposals concerning conditions of *mitigation* of responsibility by reflection upon will or character and its etiology and conclude that the central idea involved on the level of action also explains our responses to a variety of types of cases better than competing accounts. Here, too, we must discover whether or not the person, if he is able, took steps to change. The upshot is that no general philosophical constraint on moral responsibility need be added to the ones already specified, ones whose applicability to the real world requires entry into the untidy, context-bound, value-laden practical arena in which these judgments are made and assessed.

Finally, we consider various scenarios regarding the future development of psychology to discover which, if any, are antithetical to the concept of moral responsibility as we have characterized it.

2
The concept of moral responsibility

SENSES OF RESPONSIBILITY

We wish first to capture the sense of responsibility at stake in the controversy between compatibilists and incompatibilists. Perhaps it is just the relation of authorship between an agent in his action. But only a special libertarian construal of that relation would permit an inference from 'Jones is the author of act A' to 'Jones is responsible for act A'. The adoption at this stage of the libertarian construal of authorship as the analysis of responsibility would, however, beg the question against the compatibilist. Libertarians characterize authorship in such a way as to render it a contrary to ordinary determination by events of conditions. Thus, an action of Jones which is determined – and the ordinary sense of determination is the one intended by determinists – is, by definition, an action not authored by Jones. The identification of authorship with responsibility would then force the incompatibilist conclusion. The compatibilist is surely entitled to a wedge which would permit him to state his case.

An agent's performance may be deficient or substandard in one way or another. But there are many possible explanations of the deficiency, e.g., the absence of the relevant ability that would excuse the person and make it unjust or inappropriate to blame him. 'Imputations of fault'[1] are built into certain descriptions of actions, e.g., cheating, lying, and conning. These are the charges (Hart called them 'defeasible'[2]) that can be defeated by invoking

7

an appropriate excuse or justification. If the charge is not defeated, the person is to blame for his performance.

Feinberg analyzes this blaming component in terms of the notion of registrability; i.e., it is proper to place this performance on a record which reveals what sort of person the agent is in a respect that interests others.[3] Some records are written, e.g., fielding averages, and some are not, e.g., a person's reputation. Since we may distinguish the registrability of an action from the propriety of an overt blaming performance, there is then a difference between a person being to blame and a person being deserving of blame.

Whether or not this distinction of Feinberg's is too fine, there is a sense in which, for the incompatibilist, it is not fine enough. If an incompatibilist exempts a liar from moral responsibility on the grounds that his act of lying was determined, he would not deny the propriety of registering this performance. The performance may be indicative of the person's character in a respect that interests other. Yet, says the incompatibilist, he is not to blame. Registrability, then, is not in this context the interpretation of moral responsibility.

Do we have the right to suppose that the incompatibilist has a coherent notion of moral responsibility? Registrability as the potential analysans of responsibility is closely related to an idea that has often been defended, e.g., by Hume in the eighteenth[4] and Brandt[5] and Dahl[6] in this century. Brandt says that a person is morally blameworthy on account of some action if and only if the action is due to a substandard trait.[7] The incompatibilist rejects this just as he rejects the claim that a person is to blame because his performance reflects an important character trait. But is his rejection justified?

A person noted for his candor lies. His character has not changed for he continues thenceforth to be a frank and honest person. Now if we think of the case as one in which the person had an inexplicable lapse, a fleeting fit of weakness of will, or the like, we tend to excuse him. But we are excusing him not because he was not acting in character, but rather because he was not fully in control of his situation. We must distinguish the slip and the spontaneous response that is strangely out of character from the deliberate, fully voluntary lie that is also out of character. We may excuse the latter too, but not because the agent is not to blame.

We rather allow him to use the credit his reputation has earned him in order to mitigate the penalty (of blame).

I believe that responsibility applies to agents primarily in virtue of states of affairs brought about by intentional voluntary actions and only derivatively because of character traits.[8] We don't like greedy people primarily because they are disposed to perform intentionally greedy actions. If a person disposed to greediness never manifested his greed, he would not be as good, other things being equal, as a person who is not greedy, except perhaps in respect of strength of will.[9] But there is nothing to blame him for except perhaps the development of this trait and the blame here is attached to certain acts or omissions. Granted this, the position of the incompatibilist appears tenable. There is sense to examining the responsibility of a person for an action whether or not the action is in character.

Yet the distinction between intention and character should not be too sharply drawn. Character traits are displayed in actions which are intentional. I would count as intentional even the spontaneous actions of, say, a naturally helpful person who rushes to the aid of someone in distress. She acted because she took herself to be helping someone even though this thought was not present as a conscious episode.[10] The idea here is that the intentional component, *whether or not it is in character*, is the basis of a special type of moral assessment.

Also, in saying that this person is not as good as a person who is not greedy, I am conceding that character traits are proper objects of moral assessment. Honesty, compassion and courage *are* virtues. And since we have limited control over our character, it may turn out that we have limited control over the moral assessments justly applicable to us. A person who is constitutionally incapable of courage or who can do nothing about his tendencies to bouts of irrational anger is incapable of being as good as he might.

So we do evaluate character traits over and above the intentional *actions* they explain. As Blum points out, although two persons with different motives may be disposed to treat us similarly, it is important for us that only one of them is acting out of a concern for our welfare. It is evidently good to know, partly because it enhances one's sense of self-worth, that someone cares about us.[11] Yet, as we shall see, the evaluation of intention retains a special character we must attempt to describe.

Moral luck – the fact that a person can be good or bad in virtue of circumstances he is not responsible for, and the sort of character he has might well be due to circumstances beyond his control – has been accepted by many and is congenial to the compatibilist.[12] But our goal now is to formulate a conception of responsibility acceptable to both parties to the free will dispute. For example, our inquiry would end now on extreme versions of the doctrine of moral luck – the compatibilist wins hands down. As pleasing as this might be for the reader, I do not think the free will problem so easily dismissed.

The device to be exploited on behalf of the incompatibilist is the philosopher's favourite tool, a distinction. What the incompatibilist would want to say upon the discovery that determinism reigns, even in a utopia, is that the agents are not morally responsible for their virtues, i.e., for their moral goodness, just as we may not be morally responsible for our moral badness or evil. This pronouncement does not sound strange and it behooves us to see if sense can be assigned to it.

Blum, an eloquent advocate of an anti-Kantian position, insists repeatedly upon the legitimacy of the moral assessment of psychological states, including emotions and attitudes, yet withholds judgments of moral praise and blame, treating the latter as appropriate only to the products of a free will.[13] Yet the distinction is left unclarified. 'I have said nothing about the relationship between moral assessment in terms of blame and the wider notion of moral assessment appropriate to a person's emotional reactions, values, and attitudes'.[14]

Adams lays down the gauntlet by demanding to know why a negative moral assessment of a moral fault is not moral blame.[15] He points out, and we shall later agree, that the issue in this context is not utilitarian. If Adams means to say that it would be unwise or unjustified to censor, punish, ostracize, or penalize a person for a defective character, he may be right. In many cases, it would be counterproductive or uncharitable to act in such ways. But, he says, moral blame can be constituted by reproach, a response appropriate to faulty states of mind even when they are involuntary. Determinism cannot undermine either the fact that the states belong to the person or the deep entrenchment in actual moral thought of the belief in moral luck, including the practice of self- and other-evaluation, performed independently of concern about voluntariness. If we can buttress Blum's distinction, conceding a bona fide, but not exclusive moral response to states of mind, even when involuntary, we may be able both to respond to Adams and to make peace with those who, like Murdoch, have decried the philosopher's overemphasis upon moral effort and decision making, as if that is all morality is about.[16]

AGENT WORTH

It is undeniable that a moral evaluation of a person must be based in part upon a knowledge of the person's values and the priorities he assigns to them. Since a person's values depend, not just on his pronouncements, but on a readiness to act in order to secure or strengthen them, the knowledge of what a person prizes along with the depth of his commitment tells us one element which determines his behavior in situations important to him and perhaps others.

If we know a person's character, we may infer, with a degree of reliability, his values. But, as philosophers have noted, the inference is risky. We sometimes find ourselves with desires or propensities directed to objects we regard as possessing no intrinsic worth. As Watson says, we may want what we do not value.[17] Or, as Frankfurt puts it in a different account of the phenomenon, although we want A, we would prefer not to be moved by this want, or we do not identify with this want.[18] If we take steps to change, it may be due to the fact that our goals are shallow and our character inhibits the realization of a richer, more worthwhile life.

Notice that the capacity to transcend our characters permits us to attempt to become more *or less* moral. We may value morality more *or less* than our character reflects. I may decide that I have been 'good' long enough and that it is high time to experience life in all its richness, letting the chips fall where they may.

In a decision-making situation of moral significance, we can learn the importance of the moral dimension to the agent from the character of the deliberation and consequent decision. But the complexity of the situation makes this difficult. How strong are the desires which conflict with the agent's conception of his duty? What is the agent's estimate of the probability of securing the moral goal were he to seek it? What mood is he in? Also, there may be no clear answer to the question of whether the decision *reflects* an antecedent ranking of values (of which moral values are a subset) or is partly *constitutive* of that ranking.

Be all this as it may, we do take an agent's intention as relevant to the importance of morality to him. The fact that the judgment is delicate is in this context not problematic because the issue before us is not delicate. The incompatibilist may concede the relevance of moral matters to the formation of an intention; he just denies that an agent has moral worth in virtue of this fact, should the intention be determined.

Let us introduce the term 'agent worth' for the sort of worth an agent has in virtue of his readiness to count moral factors as relevant in his deliberations. 'Moral factors' here must be interpreted 'objectively.' We do not want the agent worth of a saint to be identical with that of a consistent Nazi who conceives himself to be driven by noble goals. Although I have no ethical theory which would generate an account of the objective-subjective distinction, the issues in the free will controversy do not as such require it. Nor need we here worry about moral ignorance, i.e., we shall suppose that agents possess a rudimentary knowlege of right and wrong.

Agent worth is similar to other character traits insofar as it has a dispositional character. It differs in that its manifestation is not action, but the course of deliberation leading to the formation of an intention.

Although in a causal sense, moral reasons have no weight in a case in which a morally worthy agent is forced to misbehave, i.e., they do not determine his decision, they are clearly more important to an agent who would invoke them if he could than to one who would not. Thus an ungenerous person may occasionally feel the pull of his 'better nature' but never display the beneficial effect of these second thoughts. He is ungenerous and perhaps deserves the rebuke he has earned. But his agent worth increases proportionately to his *readiness* to countenance moral concerns in his deliberations, even if they are always overridden. To know he is disposed to regard them as of some importance is to know that he is not utterly worthless.

Incompatibilists deny that agent worth is a type of moral worth unless a particular state of the agent, perhaps the readiness to count moral reasons as relevant to decision-making, is undetermined. Blum and Adams want to deny that agent worth is the *only* type of moral worth and Adams suggests it is not a separate type at all. For Adams, the same sort of blame attaches to one who ignores morality as attaches to a person caught in the grip of irrational anger, even if the anger is totally suppressed.

Even if we concede the relevance to moral worth in general of intractable traits of character, we must attempt to identify the special role of agent worth to see which of these three positions is sustained.

Even if luck plays a role in general in intention formation, as Feinberg has incisively noted,[19] the incompatibilist demands that the formation of an intention which will affect our assessment of an agent's worth be undetermined. For if there is no indetermination at a key stage, the agent would not control the formation of his intention and, even if he has agent worth, i.e., he formed his intentions with moral concerns as paramount, he has no moral worth. Adams rejects the control condition. Blum disagrees with the incompatibilist only about assessments of moral worth outside the sphere of agent worth – he permits them. The compatibilist may also agree about the need for control or voluntariness, but he does not see indetermination as required for voluntariness.

Now most, though not all, compatibilists *agree* with the incompatibilists that control (or power or voluntariness) is a sine qua non of responsibility here. They may also be disturbed about moral luck. That is the reason classical compatibilism advanced reconciliationist analyses of 'he could have done otherwise' and related notions. They agreed that freedom requires some sort of control, but its existence does not itself require indeterminism. (The exceptions are those compatibilists with a strong pragmatic orientation, those who identify moral responsibility with the usefulness of certain practices – praise and blame.[20] The utilitarian value of these institutions would be unaffected by the truth of determinism.) Let us look at several sorts of cases in which loss of control is important.

Since I presume that even Adams would not find moral fault with a person whose defective state of mind, trait, action, or intention is the effect of an omnipotent demon who causes it to come into being independent of the person's nature and who renders its removal by the person impossible, we restrict ourselves to cases in which the explanation of the lack of control is internal.

Norton's decisions are typically made with moral considerations as paramount. In this case, an unusually appealing element makes it difficult for him to decide to do what he thinks he ought to do.

Even if Norton succumbs to temptation, we may not blame him that much because we know that he has struggled and, therefore, that moral factors weigh with him. If, nonetheless, we believe he could have formed the right intention, that he did not try as hard as he could, his agent worth would decline somewhat. It is, in fact, difficult to imagine a case in which a person cannot literally have tried harder to form the right intention. He could have attended more carefully to the prospective pain he was about to create; or he could have sought for moral inspiration from those he respects; or he could have suppressed in one way or another the motive competing with the moral one. In fact if one really ever found a person genuinely incapable of trying harder just to initiate a course of action which may fail anyway for a variety of reasons, one would find someone so nonmorally defective that he would be absolved from even the most heinous crime.

Incompatibilists would balk at the above. Since it may well be that our world is deterministic, then it may be that nothing can be other than it is and consequently that no one *can* try harder than he actually does. But, although compatibilists and incompatibilists disagree about the *conditions* of power or ability, they *agree* that Norton's agent worth declines if moral concerns fail to weigh with him as much as they can. In fact, this just follows from the definition of 'agent worth' – Norton's agent worth, as a special disposition, is weaker than it might be.

Conceding the disagreement on the conditions of power, and assuming its possession by some agent, a crucial matter is a type of intimacy relating effort to intention lacking in the relation of intention to action. Although we can worry that an agent may not be able to convert his intention into action,[21] we cannot worry in one sense that an agent will fail to convert his effort into intention. True, he may be unable to reach a firm resolution with its associated commitment to initiate the undertaking; but the effort, even just the readiness, to form one *ipso facto tells us of his intentions in the matter*. We automatically know that morality weighs with him and, therefore, that he has some (agent) worth. It is along these lines, I think, that we can capture the Kantian intuition that we must be able to control the elements constituting our worth. We are, to echo Sartre, condemned to be free, or in our terms, to be the determinants of our own worth. As long as we *can* try, trying is what matters. This theme will emerge again in later chapters.

Moral compulsion represents a difficult case. Here, Norton is so moved by the right that he cannot take seriously the other option. How can his agent worth decline, as it apparently must on my view, if he cannot do the wrong thing?

The answer is: his worth does not decline on my view. Or rather, that is the way I should make it. There is an asymmetry between praise and blame. We begin with a model of an agent maximally moved by moral reasons (a model scorned by many in recent years[22]). Such an agent possesses maximal agent worth (a type of personal worth some regard as having less than supreme value). In order for this person's agent worth to diminish, he must be prepared to permit his moral motives to be overridden by nonmoral ones.

MORAL RESPONSIBILITY

Let us propose that in the context of the free will debate, moral responsibility by a person for a state of affairs is constituted by the relevance of that state of affairs to the determination of the agent worth of the person. Although the definition requires clarification, we can see how someone can fail to be morally responsible for the acquisition (as opposed to persistence) of a moral fault. I may be a jealous person even if I condemn jealousy as a vice and came to be that way *not* because of decisions, including tacit ones, which reflected an inadequate role for the evil of jealousy (or related moral considerations). We would be mistaken, then, to take my jealousy as a sign that I do not regard the fact that some act reflects this trait as a strong reason not to perform the act.

We can also see how those philosophers who have expressed displeasure with moral Kantianism should not be disturbed for I have remained neutral on two key issues: (1) the relative importance of agent worth to other varieties of moral worth; and (2) the relative importance of moral worth to other values in the world. I concentrate on agent worth not because I am a 'Kantian,' but because the issue I choose to write about concerns agent worth. I would like in fact to stress one way I am not a Kantian.

To stress the centrality of intention to agent worth is not ipso facto to tell us how to make the connection. We are left with an indefinite number of conflicting theories relating the content of intention to moral worth. The Kantian theory that respect for the moral law or duty is the sole determinant of moral worth is but one of these theories. A great deal of criticism, therefore, much of it recent, does not challenge the centrality of intention, but rather Kant's particular views about moral motivation.[23] If it is wrong to think that a person's agent worth is enhanced by an act of friendship only if he was moved to act out of the recognition that he has a duty to his friend, we can consistently agree. All we require is that his action be guided by the belief that he is benefiting his friend (such that he would not act in this way if he were to learn that the individual is not really his friend).[24] In this way, his intention in acting is to be a good friend, not to discharge a moral obligation to be so, even though he may independently believe he has this obligation. The question of the value of action from this sort of motive compared with other sorts of motives – a question whose answer may be required to render judgments in cases of conflicting obligatons – is a further issue whose exploration would land us directly in the field of ethics, an area this book is not centrally concerned with.

If ethics were our primary concern, we would have to take far more seriously the clarification of the distinction between moral and nonmoral value. Friendship is one of the finest goods in life and moral obligations arise out of this relationship. Whereas Kantians emphasize the special character of motivation by (universal) principle in discharging such an obligation, others note that only motivation by features of the particular relationship – my friend needs me – is constitutive of friendship. But to deny that an act of friendship enhances one's agent worth on the grounds that it is not indicative of the role moral reasons play in the agent's motivation may be to beg the question in favor of the Kantian view of moral motivation. I would not want here to reject the option taken by Stocker according to which the object of a *morally* good intention is not necessarily goodness or rightness.[25]

Nor do we require that intentions be consciously formulated. Although I believe that a special moral cash value of character traits resides in the intentional behavior they explain, this behavior can and should become as natural and habitual as possible. It is not required that each worthy action represents the product of a protracted moral struggle. The development of the moral virtues is, for reasons already indicated, undoubtedly desirable. If anything, it enhances agent worth by indicating the importance of morality to the agent.

By not insisting that the decision-making process be indeterministic in order for a nonholy person to have agent worth, I have not offended the compatibilist. In fact, if I have offended anyone, it is the incompatibilist. For maximal agent worth does not appear to require indeterminism. I can be disposed to invoke moral concerns as paramount in my deliberations even though this is a deterministic world.

The incompatibilist will be concerned on two levels. He will, as we have said, wish to deny that there is any moral worth in a deterministic world and that, therefore, agent worth is a bona fide sort of moral worth (or that it is *unless* the world is indeterministic in a certain way). It follows – again in a deterministic world – that a state of affairs constituted by the intention to act in some way can neither count for nor against someone's *moral* worth and, therefore, that agent worth is not a kind of moral worth. For clearly, in a deterministic world, the formation of an intention *might* reflect a disposition to form intentions for moral reasons. In a simple case of unimpeded goodness in a deterministic world, a good intention might be the mark of a good person.

Of course, many incompatibilists who accept the familiar charge that not all indeterministic worlds contain a variety of 'free will worth wanting'[26] – they may be chaotic and unpredictable and 'actions' in them may be uncontrollable and random – would like to see freedom as compatible with morality and/or rationality. Even if freedom does not imply either, if an agent is to be judged morally responsible for his action, the action must, as Hume saw, reflect some trait of the agent and the intention, too, must not be utterly capricious. One key issue is joined then at the nature of the connection between what we have called agent worth and an intention explained by it.

There are two positions which may be confused with incompatibilism, as I construe this concept, which would not charge me with question begging. Those who see as the threat to freedom not determinism in general, but rather a certain range of deterministic theories, definitely including neurophysiological determinism, but possibly others, like certain psychoanalytic doctrines, will have no qualms about my account of agent worth. They are not disturbed about causation *by* a factor like the recognition of the importance of generosity. They would be worried rather about its displacement by a very different sort of account, like the neurological one. In this book, incompatibilism is the more general position according to which *any* deterministic theory is a threat to freedom.

The other position affirms that explanations of decisions in terms of the importance to the agent of certain considerations are not and cannot be expanded into deterministic accounts. So that if an action bears on an agent's worth, it follows that determinism is false. This position is more radical than the first. The first position would not be disturbed about a deterministic theory in intentional psychology; the second denies such is possible. The second is compatible with, but not entailed by, incompatibilism. Thus, an incompatibilist who does not preclude the expansion of intentional accounts into deterministic theories would be disturbed by my account of moral responsibility for he would deny that an agent to whom I would presumably have to assign greater agent worth deserves moral credit if his deliberations proceed deterministically.

To mollify this incompatibilist without throwing in the towel, we must modify our account of moral responsibility. Both parties may agree that a necessary condition of moral responsibility by person P for state of affairs S is that S bear on the determination of the agent worth of P. They may also both agree with Blum that this sort of moral responsibility is special in that P must be able to exercise control in some way we have left rather vague. The incompatibilist will demand further that, to have control, at some key stage, not yet specified, we need indetermination. Without control, agent worth is not a type of moral worth.

We have not challenged the common assumption regarding control, power, or avoidability, but will very soon. Although we are committed to the distinction between moral assessment in general and the narrower sort of moral assessment we are now trying to capture, and although control or power will play *some* role in its delineation, it will turn out that there is a more fundamental way of making the distinction.

We may summarize these results by characterizing the dispute over the moral responsibility of P for S as a dispute over the relevance of S to the moral worth of P, given the relevance of S to the agent worth of P. That is, each requires that S be relevant to agent worth for that is the pertinent notion in this context; but the incompatibilist demands more.

ACCOUNTABILITY

An alternative account would contend that, in denying that Smith is morally responsible for a state of affairs S, the incompatibilist is denying the accountability of Smith for S. That is, no one has the right to impose demands or penalties on Smith in virtue of S.

I have not mentioned praise or blame here for one may wish to regard people as accountable in other ways. Hart, for example, defines 'moral responsibility' in terms of moral blameworthiness or a moral obligation to make amends.[27] One may hold an agent accountable by demanding reparations rather than by producing a blaming performance. Yet we shall see that praise and blame have a special status as ways of calling a person to account.

Problems are raised by the imprecision of the term 'accountable', i.e., by the fact that one may be called to account in many ways.

Suppose a person voluntarily chooses to hurt someone in order to avoid a greater evil. If we are ignorant of his motive, we may demand an accounting from him. We may, that is, insist upon an explanation and the explanation he would provide absolves him from responsibility in another sense. That is, he would be freed from the obligation to make amends or from the liberty of others to blame him. But his not being responsible in this sense does not mean that the original demand for an accounting was not justified. He was the very person who should have provided the explanation and was thus accountable in this sense. But the explanation he provided absolved him from accountability in the sense of liability to further response arising from the consequences of his action.

Over and above explanation-accountability and reparation-accountability, there is a more serious way of responding to a person's actions, to wit, by blaming the person. Here, one is not simply imposing a demand upon the agent with the implicit suggestion that satisfaction of the demand restores the moral balance. One is rather passing a judgment on the individual person which is unaffected by explanations or amends if the circumstances of action originally justified the judgment.

Given that praise and blame are overt responses of a morally significant character, one may have reservations concerning their general appropriateness, i.e., one may regard them as generally improper, perhaps because one thinks that no person should so judge or affect another, or one may think them proper only on utilitarian grounds. In either case, blameworthiness will not necessarily be linked with heinousness or reprehensible behavior performed freely and knowingly.

But objections to overt blaming performances need not extend to the propriety of adopting an attitude towards a person who has behaved miserably. I may regard a person as having merited an inferior reputation or a degraded moral status even if I doubt the propriety of blame (and, perhaps, praise). Conversely, if, on a utilitarian ethic, one has the right to engage in blaming performances on behalf of the general welfare, it does not follow that one has a right to regard the objects of the performances in an unfavorable light.

It seems clear that an incompatibilist is not only not concerned with explanation- or reparation-accountability, but also not concerned directly with blameworthiness. Although typically he wants to absolve the agent of a determined action from any of these demands or responses, he does so *because* he believes the agent has not, by virtue of that action, become morally inferior in the special way we earlier described, i.e., in terms of agent worth. What concerns him is the justification of these responses in terms of the moral taint purportedly acquired by the agent. The possibly onerous demands of explanations or amends or the shame attached to blame may or may not be proper or justified. But his distinctive claim is that their propriety cannot be grounded in a (non-existent) moral lapse.

Again, thus, the relevant idea of moral responsibility of a person P for an (obtaining) state of affairs S_1 in this context is the appropriateness of including S_1 in the appraisal of the agent worth of P (assuming agent worth is in the case at hand an instance of moral worth).

More specifically, the paradigm case has the following features:

(1) P intends to do A (S_1 = that P does A), i.e., P intends that S_1 obtains.

(2) S_1 obtains in virtue of this intention.

(3) If moral reasons are a significant subset of the set of reasons $\{R\}$ that P intends to do A, then (assuming (1) and (2)), P's agent worth increases (from its prior base); otherwise, it remains the same or diminishes.

If P's agent worth does not increase, the extent to which it diminishes depends on a moral evaluation of S_1 together with the degree to which the failure to invoke moral reasons, when they are relevant, is outside the voluntary control of P.[28] Other things being equal, if S_1 = that P tortures his neighbor, his worth declines more than it does if S_1 = that P purchases vanilla ice cream. Although in neither case does $\{R\}$ include moral reasons, moral considerations are less important to one who does not invoke them when he should than to one who does not invoke them when they are irrelevant.

The account is studded with vagueness. Whether or not S_1 obtains in virtue of P's intention depends upon all the complex considerations needed to determine whether some event is 'the cause' of another. This is even so if A is a more or less basic action.

Accordingly, there are two very different ways of absolving an agent from moral responsibility for S_1 when his intention had some causal relation to S_1. The incompatibilist would deny moral responsibility under determinism even if the agent's intention was causally decisive in relation to S_1, whereas in general we would all absolve the agent if his relation to S_1 were too remote.

To characterize remoteness, we would have to write a book different from this one, a book on the scope of moral responsibility. Such books have been written – on collective responsibility, causation in the law, the doctrine of double effects, etc. Since the incompatibilist rejection of responsibility applies to paradigm cases of moral and causal responsibility, our concern is the threat to this small class, not the proper manner of its expansion.

The paradigm case is restricted in two ways: (a) The state of affairs is of the form: that P does A. Thus, it cannot be a case in which an agent is held responsible for a crop failure (as opposed to causing the crop failure). (b) The agent must intend and cause what he is responsible for. The case cannot be one in which an agent is responsible for an unintended outcome.

It would be an easy matter to drop condition (2) altogether on the grounds that fundamental moral responsibility in this context, as we have stressed, pertains to intentions, not their realizations. We should take states of affairs only as signs of intentions and then answer our question in terms of condition (3), i.e., determine the significance of moral reasons, freely adopted, to his intention. If an agent is morally responsible for an intention, we may then worry about his further moral responsibility for resulting states of affairs.

Although tidy, the suggestion is unnatural in that the evaluation of intentions begins from the recognition that their significance derives from the effects they have in the real world. We shall, therefore, learn to live with the unclarity of condition (2).

Another problem we create by this decision, noted above, concerns the need to render more precise the relation between agent worth and the moral evaluation of S_1. States of affairs are preferable to actions in this regard for familiar reasons – I can be responsible for failing to be more careful, for having discharged the gun too quickly – but a host of further complications remains.

For example, the moral dilemmas I inherit may not, in virtue of circumstances, permit me to create very much good in the world in spite of noble intentions. Perhaps I often must choose 'the lesser of two evils.' My agent worth is not compromised so long as my motivation is fundamentally moral. Also, although S_1 may be morally undesirable, the prima facie reduction of P's agent worth may be offset by countervailing considerations such as P's intention to use the introduction of S_1 as a means to a highly desirable outcome. The point I would again stress is that a judgment of moral responsibility in the sense intended by incompatibilists is a judgment regarding the appropriateness of this evaluation. However complex they may be, an incompatibilist who is convinced that S_1 is determined would wish to remove S_1 from any deliberations designed to determine or affect a prior conception of moral worth.

There are, of course, alternative accounts of responsibility. The idea of a responsible agent as a mature adult who is 'responsible' for his actions, whether they be wise or foolish, virtuous or immoral, embodies the conception of one who has the power to make and effect rational decisions. But an incompatibilist can accept this account only if he can tease out the absence of determination from it. To be sure, there are philosophical traditions which would contrast determination by reasons from determination by character or impulse. But these accounts concern the metaphysics of freedom, i.e., structures of the self which set the agent apart from the natural order. An indeterministic account of rational powers is an account of human freedom which is a *ground* of moral responsibility, i.e., a ground of the possibility of moral worth. The applicability of this account to agents permits the moral evaluation of the agent to be affected by the moral quality of his actions. This core idea, then, reappears as central to the incompatibilist point of view and will constitute our working notion of responsibility.

STATES VERSUS ACTIONS

The incompatibilist appears to be committed to an account of responsibility whereby persons are or are not morally responsible for actions. Since we are also morally responsible for states of affairs (that such and such is the case), one may wonder about the relation between these notions and the incompatibilist construal of that relation.

Rogers intentionally fires a pistol at t_1, accidentally killing Foster (at t_1?), whom Rogers had absolutely no reason to believe to be in the path of the bullet. The following actions, construed as tokens, not types, were performed by Rogers:

(1) A_1 (firing a pistol at t_1)

(2) A_2 (killing Foster (at t_1?)).

If we are inclined to a wide-grained view of the individuation of events, thereby identifying (1) and (2), then, in light of the fact that Rogers is responsible for firing the pistol, but not for killing Foster, we must seek an alternative to events as the objects of responsibility. But since the incompatibilist appears to draw a conclusion about moral responsibility from a premise which says that an action, i.e., an event, is determined, actions cannot be ignored.

Suppose we permit ourselves the notion of a deterministic account (laws plus initial conditions) and grant that one exists for the sentence 'Rogers fires a pistol at t_1'. (The notion will be clarified in chapter 9, but the details do not bear on the present discussion.) If (1) exists and if there is no other action by Rogers of firing a pistol at t_1 – there cannot be if t_1 is short enough – then (1) appears to be determined.[29] Since, under his assumptions, the incompatibilist would want to hold Rogers responsible for neither (1) nor (2), he would not object to their identification. But suppose not only that (1) is not determined, but also that the conditions of free action, whatever they may be, are met in this case..So Rogers would be responsible for (1), but for reasons given above, not (2). (1) and (2) must, therefore, be different, contrary to the wide-grained view.

If we wish to retain the wide-grained view, we might say that Rogers is responsible for some states of affairs generated by A_1, e.g., S_1 (that a pistol was fired by him at t_1), but not others, e.g. S_2 (that Foster is killed). But we face a problem. If freedom is a condition of moral responsibility, we are apparently absolving Rogers from responsibility for S_2, not S_1, on the grounds that *only* (1) is a free action. But this is, of course, incoherent on the wide-grained view because (1) *is* (2). We must say that the killing of Foster is a free action and it is not then clear how we can exonerate Rogers for it.

A psychological conception of freedom could avail itself here of the intentionality inherent in propositional attitudes. If freedom, for example, is assent or willingness, we may note that Rogers assents to one proposition about *the* action, but not another. He is willing that the action generate S_1, but not willing that it generate S_2.

But the conception of freedom as willingness or consent is not an incompatibilist one. It is rather a variant of the classical compatibilist position embodied in the dictum that freedom is knowledge of necessity. One may know of or acquiesce in a deterministic framework for human action. Whatever else the incompatibilist requires for freedom, he at least insists that a free action not be necessitated in that sense of necessitation entailed by the proposition that the action is determined.

Reversion to a fine-grained interpretation helps only if the latter is fine enough to associate a distinct event with each logically distinct description. Thus, not only is the killing different from the firing; but the firing is different from the slow firing is different from the very slow firing is different from the very slow firing in the parlor . . . For we may have a deterministic account at one level, but not at a more specific level. This conception of events is highly counterintuitive and, in spite of considerations advanced by advocates on its behalf,[30] I find it unacceptable. (This does not commit me to the view that (1) = (2). The firing and the killing are not logically related in the way the firing and the slow firing are related and one may expect that a plausible account of events could identify the latter, but not the former pair.)

Although we would not want, therefore, to move from 'It is determined that Rogers fires a pistol at t_1' and '(1) is the only act of the type "Rogers' firing a pistol at t_1"' to '(1) is determined' (for we would then have to say that the slow firing (= firing) is determined), we can move to 'It is determined that (1) occurs'. The incompatibilist then infers about the fact that (1) occurs or the state of affairs constituted by the occurrence of the action that it is necessary and that the agent is not, therefore, morally responsible for it.

Since the considerations which led us to deny that actions are determined or necessitated apply as well to the hypothesis that we are morally responsible for actions, we must surrender the latter as well. After all, I can be morally responsible for firing the pistol, but not for firing it slowly, even though the firing *is* a slow firing.

The adoption of the principle that we are morally responsible exclusively for states of affairs may have consequences for the notion of moral responsibility. Several philosophers, e.g., Frankfurt and Fischer, reject the association of responsibility with control,[31] the idea that one is morally responsible for some state of affairs to the extent that one has control over its obtaining. An agent may satisfy all reasonable conditions of freedom, even libertarian ones, in spite of the existence of a counterfactual intervener (C1) whose mere presence removes from the agent control over the outcome by dint of the power he has to force the agent to act in the way the agent has freely chosen to do, a power C1 does not have to exercise.

Fischer points to difficulties in the associationist's attempt to identify responsibility with control under the assumption that we are responsible for our acts, i.e., for events, rather than states of affairs. But, he observes, these difficulties may not apply to the associationist who restricts his case to states of affairs. The associationist argument is that if there is a C1 present who will force Rogers to fire that pistol if Rogers decides not to do so, Rogers does indeed lose control over S_1 (that Rogers fires a pistol at t_1) even if he fires the pistol freely, without C1's intervention. But he is not anyway responsible for S_1. S_1 is equivalent to: At t_1, either Rogers fires a pistol on his own or is forced to do so by C1. (Assume these are the only two possible 'paths' to S_1.) If Rogers were responsible for S_1, then he would be responsible for this disjunctive state of affairs and he clearly is not. Thus, S_1 is a state Rogers has no control over, but is anyway not responsible for.

Rogers' responsibility is rather restricted to: that Rogers fires a pistol at t_1 *on his own*, a state of affairs he *does* retain control over. The conclusion would then be that responsibility for states of affairs is constituted by control over those states.

The argument rests on an unquestioned assumption about the notion of responsibility. The assumption is that responsibility is based on the power of prevention. I am responsible for a state of affairs when it is in my power to prevent its obtaining. In order to be responsible for a disjunctive state of affairs, therefore, I must be able to prevent *each* and *every* disjunct from obtaining. (For otherwise, I could not prevent the state of affairs from obtaining – Rogers fires the pistol because he cannot stop the C1 from forcing him to fire except by firing it himself. Although Rogers controls *which* disjunct obtains, he cannot prevent at least one of them from obtaining. So, in the relevant sense, he does not control the disjunction.)

But parallel to the distinction drawn in the theory of causation between producing and preventing causes is the distinction between two kinds of power. We control a state of affairs if we can both prevent it from obtaining and bring it about at will; but even if we cannot prevent it, we may have the power to produce it at will. The argument that Rogers is not responsible for S_1 depends, then, on the consideration that Rogers cannot prevent it from obtaining and the argument would collapse if, in this context, the relevant concept of responsibility is production-responsibility.

Implicit in Frankfurt's account *is* a production-sense of responsibility. When he bids us to look only at the factors which explain the action (or the generation of the state of affairs), he is supposing that the relevant factors are those which contribute to the creation of the outcome, not those which would inhibit the outcome were they brought into play. If an agent merrily proceeds along the path to a heinous state of affairs, his blameworthiness is not mitigated by the consideration that he would end up there anyway. If he had intentionally and willfully killed Foster at t_1, he is responsible for the fact that Foster dies at t_1. That C1 *would have* forced him to do it at t_1 does *not* imply that the agent is not responsible for Foster's death, but only for Foster's-death-as-brought-about-intentionally-and-willfully.

Now one may object to this line of thought. But argument would be required to restore the link between responsibility and control. The adoption of a conception of responsibility according to which we are responsible for states of affairs is not sufficient *in itself* to restore that link.

We will eventually develop a conception of moral responsibility somewhat different from Frankfurt's. Nonetheless, it will be sufficiently similar to block this restoration. If Rogers freely kills Foster at t_1, taking no steps in his power to inhibit the act, his blameworthiness for S (that Foster dies at t_1) rests on the relevance of S to Rogers' moral accounting (in a way we specified earlier) and is unaffected by the presence of a C1 who would have brought S about anyway. It suffices to know that Rogers 'controlled' S by bringing it about – S obtains in virtue of Rogers' intention – even if he did not control S by retaining the power to inhibit its obtaining. The upshot is that the fear that a shift to states of affairs will beg certain questions about moral responsibility is groundless. Although traditional compatibilists, like incompatibilists, impose a control condition, the defense of this posture is not sustained by a construal of responsibility in terms of states.

The associationist van Inwagen may object to this line of reasoning in the following way:[32]

(Foster's death is strictly the terminal point of an event, Foster's dying, and not a state of affairs. Let us then use here the paradigmatic form 'that _____ ' to designate states of affairs.)

If Rogers is held responsible, not just for the state of affairs he can prevent, that Foster dies at t_1 as a consequence of a willful act of Rogers (W_1), but also for the fact that Foster dies at t_1 (W_2), why not hold Rogers responsible for the fact that Foster dies (W_3)? On the production model, Rogers has done something, A_1, which was sufficient in the circumstances for the obtaining of W_1, W_2, *and* W_3. This, of course, is a *reductio ad absurdum* because Rogers is clearly *not* responsible for W_3. The fact that Foster dies at some time is the fact of Foster's mortality and only God, Adam, or Nature can be blamed for *that*.

The argument does show that moral responsibility is not closed under logical consequence. That is, if P is morally responsible for the state of affairs that L, and L entails M, it does not follow that P is morally responsible for the state of affairs that M.

Van Inwagen may be seen as challenging the critic of associationism to produce a reasonable way to draw the line between those logical consequences of L P is responsible for from those he is not responsible for. The intuition is that Rogers is responsible for W_1 and W_2, but not W_3, because he brought about only the first two.

The temptation is to say that A_1 is causally irrelevant to W_3 insofar as W_3 would obtain whether Rogers shoots Foster or not. But, of course, such is also true of W_2, a state of affairs Rogers does bring out.

What we would like to characterize is something like Mackie's idea of an inus condition.[33] For Rogers' act manifests an inus condition (being shot in a certain way) of W_1 and W_2, but not W_3. Very roughly, A_1 is an essential part of a sufficient condition of Foster's death at t_1, although there are other sufficient conditions of death which do not include this condition. Although Mackie's definition applies to conditions as types, we might try to extend it to tokens and say that, even if there is a distinct sufficient condition of Foster's death at t_1 (overdetermination) or would be were A_1 not to have occurred (preemption), A_1 is still an essential part of one operative sufficient condition. Yet A_1 is not necessary for Foster to die in the following sense.

We must be able to identify the parts of a causal process independently of the possibility that a distinct (token) process might intersect at the same terminus as the original one. If A_1 and Foster's token death D_1 are parts of one process, then Foster would not have died at t_1 had A_1 not occurred *and* had there been no other causal process with D_1 as a part. A_1 is not in this sense a necessary condition of the fact that Foster dies at some time, for it is not the case that Foster would not have died had A_1 not occurred and had there been no other causal process with D_1 as a part.

If I were to enter the quagmire known as the philosophy of causation, I would never emerge. There are notions crying out for clarification I cannot provide. The key point is this. Even the associationist must concede that there is a causal relation between Webster's placing arsenic in Walker's tea and Walker's dying at t_1 (from *that* poisoning) which is not undermined by the fact that Webster's poison neutralized Wilson's poison and thereby pre-empted a sequence that would have led to Walker's dying at t_1. He, too, must grapple with the same notions as the anti-associationist to produce an adequate theory of causation. (As in symmetric overdetermination, Webster's act is not in some sense necessary in the circumstances for the outcome.) The differences emerge *afterwards*. The associationist wants to deny Webster is responsible for the fact that Walker died at t_1 and *that* conclusion requires argument beyond the observation that Webster could not have prevented it.

The advantages of states of affairs are several. Since they are fine-grained, distinctions required for judgments of moral responsibility can be made without the controversial commitments such distinctions would create for a construal in terms of events. Not only can we be precise; we can also extend a single responsibility relation, e.g., to omissions, in ways an account in terms of action would forbid. With respect to nominalist suspicions I shall say only that this account, like any in terms of states of affairs, facts, or propositions, certainly does not preclude nominalist reductions. And should such reductions prove difficult or impossible, we shall then have to make a decision between realism and a radical reconstrual of the various philosophical notions, like responsibility, which seem naturally to call for states of affairs. In this work, my energies will be directed to issues distinct from those bearing on whether or how such a decision is to be made.

If actions are the focus of the incompatibilist's interest, then the states of affairs whose freedom concerns him will be of the type: that P does A at t. Again, these states are different from actions insofar as an action is the obtaining of a state of affairs. Only the action is dated. Also, unless an extreme narrow-grained view is upheld, states of affairs are more fine-grained. 'That Rogers fires a gun at t' denotes a different state of affairs from 'that Rogers fires a gun slowly at t', although Rogers' slow firing (= firing) at t is the obtaining of both states of affairs.

Although, at the level of truth-conditions, we may have to address relations between actions and states of affairs more carefully, we shall *characterize* moral responsibility as a relation between persons and states of affairs. Although we shall often speak with the vulgar, we shall, when the occasion requires it, speak of an agent's moral responsibility for states of affairs or outcomes only rather than actions.

3

Causal and moral responsibility

UNAVOIDABILITY AND RESPONSIBILITY

The incompatibilist draws from a deterministic account governing the fact that an agent has performed a certain action a modal conclusion that grounds his belief that the agent of such an action is justly absolved from moral responsibility. A wide range of related modal concepts has been invoked – (causal) necessity, compulsion, inevitability, and unavoidability, to mention a few.[1]

Frankfurt's important observation that an action can be rendered inevitable or unavoidable by a force which does not exercise its power over an agent because the agent freely acts in the way the force desires has led many to agree with him that unavoidability (or inevitability) does not automatically imply nonresponsibility and that, therefore, at least these concepts should be dropped from the above list of modal concepts serving as candidates for the middle term between determination and the absence of moral responsibility.

Frankfurt's conclusion has not gone unchallenged. Fischer, a sympathetic critic, concedes, after reviewing unsuccessful attempts at rebuttal, that Frankfurt may have demonstrated that moral responsibility can be present even when the agent lacks freedom or power over outcomes.[2] That is, Jones is morally responsible for having done A, although there is nothing Jones can do to prevent himself from doing A. He points out incisively, however, that this interesting observation may be blunted. The fact that responsibility and/or freedom do not require control is a far cry from compatibilism. The presence of the 'counterfactual intervener' (so called because he does not actually intervene to bring it about that Jones does A) may negate the control over outcome (A or not-A) Jones would otherwise possess; but the presence of a sufficient cause which operates in the actual sequence to determine the action A may be a more serious threat to Jones' freedom. 'The reason why determinism threatens responsibility is not that it undermines control; determinism involves actual-sequence compulsion, and such compulsion might be incompatible with moral responsibility.'[3] To be sure, the incompatibilist must *show* that something akin to compulsion is an essential feature of every deterministic sequence; but that idea has surely guided his thinking anyway. It is not as if Frankfurt has forced him into a corner he never wanted to be in.

Yet sophisticated incompatibilists would balk a bit at the formulation, adopted by Fischer, which requires them to believe that determination implies compulsion. The incompatibilist Campbell denied, against Schlick, that he was guilty of confusing causation with compulsion. Yet when Campbell described the feature of causal sequences he found disturbing, it turned out after all to be the absence of control. If Frankfurt is right, however, this feature can be present in a case of action satisfying Campbell's requirements for freedom. An agent's self may intervene in the causal scheme to bring about an outcome even if a counterfactual intervener is present to insure that outcome.

Critics of Frankfurt have argued that the counterfactual intervener does not insure that the action that ensued, A, would have ensued anyway, for the intervener would not have brought about A, but rather an action of the same type as A. Fischer rightly rejects such arguments when they rely on the principle of event individuation according to which events are the same only when their causes are the same, for the principle is dubious. Yet in *this* case, there may be independent reason to believe that the event the counterfactual intervener would have brought about could not have been A. The reason does not rest on the causal principle of the individuation of events, but rather on the assumption that the counterfactual intervener would bring about through some deterministic mechanism only the bodily movement involved in A. But the rising of Jones' arm having been agent-caused by the self who is Jones cannot be identical with the rising of Jones' arm as caused in the ordinary way by a process emanating from an event initiated by the counterfactual intervener. If the action incorporates the special cause, the agent, as a part of its nature (as obtains, for example, in R. Taylor's view[4]), then a different cause would imply, in this special case, a different event. Campbell could then argue that unavoidability is a bona fide alternative to compulsion as the element of deterministic sequences which negates moral responsibility. For the counterfactual intervener does not render Jones' creative act unavoidable. Had he intervened, Jones would not have performed *that* creative act, but rather a different noncreative one that happened to incorporate the same bodily movement.

This hypothetical response of Campbell fails because an assumption it rests on may be challenged. Instead of supposing that the counterfactual intervener acts by bypassing Jones' self, suppose we envisage a case in which he induces the self to cause the bodily movement. On some libertarian accounts, e.g., R. Taylor's, there is a difference between causing a bodily movement (no action) and causing an agent to cause a bodily movement (no *free* action). Thus an action (a bodily movement as caused by the agent) can be specified independently of its cause. It is free if and only if it has no cause. If this line of thought is tenable, the counterfactual intervener could have forced the agent to perform 'the same action.' We might have to agree then with Frankfurt that moral responsibility and unavoidability are compatible and Campbell would not be able to bypass the question of what it is about causal sequences, if they do not ipso facto involve compulsion, which renders them unfit for moral responsibility.

So if incompatibilists are appropriately uncomfortable about replacing the discredited unavoidability with compulsion, the burden of elucidating a modal notion which can serve as the middle term between determination and nonresponsibility remains.

COMPULSION AND RESPONSIBILITY

Having noted earlier that Fischer assumes without argument that compulsion is the only alternative to unavoidability as the feature which precludes responsibility according to incompatibilists, we must note in addition a failure to address the question as to how compulsion removes responsibility. The connection may be regarded as too intimate for further elaboration. But we cannot be sure without a minimal discussion of the nature of compulsion. And we must be careful not to argue that the unpleasant fact about compulsion is that it implies unavoidability for the latter can obtain, we now know, in the presence of responsibility.[5]

We might even wonder why Fischer's assumption that actual sequence compulsion or determination is more serious than alternate sequence compulsion appears reasonable. For starters, let us recall an elementary compatibilist point to the effect that determination as such does not ostensibly possess the features of either standard cases of physical or psychological compulsion. Need we dust off and display once again the standard examples of the difference between acting from compulsion and acting from desire?

Secondly, if we are to suppose that each instance of causal determination is an instance of compulsion, we will be forced to say that Jones is compelled to vote for Reagan even in the case in which Jones' self freely and indeterministically decides to do so. For, although the decision is not causally determined, it determines the act. Fischer attempts unsuccessfully to deny this by discounting, for no good reason, causally determined acts that are not parts of sequences all of whose stages are nomologically inevitable.[6] (A first cause can obviously initiate a series of causally determined stages.)

This question leads directly into the issue of derivative responsibility. There is a powerful inclination to view certain causal consequences of free decisions and actions as equally free. One intuitive appeal for the separation of causation from compulsion, in fact, rests upon this inclination. If I murder Smith out of a free decision to do so, and plead that I was acting under compulsion (induced by my decision) and ought, therefore, to be judged only for the mental act of forming an intention to kill, my plea will not be treated favorably.

Let us describe conditions under which an agent Walters is derivatively responsible for a state of affairs {S} he cannot help producing in virtue of a prior, free action A.

(1) Walters performed A in order to bring {S} about.

(2) Walters believed that the probability that A would lead to {S} is very high.

(3) {S} is not causally remote from A.

(4) Walters freely undertook as part of his responsibilities the avoidance of states of affairs of which {S} is an instance.

(5) Walters believed that he would be unable to prevent {S} once he did A.

(6) {S} is morally significant.

These conditions may not all be necessary for derivative responsibility; but if they are sufficient, we have many cases of responsibility for actions we cannot prevent at some time prior to their performance. We shall suppose here that the incompatibilist would be prepared to give ground to save his central thesis, i.e., that he is prepared to allow derivative responsibility only where the outcome is the result of an intentional action that is not determined. Actions we are responsible for in spite of our inability to prevent them derive their special status from paradigm cases of responsible actions, all of which must be free of compulsion. We would consequently be in error if we held an agent responsible for $\{S_1\}$, but were unable to uncover a bona fide case of a responsible action, i.e., one that is, among other things, undetermined, in the causal ancestry of $\{S_1\}$.

Although difficulties attend the attempt to defend the view that actual sequence causation is invariably compulsion, it is a simple matter to show why actual sequence causation might have a bearing on responsibility in a way alternate sequence 'causation' or 'compulsion' cannot. The case of the counterfactual intervener is one of preemptive overdetermination. Jones preempts the intervener by doing what the latter wishes and thereby renders the intervener's disposition a part of a sufficient condition of Jones' action that is not completed. Hence, the intervener is causally inefficacious, though he could become causally efficacious by instituting a separate sufficient condition of Jones' action.[7] So we are justified in directing our attention to the actual sequence, concluding either that Jones is morally responsible because the causal sequence exhibits certain features (compatibilism) or that Jones is not morally responsible just because there is a causal sequence leading to the action (incompatibilism). (The matter has nothing to do with the fact that the intervener performs a negative act for (completed) sufficient conditions often include absences or failures.)

It is natural, thus, to suppose (and Frankfurt among others does) that the only factors bearing on the moral responsibility of an agent are those entering into the causal explanation of that action. Some causal factors, of course, have no relevance to moral responsibility. But only causally relevant factors are morally relevant. We shall see that adoption of this principle will eventually create problems serious enough to require significant modification of it.

Although it, therefore, appears to be obvious that we should look to features of the actual sequence for ones that determine the moral responsibility of the agent for the outcome of the sequence, the action, we do not yet know the best way for an incompatibilist to charaterize the feature that eliminates responsibility. Although compulsion is, we have argued, problematic, no alternative has yet been specified.

IRRESISTIBILITY

Although there is deep disagreement about the implications of the fact that the actual sequence is deterministic, one might have supposed that all would agree that, if that sequence contains a motive or desire that is genuinely impossible to resist, the agent is not responsible. For here, the irresistible force is operative, not just, as in the case of the counterfactual intervener, potential. Surely a compulsive desire absolves one of responsibility.

Frankfurt has raised questions here, too. A far more serious blow to incompatibilism would obviously be provided by a demonstration that one's moral responsibility for A is not even necessarily undermined by the fact that one is compelled to do A. For the character of causal sequences which renders them compulsion-like is the basis of the incompatibilist's indictment.

The above idea here is that, since a person's moral responsibility for A rests on his causal responsibility for A, we must look to features of the causal explanation to ascertain the person's liability. And we may then discover that, although the agent's desire to do A was irresistible, its being so played no explanatory role. The explanation may allude to character traits or experiences of an anticipatory sort, e.g., the expectation of satisfaction, the possession of which does not imply that the agent is a victim of compulsion (though he may be), but does imply that the action may be legitimately charged against the agent. This explanation is compatible with the premise that the agent could not resist acting on the desire or manifesting the character trait. The agent may even be unaware of the irresistible character of his motive for, say, he has never attempted to resist it. The key point is that the agent should be treated, from the point of view of his moral responsibility, like a person who is not an addict, but does A because he likes to, for the explanations, insofar as the difference vis-à-vis irresistibility is irrelevant, are similar.

The addict is absolved from moral responsibility, according to Frankfurt, only if his action is *explained* by his inability to do otherwise or his belief in an inability to do otherwise. We can picture a case of one who is driven by an urge whose irresistible character is virtually a phenomenal feature (although this description may, nay should, be challenged[8]) or one who does not feel this irresistible character, or even one of great intensity, but acts on the basis of the belief, perhaps mistaken, that he cannot resist the urge, no matter how hard he tries.

In the case of the person who acts out of the belief that he cannot do otherwise, whether the belief is true or false, his exoneration would presumably be based on the fact that the action does not represent his underlying propensities. He acts out of resignation, not anticipation, and is, therefore, unlike the paradigm of a responsible agent, that is, one who freely chooses to do A because he overall prefers A to all other options and in no way minds being that kind of person.

Yet it is important to notice that a desire, resistible or not, is causally necessary, even in action from resignation. Even the agent who has an unconscious motive and feels no urge, but just acts from resignation, is doing so in order to avoid the intense pain he believes, perhaps falsely, he would experience were he to attempt to resist. It is misleading to suggest that an addict, unwilling or otherwise, is not moved at all by the affective or volitional portion of his nature, and that his desires are entirely opposed to the direction of his behavior, where the latter results entirely from cognitive sources. Although one may wish to downgrade the role of a first-order desire where there is a contrary second-order one, even a person who acts from resignation acts partly from a desire whose content is relevant. There is an inauthenticity, I fear, in the attitude which would have us avert our eyes from the attractiveness of objects of desire for the motivated agent who may happen to be an addict.[9] This attitude is also found in Frankfurt's description of the process of refusing to identify with a desire as expulsion from self, an outlook I have criticized elsewhere.[10]

A willing addict's action, however, cannot be explained by the irresistibility of his desire. For if he is willing, i.e., if he is content to act from that desire, why would he not be content to act from that desire if it were slightly less compelling? But then irresistibility is not a sine qua non of the efficacy of the desire which issues in action and we are forced to conclude that the willing addict is responsible just because he is willing.[11]

For an unwilling addict, however, the important consideration is that, in virtue of the causal necessity of the belief that he cannot do otherwise, the agent would do otherwise if he thought he could. But then there must be some conflict within this agent. He would not act otherwise if he could unless he has a propensity to do so alongside the desire he regards as overwhelming together with a second-order desire that the strength of his first-order desires be reversed. Since he would not do otherwise if he could in the absence of this second-order desire, Fischer's contention that this agent might not mind being the sort of person he is cannot be right.[12] If he were content with his nature, he would act on the desire perceived to be irresistible even if it were believed to be resistible. For this person, the belief in the desire's irresistibility is not really essential in the circumstances and he cannot appeal to it, even if it is present, as an excuse. For he has no rebuttal to the charge that he is the sort of person who would perform that action whether or not he can refrain from doing so.

I would like now to suggest that this position is more radical than Frankfurt appears to recognize.

We first eliminated as irrelevant to moral responsibility alternate sequence compulsion. Actual sequence compulsion is similarly irrelevant unless the compulsive desire is not simply present, but also explanatory *qua compulsive*.

Now if compulsiveness vis-à-vis action A absolves, as we have just said, the agent would act otherwise even if he had a very powerful, but not irresistible urge to do A. He might, therefore, have a very powerful inclination contrary to A that his compulsive desire thwarts in the actual circumstances and that is the basis of his exoneration. Or he might have a weaker desire to refrain from doing A that can be reinforced by an effort of will à la libertarianism once the inclination to do A is merely powerful, but not irresistible.

Even if compulsiveness under special conditions exonerates, we need not suppose that a very powerful, but resistible desire can never exonerate. Perhaps one is absolved of moral responsibility because, though one can resist the desire, its intensity renders the act of resistance noble rather than morally mandatory. Nevertheless, we would certainly hold an agent morally responsible if he knowingly acts out of a weak immoral impulse even if he has an even weaker desire to act morally. But then why does compulsiveness exonerate just because the agent has a weaker desire to do otherwise? (We saw above that an addict is excused in virtue of a desire which would be manifested were the addictive desire weaker.) If unavoidability is irrelevant in other cases, why is it relevant here? And if it is not, is there any morally relevant difference between an agent who knowingly acts immorally out of a weak desire and one who does so out of an irresistible desire when each has a somewhat weaker opposing desire?

It is tempting to exonerate the 'victim' of the irresistible and immoral desire by taking second-order volitions into account. For if the agent would prefer not to be moved by that desire, he can, according to Frankfurt, refuse to identify with it. Thus, the unwilling addict's behavior is excused because it is a consequence of a state that does not truly represent the agent. The person, as an outsider, watches his body go through certain gyrations he wishes he could control.

I have criticized this line elsewhere.[13] I need only note here, where the issue is the relevance of compulsiveness or unavoidability, that it is utterly irrelevant. For an agent who can refuse to identify with an irresistible desire can just as easily refuse to identify with a resistible one. Nonidentification is not a necessary difference between the victim of an irresistible desire and the victim of a resistible desire.

We do not, in other words, know why an agent is absolved of moral responsibility even if he acts *because* he could not have done otherwise. To be more specific, let us describe this purported paradigm of nonresponsibility in order to see if we can discover the grounds of this characteristic. Jones does A out of an irresistible desire to do A. The irresistibility of the desire is causally relevant in that he would refrain from doing A if the desire were just powerful, but resistible. He, therefore, has a desire to refrain from doing A that he wishes were the predominant motive. (In the absence of this second-order volition – the desire that the desire to refrain be predominant – the irresistibility of his first-order desire to do A would not be causally necessary and he would, as a consequence, be morally responsible. For example, were the two competing desires roughly equal in strength, a second-order endorsement of the desire to do A should make the difference.[14] So that in the original case, the irresistibility of the desire to do A would not be causally necessary and he would, as a result, be morally responsible for having done A.)

Is Frankfurt trading on the nonidentification of Jones with his desire to do A in order to draw the conclusion that Jones is not morally responsible because he is acting out of an irresistible desire? Are we responding then to the fact that the addict must be unwilling and not to the fact that he is an addict? Unavoidability alone, Frankfurt has taught us, is apparently of no moral relevance. Yet, as we have just seen, nonidentification is similarly irrelevant or we would be unable to pass judgments on weak-willed persons, i.e., those who can and wish to resist temptation, but fail to do so.

The direction of this line of thought is radical. If compulsiveness or irresistibility per se has no moral relevance, then incompatibilism fails even if causation implies compulsion. We must, therefore, proceed carefully.

CHARACTER VERSUS ACT EVALUATION

A case might now be advanced that Frankfurt has confused two separate matters: moral responsibility of an agent for an action A and relevant aspects of the moral character of an agent who performs action A. Consider three persons, Smith, Robinson, and Green, each of whom is driven by an irresistible desire to do evil. Were the desires merely very powerful, Smith would, in virtue of a very strong desire to be good, resist evil; Robinson, possessed of only a moderately strong desire to be good, would suffer from weakness of will and succumb to his evil nature; but Green, also laboring under the same discrepancy of strength of desires, would exert an effort of will on behalf of the good and rise to duty.

Although Robinson's character is worse than Green's, why should he be blamed in the actual situation because he would not have done otherwise if he could? Why should Robinson's disposition to succumb to temptation be relevant to an ascription of responsibility in a situation in which it plays no causal role, especially in light of the working assumption that only causally relevant factors be considered? It is surely unfair to Robinson to point to character defects in such an indiscriminate fashion. If his character is the subject of inquiry, it is important to know about his intemperance. But this consideration is not relevant to the evaluation of the action. If it were, we might just as well hold Robinson responsible if, at the last minute, he is forced from without to act in the way he was about to act. For there, too, we may say that, due to his intemperance, he would have acted in the same way had he been able to do otherwise.

41

It may be objected that ascriptions of causal relevance always require appeal to distinct situations some of which may be counterfactual. We learn that P is causally relevant to Q in S when we have a right to conclude that Q would be absent in a counterfactual situation S′ which fails to include P, yet is relevantly similar to S. Thus, in spite of the causal irrelevance of Robinson's intemperance, the fact that he would display weakness of will is the basis for our knowledge that the irresistibility of his desire in the actual state of affairs is causally irrelevant. Robinson's culpability, Frankfurt could contend, is not based on a causally irrelevant character trait, but rather on the failure to be able to exonerate him by reference to the causal necessity of irresistibility. Our *evidence* that the irresistibility of his desire is causally irrelevant is provided by reference to a character trait which would be manifest in situations different from the actual.

And in the case in which Robinson happens also to be subjected to an irresistible *external* force driving him to the same outcome, Frankfurt is prepared to bite the bullet and to conclude that Robinson is still guilty. So long as the case is one of genuine or symmetrical overdetermination, Robinson's desire is causally relevant and, had he been able to do otherwise, that is, had neither his desire nor the external force overwhelmed him, he would still have done A. So it matters not at all to his responsibility that he is driven both internally and externally by forces of an irresistible character.

EFFORT AND RESPONSIBILITY

Without claiming then to have refuted Frankfurt's position, I would like to explore an alternative line of thought on the criteria of moral responsibility.

Imagine that Robinson, in the original situation in which he has an internal, irresistible desire to do A, wants desperately not to be held responsible for A. As intemperate, Robinson would fail to bring himself to exert sufficient effort in a hypothetical case in which the desire is resistible. Yet his intemperance is of such a nature as to permit him to try as hard as he can to prevent himself from doing A when he knows he will fail. In the secure knowledge that he is bound to fail, Robinson proceeds to try as hard as he can (or as hard as can reasonably be expected of him) to refrain from doing A, but, of course, in light of A's irresistibility, fails. I would submit that no one can be held responsible for a state of affairs arising from an action he tries as hard as he can to refrain from performing (unless he is derivatively responsible in that he knowingly and freely placed himself in circumstances which lead to his being unable to do otherwise, a condition we may suppose not to be present here). Robinson is absolved of responsibility, then, in spite of the fact that he exerts an effort to refrain from doing A *only* because he knows he will fail. Since Robinson would not do otherwise if he could, the basis of his exemption is different from Smith's for Smith's innocence is grounded in the fact that he *would* do otherwise if he could. Robinson's maximal effort absolves him of responsibility whereas his failure to try as hard as he can to refrain from doing A in the original situation is the reason we consider him a possible candidate for moral blame in spite of the irresistibility of his desire.

If the concept of effort is not introduced, the moral difference between Smith and Robinson, resting on the causal relevance of irresistibility, remains obscure. To summarize the reasoning which led to this conclusion, we note first the concession to Frankfurt of the principle that unavoidability alone or even the presence of an irresistible desire is not a sufficient excuse. With this concession, Frankfurt may then seek to identify a relevant difference between the two. Yet he cannot find it in the character of the motivational process. For, as we earlier insisted, Smith need not be acting purely out of resignation. The attractiveness of the object of desire is as important to him as it is to Robinson. Also, we saw that it matters not to the assessment of their responsibility which desire they identify with. Both might prefer to be different sorts of persons. Moreover, if a person is absolved from responsibility when, in virtue of a powerful, countervailing desire, he would have acted different had the actual motivation been resistible, we have no way to explain why we hold weak-willed persons responsible (perhaps not all the time) for their actions. They too act from strong impulses (to do evil) which are set alongside weaker impulses (to do good) such that they would act differently had the stronger impulse been less strong. Here too, their responsibility does not rest upon the decision as to which desire to identify with. If the weak-willed person had preferred to be as he is, viz., evil, he would be a worse individual than the one who identifies with the better part of his nature. But they are equally responsible for the evil actions. Why, then, in light of the irrelevance of irresistibility per se, should we permit the agent acting *from* an irresistible desire to be let off the hook? He is not let off the hook if the contrary desire fails to be almost as intense as the irresistible one (and he is disposed of weakness of will). Why should it matter so much that the inefficacious desire is a little stronger? If we think that it matters that the agent is disposed to weakness of will, why should we not simply think of that as a character defect which reduces our overall appraisal of the person, but plays no moral role, since the agent is not succumbing to temptation, in the assessment of A?

In other words, why should anyone, acting as his nature dictates, even under the influence of external coercion, fail to be morally praiseworthy or blameworthy? Why should we draw any distinction between causal and moral responsibility? To deal successfully with these questions and to develop the answers suggested in the above discussion, we must probe more deeply into issues left untouched in this chapter: the analysis of irresistibility and ways in which the concept of moral responsibility imposes constraints upon relations among character, effort, and action.

4

Intention and moral responsibility

CHARACTER AND ACTION

In the previous chapter, we saw that a reasoned extension of Frankfurt's views would result in a virtual identification of moral responsibility with causal responsibility. Since we all wish sometimes to exonerate a person who is causally responsible for his deed, even when we disagree on the conditions of exoneration and on many actual cases, no one would find this result satisfactory. We wish then to see whether a less extreme way can be found to preserve Frankfurt's insights. Only then can we reconsider the question which originally motivated this discussion: is there a middle term between determination and the absence of moral responsibility which permits a prima facie plausible incompatibilist argument, and, if so, what is it?

In chapter 2, we advanced as the core idea of moral responsibility for action A the principle that A is proper to cite in a moral evaluation of the agent. If A is objectionable, our estimate of the agent's worth declines, whereas it, of course, increases should A constitute, say, a supererogatory act or even the fulfillment of some obligation on the agent's part.

An action may be indirectly relevant to the moral evaluation of an agent by revealing a character trait whose presence is directly relevant. Since it is important to know that an individual is selfish or courageous when we draw up a moral accounting of him, it may, consequently, not be important that this information is

45

acquired by observing a compulsive expression of the pertinent trait (except in those cases in which the trait is of a nature which precludes compulsive manifestations).

If an action is only relevant in this way, the agent may not be morally responsible for it. Not only may the manifestation of the trait be a compulsive one; but the agent may want to be rid of this trait and be taking all steps in his power to effect this end. Not even Frankfurt would then regard him as morally responsible. To be morally responsible for A, therefore, A must be directly relevant to the agent's evaluation in that, even if, following many philosophers, e.g., Hume, Brandt, and Dahl,[1] we require that A reflect a defective character trait, the fact that the agent acted on this trait is important independently of the possession of the trait. That is, certain features of the action or its relation to its psychological matrix must be present in order for the agent to be blameworthy *for* A. Yet we cannot blithely assert that the relevant trait is a noncompulsive manifestation in light of the difficulties we confronted in the preceding chapter trying to discern the relevance of compulsiveness or irresistibility. We may, for example, regard a killer as blameworthy for a killing he was irresistibly drawn to perform when we learn that he endorses his way of life and the actions flowing inevitably from his personality. We may concur with Frankfurt's observation that, since he would have acted in the same way had he not been held sway by an irresistible impulse, he is to be judged as we would judge a person who can control his murderous impulses, but chooses not to do so.

As I indicated in the previous chapter and am here reiterating, the plausibility of some views of Frankfurt may require a theoretical grounding in which a more careful distinction between character evaluation and act evaluation is made. Imagine that Dunsley is uncertain as to the irresistible or resistible status of his murderous impulses and decides to test himself by trying as hard as he can not to kill his present victim. In spite of absolutely heroic, maximal efforts, he succumbs, thereby learning that he is unable to refrain from giving vent to his evil desires. In light of his approval of his lifestyle, he should not be upset at this discovery.

As reprehensible as Dunsley is, he cannot be judged morally responsible for the killing, although, of course, he may be derivatively responsible for having evolved into a compulsive killer. It is surely a sufficient excuse that he tried as hard as he could to refrain. Frankfurt might agree on the grounds that Dunsley discovered, through his maximal efforts, that he acted in the way he did only because he could not have done otherwise. But the aptness of this description should not conceal its basis, viz., the presence in Dunsley of a desire to murder the satisfaction of which is so prospectively appealing to him that he can do nothing to inhibit its manifestation.[2]

Frankfurt might also treat Dunsley like any unwilling addict who is absolved because his higher-order desires are inefficacious against an unbending first-order nature. If we suppose that Dunsley has decided in this single case to attempt to abstain either just to see if he can or because he can acquire some personal gain by so doing, but in no way as the result of a change of heart, his desire to thwart his first-order desire attests in no way to his nondepravity. Yet regardless of the state of Dunsley's desires, despicable as they are, he is off the hook in this case just because he has done everything that can reasonably be expected of him.

If this is right, it can surely make no difference to Dunsley's lack of responsibility that he happens to know his efforts will fail, assuming this knowledge does not affect the genuineness or depth of his efforts. But it is then a short step to the conclusion that Dunsley is not responsible for the killing even if he does not try to prevent it so long as he knows he will fail. For he may surely charge that he does not become absolved of responsibility by undertaking efforts he knows in advance will be unsuccessful. How can someone be required to go through these motions, unless, of course, there is some genuine doubt concerning the futility of the efforts?

It cannot be overemphasized that such doubts are almost always genuine. In chapter 5, we will explore the nature and existence of addiction and will simply assert here that, in the relevant sense of 'addiction', we shall learn that addiction is rare, very difficult to detect, and, therefore, very difficult to be certain of.

Suppose, though, we have a genuine case, one in which the agent knows for certain his efforts will fail. We might nonetheless require of this individual that he be fully prepared to expend as much energy as he is able if he acquires any reason to believe he might be successful.[3] Thus, a person is not blameworthy for some action A if either he tried as hard as he could to prevent himself from doing A or would have unless he knew there was no chance of success.

THE EFFORT-THESIS

Before this doctrine, which we shall call the Effort-Thesis, is applied to various other cases, two clarificatory remarks are in order. First, he may fail to be blameworthy under weaker conditions as well. For example, circumstances may be such that a serious and sustained effort suffices as excuse – maximal effort is not required. We are not saying then that exoneration *requires* maximal effort. The position so far describes a sufficient, not a necessary, condition. Second, a person is not exonerated just because he knows he is an addict. He must be disposed to make the effort such that he would try not to succumb if he were to believe he has any chance of success.

(1) Webster is addicted to killing, contrary to her second-order volitions, but has only a moderately powerful desire not to kill which would still emerge the loser were her murderous impulses a bit weaker. I suggested earlier that someone like Webster is as morally responsible as a person like Smith[4] in spite of the fact that Smith, but not Webster, would do otherwise if he could. Webster does not have as good a character as Smith, but that is a different matter. In spite of the fact that the irresistibility of Webster's impulse is causally irrelevant to her action, she is surely exonerated if she did everything in her power to refrain, motivated by her second-order desire to be a different sort of person combined with an erroneous belief she is not in the grips of an addiction.

If we regarded her efforts as relevant only to the obligation to *try* to refrain from immorality, we would lack the means to absolve her from responsibility for the action. We know, for example, that the doctrine that inability to do otherwise suffices for exoneration is problematic. Nor can we exonerate her on the grounds that she would have done differently had she been able to do so, for that is not so. Thus, her efforts must play a crucial role in this regard.

(2) Burton enjoys killing enormously, but is neither addicted nor content with his lifestyle. He would refrain from killing were it

not so gratifying, but fails always to summon up sufficient will energy to achieve his second-order desire. Recall that Frankfurt's position fails to explain why we might hold someone like Burton responsible for a particular act of murder. Insofar as he prefers not to act on his desire to kill, he does not kill freely, i.e., willingly. To be sure, since he can, but does not refrain from killing, what is true of some unwilling addicts is not true of him, i.e., it is not the case that Burton would refrain if he could. He can refrain, but does not. What is morally objectionable is his failure to attempt to refrain.

Responsibility and avoidability appear to be logically indepen-dent. As we have frequently noted, a person who avoidably harms another may not be blameworthy if, say, the harm is minor and abstention would have made inordinate demands of the agent. Conversely, Frankfurt may be right that there are instances of unavoidable acts for which the agent is morally responsible. Nonetheless, it is also possible that, under certain circumstances, avoidability implies responsibility. If these circumstances obtain in the case of Burton (for example, it would not be enormously difficult to control his murderous impulse), his blameworthiness may hinge on the avoidability of the act.

The moral relevance of avoidability is bound up with the relation between avoidability and the effectiveness of effort. Specifically exoneration is based on unavoidability which, in turn, is based either on unsuccessful maximal efforts at abstention or the knowledge that any efforts at abstention would be unsuccessful. We may wish to add, as a third basis of unavoidability, the inability even to undertake such efforts, where this condition can be present.

(3) Tudor kills because he wants to, although his act is, due to the presence of a counterfactual intervener, unavoidable. For Frankfurt and me, Tudor is blameworthy. For me, he failed to take steps to inhibit his action and this failure is due not just to his (possible) knowledge of the counterfactual intervener. Suppose, though, that the counterfactual intervener would have rendered even an effort physically impossible in the event the thought of abstention merely crossed his mind. There is the familiar ambiguity of 'can' which permits opposing truth values for 'Tudor could not try to abstain' in light of the actual non-intervention of the counterfactual intervener. If we decide that Tudor could not

have tried to abstain, then, if we add this power to the list of sufficient conditions of nonresponsibility, we shall have to say, contra Frankfurt, that Tudor is blameless.

There is no need now to enter this modal quagmire since we repudiate the suggestion of Tudor's innocence by noting that the cause of his failure to put forth the required effort is his desiring nature, a condition which preempts the counterfactual intervener.

Yet we would wish to accommodate the case of one who is so incapacitated that he is actually incapable of undertaking any effort to do or prevent the doing of A. Let us then revise the Effort-Thesis to read: a person is not responsible for some action A if either he tried as hard as he could to prevent himself from doing A or would have had he been able to (unless he knew there was no chance of success).

Does this emendation subject the thesis to the same difficulty which plagues Frankfurt's formulation? We saw there that it is arbitrary to blame Robinson but to exonerate Smith because it is only true of Smith that he would have done otherwise if he could. If they are both acting from compulsion, the fact that Robinson's countervailing desire is a little weaker than the corresponding one in Smith does not appear to be able to carry the weight required of it. This consideration does not affect the Effort-Thesis because, again, it states only a sufficient condition of the absence of blame-worthiness. Thus, if Tudor cannot try to prevent himself from doing A, and would still have failed to try even had he been able to do so, although the Effort-Thesis may not be invoked to exonerate him, other grounds of exoneration may exist. Given the circumstances, the putting forth of effort may not be morally required of him.

The Effort-Thesis is being advanced as a corrective which would prevent the identification of causal and moral responsibility. The blameworthiness of an agent who fails to satisfy the conditions stated therein (as well as all other conditions which would excuse him) is not based directly upon the defectiveness of his character even when his action is due to a defective trait, but rather upon a defect of will, even if this latter defect is due to a defective character. He is guilty because he failed to take steps to inhibit the manifestation of his character. Hence, the action has an independent role to play in the assessment of the individual's worth. His personal worth declines further than it would were one to base an assessment just on character.

The role of the individual context of action may further be underscored by noting the irrelevance even of such elements of character as strength of will. What matters is the exercise, not the presence of such a trait. Hence, we may even overlook the absence of such a general propensity so long as the effort was forthcoming in the particular case.

Conversely, an agent whose reprehensible behavior is the result of an immoral nature may be exonerated by sufficient effort[5] even if, as in the unusual case of Dunsley, he has no objections either to his behavior or his character. A special action, maximal effort to prevent A, defeats the charge of responsibility for A which would normally be forthcoming. The causal account of A, which may not refer to this effort at all, establishes internal causal responsibility on the part of the agent, while the effort absolves him of moral responsibility.

We are, therefore, modifying the assumption that only factors which play an explanatory role are relevant to a moral evaluation of A. A causal account of A may fail to refer to the morally relevant exertion of effort in two different cases: (1) the agent failed to exert effort and, for this reason, bears responsibility; (2) the agent exerted effort and is, therefore, absolved of responsibility, but the effort is inefficacious. We hope, as a consequence, now to be able to disentangle causal from moral responsibility.

The conception of responsibility which emerges when the Effort-Thesis is included in the account coheres with an overall ethic of intention. To exert maximal effort to prevent A is to perform an action B, perhaps a quite minimal one, e.g., the contraction of certain muscles, guided by a (correct) belief that B is the most likely action among the available ones to prevent action A.[6] A person who exerts maximal effort to prevent A is acting with the intention of preventing A and cannot, therefore, be judged a lesser person on the basis of A (unless his efforts are half-hearted) no matter how despicable an individual he happens to be. This account coheres better with our intuitions regarding the various cases we have described than does the account based on a moral review restricted to the facets of character which play a role in the explanation of A.

The incompatibilist outlook on this result is that the Effort-Thesis states a sufficient condition of exemption from moral responsibility which is logically independent of another such condition, determination. An agent is absolved of responsibility for A if A is determined whether or not he exerts or is disposed to exert maximal effort to prevent A. This position is compatible with the Effort-Thesis insofar as the latter is not presented as a necessary condition of exemption from moral responsibility. Thus, the agent who fails to put forth the effort, even where he believes it would have some chance of success, may anyway be absolved of responsibility and the incompatibilist proposes that he is so absolved under the condition that it is determined that he do A.

The incompatibilist would disagree with our conclusions concerning Tudor in the following respect. Assuming that the particular act A of killing by Tudor is determined by his own character traits, and assuming that the counterfactual intervener would have forced Tudor to kill, but would not have rendered it impossible for him to exert maximal effort to refrain from doing A, the incompatibilist would regard Tudor as free of moral responsibility for the killing, whereas we counted his failure to try to prevent A, in light of his ignorance concerning the futility of this effort, as decisive grounds for culpability.

We argued earlier that the exertion of effort must be construed as both satisfying the obligation to try not to do evil as well as exonerating the agent from blame for the action. In a parallel way, we are now insisting against the incompatibilist that the failure to exert effort bears also on responsibility for the action itself.

The incompatibilist could agree that this failure can, under certain conditions, have this consequence, but fails to do so when the agent is anyway absolved by dint of the presence of determining conditions. And, of course, the determining conditions which matter here are the internal ones, not those created by the presence of the counterfactual intervener. He could point out that his view is compatible with our conclusion that the exertion of effort exonerates an agent not just from the charge that he has not tried to prevent evil, but also from charges arising directly from the performance of the heinous act. The incompatibilist objects to attempts to find people responsible when their acts are determined, not to attempts to formulate sufficient conditions of exemption from responsibility separate from determination.

UNAVOIDABILITY AND NECESSITY

We are now in a position to reconsider the question which initiated this lengthy discussion. What precisely provides the link between the determining conditions and the absence of responsibility, according to the incompatibilist?

Earlier we argued that the counterfactual intervener's failure to complete a sufficient condition leading to the action warranted us in looking only at the actual sequence which terminates in the action for features relevant to the agent's moral responsibility. Since the agent preempts the counterfactual intervener, the latter plays no role in the causal explanation of the action and may, therefore, be ignored. But the presupposition that only causally relevant features bear on moral responsibility was abandoned when the Effort-Thesis was adopted. We there decided that the agent's failure to attempt to inhibit his activity is morally, though possibly not causally, relevant to his behavior. Does this mean that the unavoidability of the action (more precisely, the state of affairs constituted by the agent's performing a certain action) as the result of the presence of the counterfactual intervener *is* relevant?

In defense of the view that the counterfactual intervener may be dismissed, we may note that the acceptance of the Effort-Thesis does not constitute a complete abandonment of the principle linking causal to moral responsibility. Given that conditions are leading to a morally objectionable outcome, we may reasonably expect an agent to take steps to prevent that outcome if it is in his power to do so and if he estimates he has some chance of success. A failure to take such steps is a moral failing which permits us to regard the agent as blameworthy on a conception of moral responsibility which focuses on the effect of such actions on the overall moral appraisal of the person. It is not as if we are going entirely outside the context of the causal nexus of action. We demand of the agent that he do something about the actual path leading to the action, about the constellation of potentially effective factors which his efforts might bear upon.

It is nonetheless true that the counterfactual intervener renders the action unavoidable and the incompatibilist still owes us an answer to the question of why that is not disturbing in a way he is disturbed by the unavoidability created by determination.

Perhaps unavoidability is not the concept the incompatibilist wants. Since we saw earlier that compulsion is also problematic as the middle term between determination and the absence of responsibility, we must explore further the requirements on the modal notion he seeks.

One fact appears to be of crucial importance here. Although the disposition of the counterfactual intervener renders the action unavoidable, it does not necessitate the action in one sense of 'necessitate'. The disposition guaranteed, but did not determine the action. The incompatibilist is concerned about the consequences to the agent's moral responsibility of the operative sufficient condition, not merely of some condition whose presence insures the outcome. But how may we clarify the distinction between determining and insuring?

The disposition of the counterfactual intervener insures a disjunctive state of affairs, either the agent will decide on his own to do A or he will be forced to do A, which itself insures A. The situation is similar – but also different as we shall soon see – to one in which a painting contractor insures that his client will love the dining room walls by ordering his painters to paint the room green. He leaves it to them to choose the shade because his client is so enamored of that color that it matters not what shade of green is chosen.

We shall adopt the following abbreviations:
  d: the disposition of the counterfactual intervener
  f: the forcing of the agent to do A by the counterfactual intervener
  a: the action done by the agent
  o: the agent's decision on his own to do A
Ox: x occurs (or comes into being)
In the actual world, all but f obtains. In addition, the following are nomically grounded truths:
$$Od \supset (Of \lor Oo)$$
$$(Of \lor Oo) \supset Oa$$
Although, therefore, $Od \supset Oa$, we speak of insuring, rather than necessitating because Od drops out of the picture in the

following way. At some level of specificity in the causal account leading to a, d is no longer a factor. Although $(Of \lor Oo) \supset Oa$ and $Oo \supset Oa$ may be involved, d is causally relevant only for the less specific account, viz., the former. The causal history of o makes reference neither to d nor even to d by a less specific description. The factors which comprise the sufficient condition which determine an outcome, therefore, are those which appear in the most specific causal history leading to that outcome.

The reason we regard the painting contractor's orders as determining the pleasure experienced by his client as he surveys his dark green dining room walls is that reference to those orders is relevant to the painters' decision to paint the walls dark green. To be sure, the orders are not sufficient insofar as the painters were given some leeway. But the orders narrowed the selection and, therefore, play a contributory role in a way d does not (in relation to a).

If (a big one) determination is a form of necessity, what is it about this sort of necessity that precludes moral responsibility? We need to know more about this notion of necessity to answer this question because, sadly, we have hitherto failed to discover a middle term illuminating the link alleged by incompatibilists to obtain between determination and moral responsibility which could, by virtue of this illumination, become the analysis of necessity in this context.

Before we directly address the nature of necessity in this context, we shall attempt to understand better two key notions we have shamelessly availed ourselves of, irresistible desire (addiction) and power. The latter, a synonym of freedom in one of its senses, is a central contender for the feature whose absence serves as the middle term between determination and the absence of responsibility.

5

Addiction

ANALYSIS OF ADDICTIVE BEHAVIOR

We conceded to Frankfurt and other participants in these discussions the actuality of action from irresistible desire (addiction) in spite of the serious unclarity of the notion of irresistibility and related skepticism regarding the existence of addiction. (We shall use the term 'addiction' as a synonym for the state of one who is in the grip of an irresistible desire rather than using it as a label to set off a group of persons whose existence is virtually uncontroversial.)[1]

Our quest is not 'the' analysis of addiction, for there is no such thing, but rather an analysis that may reveal important relationships to moral responsibility. Our primary concern is not the time period during which Jones is an addict, but rather the episodes during that period when Jones has the pertinent desire. Also, it suffices for addiction that irresistibility is temporally coextensive with the presence of the desire. We are not here concerned to require that Jones be unable to take steps to control his behavior prior to the onset of the desire.

Consider the following proposed analysis of 'Jones is addicted to heroin during t_n to t_{n+m}':

(1) Jones is in the state [Jones desires heroin] from t_n to t_{n+m} and, due to the strength of this state, there is no time t during t_n to t_{n+m} and no act type a such that if Jones believes during t_n to t_{n+m} that he has some chance of acquiring heroin and believes that if there were a token of a with Jones as agent, it would prevent heroin-seeking behavior by Jones from t_n to t_{n+m}, then Jones can do a at t. Moreover, if Jones is not prevented from engaging in

heroin-seeking behavior by events other than his own actions (and inactions) or by the knowledge that he has no chance of acquiring heroin, he seeks heroin at some time between t_n and t_{n+m}.

We surely intend, in talking of an irresistible desire, that the strength of the desire play a causal role in the irresistibility.

Suppose that Ripley has a mild desire for heroin to which he would succumb were its satisfaction permitted by outside forces. Although Ripley can normally perform some act which would inhibit heroin-seeking behavior, a counterfactual intervener (CI) looms in the background in this situation to render him impotent if he were to set out to perform one of these acts. Thus, Ripley cannot do anything he believes would prevent him from seeking heroin. Yet, in the actual case, Ripley never contemplates abstention from heroin-seeking behavior. He is clearly not acting from an irresistible desire for he does not have an irresistible desire at all.

If one feels that CI's nonintervention permits Ripley to retain in some sense the power to abstain, we may simply describe a different case in which Harris is actually rendered impotent by an outside force who interferes with Harris' brain process by emitting signals from a sophisticated and secret electronic device. Harris can do nothing which he believes would bring about his abstention from heroin-seeking behavior, but may have no inkling of this limitation. Yet he succumbs to a mild, non-irresistible desire for heroin. If he were to attempt to desist, he would discover his inability, but not the irresistibility of his desire. That he cannot fail to act does not imply that the desire is irresistible unless the strength of the desire explains his inability.

We can also make sense of the idea, used by Frankfurt, of an action of an agent who has an irresistible desire to do what he is doing, but would do it even if the desire were resistible. He is an addict although the last sentence of the analysis would be true even if the state [Jones desires heroin] were sufficiently weaker so that *it* no longer renders impossible an act type *a* which Jones can perform in the belief it would prevent his seeking heroin. (The italics indicate the possibility that Jones is still compelled to seek heroin, even with the weaker desire, by dint of outside forces.)

Suppose Jones is forced to acknowledge that there is no available heroin. He cannot engage in heroin-seeking behavior because he knows there is no heroin to be sought. Environmental conditions of various sorts are necessary for successful goal-seeking behavior – a partner and social conventions for the desire to play chess, a typewriter and certain historical constraints for the desire to be the first person to type this sentence. To be sure, such things can be sought in ignorance of facts which preclude success. But, unless we suppose a person so tyrannized by his desire that he is incapable of coming to believe that its satisfaction is impossible, we shall want to permit a person who has an irresistible desire to be thwarted by the knowledge that it will remain unsatisfied.

There are, of course, responses of varying desperation. But even if such persons cannot act on their irresistible desires, they are addicts for their desires are sufficiently strong to impel them to action should they acquire the slightest hope of success.

A desire is rendered irresistible, through its strength, in two ways. Either the range of actions within the capacity of the agent is reduced or the belief that an action would inhibit (object of) desire-seeking behavior is expanded with the consequence that of the actions the agent can do, none is such that he believes of it that it will prevent behavior whose goal is the desired object.

We have explained the significance of the first occurrence of 'believes' in (1). The second is prompted by the thought that an addict is one whose acquisition of certain beliefs is sufficient for his being incapable of performing a certain type of action, i.e., a state whereby the recognition that a certain action on his part would result in his desire not being satisfied literally paralyzes the agent with respect to that action.

The sort of paralysis in question here, since we are not dealing with physical paralysis, is most plausibly thought of as the inability even to try to undertake in a serious and wholehearted way the action in question. If expanded, his efforts fail because he cannot bring himself to try as hard as one who is not addicted. The strength of his desire sets limits on his perseverance, resourcefulness, psychological and physical strength, energy, and 'will power.' But the limits are not general – he may be able to persevere in certain tasks, though finding himself unable to persevere in efforts directed against his own goal-seeking behavior.

For example, suppose that Smith forces Jones to submit to a needle which must remain in Jones' arm for five minutes in order to induce a state which will inhibit heroin-seeking behavior, but not the associated psychological state, i.e., the felt urge.[2] Jones is not physically prevented from removing the needle, and his failure to remove it would lead to the abstention (presumably by doing something a lay person would describe as strengthening Jones' will power). If we count such failures as acts – and I see no reason not to – then if Jones can refrain from removing the needle, his desire for heroin is not irresistible.

In one sense, obviously, Jones can refrain from removing the needle. There is nothing physically preventing him from so doing and, if he erroneously believed the drug being administered is a different one, one which is quite beneficial in an entirely different way, he would choose freely to leave it in. We normally preserve the *physical* ability to prevent ourselves by action or inaction from doing something we desperately, even irresistibly want to do. What we cannot perhaps do is to refrain from removing the needle in the belief that its effect is the inhibition of heroin-seeking behavior. Hence, the second occurrence of 'believes'.

Consider the last sentence of (1). If I refrain from heroin-seeking behavior because you threaten me, the desire is resistible since, in my compliance, I have prevented myself from acting, although I did not initiate the chain of events leading to the abstention. The relevant consideration is that an act of mine, compliance with a threat, appeared in the causal chain. Thus if my abstention is due to a sudden illness, an event arising in me, the desire may still be irresistible since no action of mine played any causal role. We must, of course, extend these considerations to sudden bouts of 'mental illness' *if such is possible*. Jones may be about to plunge into heroin-seeking behavior from an irresistible desire and be thwarted by a non-induced bout of depression or melancholy.

Of course, the preferred description in most of these cases is that the desire has been rendered resistible insofar as the agent can abstain once the illness begins its course. This situation is to be distinguished, therefore, from one modelled upon an example in which the agent abstains only because he is bound and gagged or, to take an example of an internal cause, he suffers a paralytic seizure. Here, he is still in the grips of an irresistible impulse, one whose strength has not diminished, because *he* can do nothing to control his behavior. No doubt, there are many borderline cases.

Note that, although '*x* prevents *y*', since it is causal, may then be extensional, the relevant sentence in the analysis is embedded in an intensional belief context. We have: there is no act type *a* such that, if Jones believes that if there were a Jones-token of *a*, say *j*, *j* would prevent heroin-seeking behavior on his part, Jones could do *a*. Suppose that 'heroin-seeking behavior of Jones' is coextensive with 'Jones' waiting on the corner of Fifth and Grand'. Thus, if *j* prevents one, it must prevent the other. But Jones' beliefs may diverge in the following way. Incorrectly placed street signs induce in him the erroneous belief that his contact is on the corner of Fifth and Baker each day. If the error were to be corrected, Jones might engage in heroin-seeking behavior by doing something, running confusedly through the city (looking for Fifth and Baker), which would prevent his waiting on the corner of Fifth and Grand. Thus, even if there is nothing Jones can do which he believes will suppress the urge to seek heroin, there is something he can do which he believes prevents his waiting on the corner of Fifth and Grand. (The assumption of extensional equivalence tells us this will never in fact happen, that there will be no divergence between heroin-seeking behavior and waiting on Fifth and Grand each day.)

TYPES OF ADDICTION

Perhaps an analysis even weaker than (1) would do. Consider, as (2), (1) with the proviso that act type *a* not include acts which render heroin-seeking behavior by Jones physically impossible. In other words, Jones is under the influence of an irresistible desire even if he can prevent himself from acting on it by killing himself, taking an anaesthetic, inducing others to tie him up, etc. The desire is irresistible because he cannot resist it through 'the power of his will.'

The analysis must specify that the behavior induced by the desire be characterized in terms of that desire. One is driven to behavior out of the belief that it has a chance to eventuate in the satisfaction of the desire. Since action from irresistible desire requires both a certain kind of behavior as well as a belief guiding that behavior,[3] one can render the result impossible by insuring the physical impossibility of just the behavior (anaesthetizing, killing, etc.) or, perhaps, if such is possible, the belief (neurological inducement of an unalterable belief that any action one can perform has no likelihood of bringing about the satisfaction of the desire).

There is another dimension along which one may consider weakening (1). One may regard a person as a victim of an irresistible desire even if he can resist it, so long as the conditions under which this can happen are extreme, e.g., life-threatening ones. If we liberalize the definition in this way, we approach more closely the ordinary meaning of 'irresistible' which is 'resistible only under extreme conditions', where 'extreme' itself may have to be relativized to features of the context, including the moral dimensions of the situation. A desire is irresistible in this sense if the costs of the action required to prevent the realization of the desire are so great that, even though the agent can perform that action, it is (highly) unreasonable to expect him to do so.

Let us designate (1) and (2), respectively, as total and psychological irresistibility, and the type just described as moral irresistibility.

Another distinction invoked in these discussions may be designated as phenomenological vs. dispositional irresistibility. Frankfurt and Fischer speak of persons acting out of irresistible desires they may not be aware of as irresistible. If they attempted to abstain, they would 'experience an irresistible desire'.[4] If such experiences exist, it is an easy matter to define 'irresistible' as a simple, phenomenological feature of experience. A person would be acting from an irresistible desire if he has such an experience or is disposed to were he to attempt to abstain from acting on the desire.

Yet it is difficult to deny that irresistibility is not a phenomenological feature of experience for one can at best infer from the qualitative content of an experience that one *cannot* resist it. The manifest content is surely only the *basis* of an inductive inference – one can always be surprised at the resources of the human animal. How many of us have risen above a firm conception of our limitations?

Let us then describe the phenomenological content of an experience that is the basis of a belief in its irresistibility as maximum craving. Although many irresistible desires display actual or dispositional maximum cravings, they need not do so. The important consideration is not how one feels, but whether or not one is impotent to prevent the action. A person may have an irresistible desire and believe erroneously, perhaps because he does not undergo maximum craving, that he can abstain, or, more commonly, a person may fail to have an irresistible desire, but take an experience as one of maximum craving and form the erroneous belief that he is impotent in the face of his own psychological condition.

The core idea in all these accounts is that a person is rendered (totally, psychologically, morally) impotent by the strength of his or her desire. However strength of desire is characterized, two extremes must be avoided. As we have just argued, the strength sufficient for this incapacitation cannot be identified with maximum craving. At the other extreme, we do not want to base a judgment of strength solely on the effects on the person's capacities. We want to permit a weak desire to be part of a causal sequence which terminates in the inability of the agent to prevent himself from acting on it. (Recall external agents who 'force' people to act on mild and fleeting desires.)

Perhaps, though, we are trading on difficulties in making the distinction between standard and deviant causal chains. We balk at describing the behavior of Jones as action from irresistible desire when some outside force is an intermediary. The desire is under those circumstances perceived as an occasion for intervention by the force who is the genuine cause of the action (or the inability to refrain from the action). We could rule such causal chains out if we could identify the features of a normal case of acting 'on' desire. If this could be done, would it not *then* make sense to identify irresistibility with a property of the effect of the desire? Surely, in a nondeviant case, a desire cannot have irresistibility as an intrinsic feature when the agent retains the power to resist it!

Also, however we analyze notions like irresistibility, whether by retaining a modal primitive or by attempting an analysis in terms of the hypothetical effects of (hypothetical) efforts, it is plausible to believe that an intrinsic state of the agent, perhaps neurological, is nonaccidentally related to irresistibility.

ADDICTION, COMPULSION, IMPOTENCE

If the notion of an intrinsic state N makes sense, we have the following cases: (1) *Behavior of an addict*:[5] Goal-seeking behavior by an individual in state N where N is the nondeviant result of the strength of the individual's desire for the goal; (2) *Behavior of a compulsive*: Goal-seeking behavior by an individual in state N regardless of the causes of this state; (3) *Behavior of an impotent*: Goal-seeking behavior by an individual, whether he is in state N or not, such that if he is not in state N, the attempt to desist from seeking that goal would lead in some way or another to his entering state N.

All addicts are compulsives and all compulsives are impotents, but not conversely. Impotents do not have the freedom or power to do otherwise, but some of those who are not compulsives may be said to act freely and can be morally responsible for their actions. (An impotent would be blameworthy if he performed a heinous action and failed to take steps to inhibit himself when he did not know these efforts were doomed to failure.) Advocates of a hierarchical conception of freedom would permit even addicts to be described as acting freely, so long as they endorse their status and are not unwilling to be moved to act by their overwhelming desire.

Incompatibilists believe that compulsives are not morally blameworthy for their evil acts even if they fail to try to take steps to prevent themselves from so acting – assume they are unaware of their compulsive states. But this belief receives no support from our analysis. For even if compulsives act out of necessity, i.e., act in virtue of a state, N, whose presence insures that, should the agent have certain beliefs, he must act in a certain way, the necessity in question is not implicit in the nomic or deterministic character of the connections, but has rather to do with a feature special to compulsiveness. Or at least the incompatibilist would have to show otherwise. We have not even claimed the irreducibility of the necessity embodied in compulsive action to nonmodal notions, although reducibility claims of this sort are notoriously difficult to make out.

The burden of proof would also fall upon the incompatibilist to demonstrate that ordinary action out of desire, i.e., the action of a non-impotent, so long as it is determined, is action for which the agent is not responsible. The compatibilist can cite the above distinctions to indicate that people fall on different sides of a line, depending *not* on simple determination. The incompatibilist would then have to appeal to the primitive link he contends obtains between necessity and responsibility.

Before we turn to that issue, I must remind us of the significance of the empirical fact that total addiction is extraordinarily rare. Few desires render a person literally impotent to take any steps to inhibit the desire's expression. To be sure, the modal character of the concept of impotence permits a vagueness which itself allows for disagreement about actual cases. But surely the vast number of cases identified as addiction are ones of moral, not even psychological, irresistibility. Moral questions, therefore, play a very large role in the evaluation of the behavior of people called 'addicts'. These facts explain in part the appeal of views about addiction like those of the psychiatrist Thomas Szasz.[6]

6
Power

POWER AND CONTROL

A traditional way of formulating the incompatibilist argument incorporates the notion of power, possibly as the analysis of freedom. Determination is conceived as narrowing an agent's power to the actual. If it is determined that Jones does A, he lacks the power to perform any contrary action.

The idea is closely related to the notion of control, discussed briefly in chapter 2. The logic of the notions may be developed differently. For example, it is natural to think that power has to do with actions and control to states or outcomes. Thus, I lack the power to fly (unaided) and the control over the outcome: that I fly. But the difference here is deceptive since, given that I did not fly, no action enters the analysis of the judgment of power anyway. And should one try to introduce the notion in the following way,

(1) Jones lacks the power to do A $=^{Df}$ There is no action b such that b is of type A and Jones can-do b,

the result is unacceptable. For if a particular act of some bird or Superman counts as an act of type A, surely it is *trivially* untrue (it may be meaningless) that Jones can-do *it*. Evidently in denying that Jones has the power to fly, we are not denying that he can have performed the very token acts of flying of that bird or Superman. If Jones unsuccessfully tries to fly, he is not trying to perform one of the particular feats of another being. If, on the other hand, only an act of flying by Jones is a possible value of b, we again get the right result for the wrong reason. Since there are no values of b, the right-hand side of (1) turns out to be true. So, therefore, does the left-hand side and that is as it should be. The problem, of course, is that this sort of result would obtain for any type of act Jones never does. We would, thus, be forced to say that Jones can-do only the things he does. For example, even if Jones can ride a bicycle, we may be curious as to whether he can ride a bicycle in Caracas (at noon, on Friday, . . .). If he never rides a bicycle in Caracas, there is no action of the type 'riding a bicycle by Jones in Caracas' and the result is that Jones lacks the power to perform an act of riding a bicycle in Caracas.

Thus, although the logic of power is similar to that of control in that neither concerns action-tokens, the fact that we have the power to *do things* and the control *over outcomes* indicates that the concept of power is restricted to action-types. I lack control over my mortality; but the relevant impotence here concerns acts of the type 'making myself immortal', or 'making myself mortal'.

Although an improvement, this suggestion is not problem-free. The analysis now would look something like:

(2) Jones lacks the power to perform an act of type $A =^{Df}$
There is an act type A such that it is not the case that Jones can-do A.

What is it to be able to perform an action type? If 'Jones does A' means 'There is an act token of type A of which Jones is the agent', we may try to construe 'Jones can-do A' as the possible truth of this sentence. Yet any reasonable clarification of possibility in this context is likely to result in a doctrine too weak for our purposes as we shall see shortly.

Another difference emerges from reflection on cases, like ones involving a counterfactual intervener, in which we control the path to an outcome, but not the outcome itself. I must do R either on my own or, failing that, through the intervention of the counterfactual intervener. In this case I do not control R, but I have the power to do R. What I lack is the power to refrain from doing R. In the case of control, however, I cannot control the state S without controlling not-S. I have control over S only if I have the power to do something which realizes S and the power to do something which realises -S.

THE COMMON CONCEPTION
OF FREEDOM

Whatever other problems pervade the attempt to analyze the notion of power and its relation to control, the idea that determinism reduces power invokes a conception of the implications of determinism, powerlessness, very close to the common conception of freedom. When we think of political, religious, or artistic freedom, we think of the availability in each domain of a wide range of options or alternatives. The imposition of the reduction of alternatives – limits – by a totalitarian regime is a model of the imposition by determination of limits on human action.

The model has its limits. It is probably best to construe the common conception as a characteristic of agents, not individual states or actions. Agents possess (more or less) freedom in sphere S (politics, religion, art) to the extent that a range of alternatives in S is available to them. The amount of freedom would be a function not just of the number of options – the fact that you can be any sort of Mormon you wish does not constitute a high degree of religious freedom – nor even of the 'variety' (many types may be uninteresting generally or unattractive to many or all agents).

I may be a free agent in this sense ('common freedom'), yet lack the freedom or power to act on this freedom. The fact that there are no political or social barriers to my conversion to Mormonism does not imply that I have the power to convert. A number of psychological impediments may render this impossible – an inability to believe in its precepts, a fear of alienating my family, etc. (For an incompatibilist, of course, determination is always a sufficient reason. But one need not be an incompatibilist to find numerous examples of impotence not due to limits on common freedom.)

The common freedom of agents has to do with just one set of restrictions on action (or decision), namely, those of a political or social character. Common freedom, thus, is implicitly incorporated in the notion of power as a necessary, but not sufficient condition.

A separate notion of freedom is implicit in an earlier remark

67

concerning the qualitative and quantitative importance of the range of options available to an individual. This notion is similar to that of common freedom since it applies to an agent and admits of degrees. Yet, unlike common freedom, two individuals possessing equal amounts of common freedom (by virtue of membership in the same society and the possession in equal measure of capacities permitting them to compete for social goods) may vary greatly in this other respect. There are limitations which do not adversely affect a person moved by the passion for success, wealth, or prestige. Indeed it may well be that, for example, certain sensitivities which enlarge a person's capacity for enrichment and appreciation are positively detrimental to the pursuit of standard goals. If a person's freedom is conceived of as a function of the power to appreciate or respond in a significant way in any domain which can serve the person's interests or create new ones by enhancing his perceptual powers, knowledge, sensitivity, and insight, the notion is more wide-ranging than common freedom. It is a romantic idea in its identification of an increase in freedom with an expansion of an individual's capacity for zestful and varied living, not just by the removal of social barriers, but by the elimination of ignorance, individual fears, neurotic blocks, and habits designed to promote security and reinforce stagnant modes of response, as well, of course, as the development of appropriate skills and sensitivities. Although it is coextensive neither with mental health nor happiness, it is rich enough to sustain a conception of a central human ideal.

Again, a crucial difficulty in the clarification of this ideal concerns limits one might wish to impose on the value attached to certain improvements. A person who can discriminate among a vast number of beers may be far more narrow, other things being equal, than one who can discriminate among subtly different human emotions. The relation among capacities and sensitivities is, of course, important in this regard. In fact, some people are 'too' sensitive in certain ways and find their lives are hampered and their freedom in general reduced by the havoc caused by a particular sensitivity. It is clear that value judgments enter in, although it may be that these judgments concern limits *upon* freedom and do not enter directly into the analysis of freedom. Certain abilities are more valuable than others, not because they make you more (or less) free, but rather because the enjoyment of certain freedoms is less trivial than the enjoyment of others. It is preferable to be a discriminating listener of fine music or viewer of fine paintings than a connoisseur of squids (for eating).

Notions such as these play a small role in the concern of the incompatibilist. His focus is upon a particular action of an agent, not a general feature of the agent. Determination of the action is alleged to remove a feature – power is the one we are currently considering – the presence of which would normally permit us to revise our estimation of the moral worth of the individual in light of the action.

TWO NOTIONS OF POWER

Before spending more time on the concept of power, we would be well advised, in light of our qualified endorsement of Frankfurt's view that the absence of the power to do otherwise is not an automatic ground of exemption from moral responsibility, to consider the relevance of power in this context.

We have advanced the position that an agent whose action, A, is determined is morally responsible for A even if the incompatibilist is correct in his belief that the determining conditions render it necessary that he do A in a sense which implies his incapacity in relation to any action contrary to A so long as he fails to exert sufficient effort to refrain from doing A, where he is able to exert this effort and is unaware that the effort would be futile. We have not, however, established this position even if we have successfully defended the converse, to wit, that maximal effort to prevent A exonerates an agent from moral responsibility for A.

If power is a crucial element in the incompatibilist's case, he must analyze the notion so that it is distinct from the notion embodied in the claim that a counterfactual intervener renders an agent impotent. Recall the case of Tudor who kills because he wants to, although a counterfactual intervener renders the action, but not any effort Tudor might have expended to prevent the action, unavoidable. We concluded that the failure to attempt to desist renders Tudor morally responsible and the incompatibilist might agree unless the killing turns out to have been determined. Hence if the fact of determination matters because it implies that Tudor lacks the power to have refrained from the killing, we must acknowledge two senses of 'power'. For it is true independently of the fact of determination that he lacks the power to have refrained from killing (because of the counterfactual intervener) in a sense which still permits us to regard him as morally responsible.[1]

Thus, a condition of adequacy on an indeterministic analysis of power is that it permits these two distinct notions.

COMPATIBILIST ANALYSES OF POWER

Compatibilists have advanced analyses of power, the so-called hypothetical analyses, designed to permit judgments that an agent had the power to perform an action he failed to perform in a sense which permits one to regard him as morally responsible for the act he did perform, even if determinism is true.

There are, to be sure, senses of 'power', 'can', and 'ability' which apply in a deterministic world. The can of opportunity, exemplified in 'He could have killed that pitch, if only he knew how to hit', is one such sense. But since the agent is not morally responsible for his failure by virtue of his not possessing the relevant ability, the incompatibilist need not be perturbed by the existence of such compatibilist readings, plausible as they are, of uses of terms in this family. He would be disturbed only if the compatibilist produced an analysis of power which does permit pertinent judgments of moral responsibility.

Since Harry is an instance of the law of falling bodies, to take the clearest sort of case, he lacks the power to reverse direction in a responsibility-absolving sense. What, according to the compatibilist, does he lack?

Perhaps his impotence is grounded in the fact that any effort of his would fail. One of the merits of this suggestion is that it limits power to agents, i.e., beings who exert effort (even though, to be sure, inanimate objects have powers in a different sense.) Another merit of this analysis is its coherence with the compatibilist insistence that certain conditions of an action A are, and some are not, conditions of the power to do A. An intact nervous system is, but a desire to do A is not, a condition of the power to do A. Though I was not motivated to try to do A, I could have done A because I would have had I tried.

(It is evident why the compatibilist needs a condition which is of A, but not of the power to do A. Under determinism, but not indeterminism, a type of event always occurs if all its conditions are present. If action A fails to occur, therefore, a condition of its occurrence is absent. If all conditions of A are conditions of the power to do A, a condition of the power to do A is, therefore, also absent. Thus, under determinism, we lack the power to do that which we do not do. The compatibilist must, therefore, seek a condition which is a condition not of power, but rather of its exercise.)

The analysis is, however, subject to many difficulties, a number of which were cited by Chisholm.[2] Chisholm concluded that these objections can be surmounted by the following analysis of power in terms of effort:

'P could have done *a*' just in case '($\exists b$) (P could have tried to do *b* and, if P had, he would have done *a*)'.

Chisholm was concerned to note how this analysis fails to reduce 'can' to 'will, if' since 'can' appears again in the analysis. The appearance of 'can' in the analysans is a significant one, he argued, because there are actions a person cannot even try to do.

To deal with this familiar problem, Davidson replaces efforts with desires and beliefs because, as states rather than actions, one cannot ask whether one could have done them.[3]

One might object as follows. If I can deny that Jones could have done A because, although he would have done A had he tried to do B, he could not have tried to do B, I can just as plausibly deny that Jones could have done A because, although he would have done A had he wanted to do B, he could not have wanted to do B, i.e., he could not have been in the state of wanting to do B. In fact it is usually more plausible to deny that a person can have a certain desire he does not have than to deny that a person can try to do something he in fact does not try to do. We can try to do most things.

But a convincing rebuttal to this line of argument can be made. Although we regard the inability to try to do A (or, more carefully, the inability to try to do something such that if one tries to do it, one does A) as conclusive grounds for the conclusion that one cannot do A, one does not regard the impossibility of having the desire to do A as even a weak reason for believing one cannot do A. The reason is simple. One can do A without having the desire to do A (as an antecedent state), whereas one cannot do A if one cannot try to do anything B such that if one tries to do B, one does A. So one is not incapacitated by the absence of a desire to do A, though, of course, it may be much harder to do something one does not want to do.[4]

Ultimately, however, Davidson confronts what he concludes is an insurmountable obstacle to a causal analysis of 'P is free to do *a*'. The proposed analysis, 'P would do *a* intentionally if he had attitudes that rationalize his doing *a*', read causally, is inadequate, Davidson says, because P may have attitudes that rationalize his doing *a* and which cause him to do *a*, yet *a* would not be done intentionally. There are, as Chisholm, Taylor, Goldman and others have pointed out, wayward causal chains. In the normal case, desires and beliefs lead to intentional action; but they can also lead to the desired action where the latter is, however, unintentional. Chisholm's case will do for illustration. A young man wants to kill his uncle in order to inherit his uncle's money. This state unnerves him so much that he decides to go for a drive to make himself calmer. He unintentionally runs over and kills his uncle while driving. In the literature, several proposals to characterize the difference between normal and wayward causal chains have been advanced. Davidson, however, cannot see how the distinction can be satisfactorily defined. He agrees with Goldman that the best we can do is wait to see if a genuine law linking desires and beliefs to intentional action can be produced. The difference between normal (Goldman uses the term 'characteristic') and wayward causal chains will only be specifiable empirically.

Though we therefore cannot produce the right hypothetical statement now and cannot, consequently, advance a satisfactory analysis of 'P is free to do *a*' which would establish the truth of compatibilism, incompatibilism does not follow. The failure to produce an analysis of freedom does not preclude the existence of laws of freedom. Even if determinism is true, we are free when our intentional actions are caused in the normal way by the attitudes that rationalize those actions.

Now, if one means by a causal analysis of freedom a statement of the sufficient condition of intentional action, Davidson is certainly right in saying that we cannot now provide such an analysis. But we can formulate a statement that we might call a causal analysis of freedom along the lines of this proposal: P is free to do *a* if there is a set of conditions *c* and a law *l* according to which people under conditions *c* do *a* intentionally if they have attitudes that rationalize the doing of *a* and P is under *c*. The analysis enables us to say of P, who is under *c* and who does *a* intentionally because he has attitudes that rationalize the doing of *a*, that he does *a* freely, and also enables us to say of Q, who does not do *a* because he does not have an attitude that would rationalize the doing of *a*, but is under condition *c*, that he is free to do *a*.

The nephew, while driving, has an attitude that rationalizes an action of the type 'killing my uncle'. Suppose, to change the case, that he had noticed a man crossing the street and, in his unnerved state, intentionally swerved in order to hit this man. He kills this man, and one may even say, if at the time the nephew's impulses were murderous, that he killed this man intentionally. Now, even if it turns out that the man is, unbeknownst to the nephew, his uncle, we need not say, in virtue of the intensional nature of intentionality, that he killed his uncle intentionally. So the desire to kill his uncle caused him to kill a man intentionally who was his uncle, but did not cause him to kill his uncle intentionally. According to an analysis I have defended elsewhere,[5] the nephew failed to kill his uncle intentionally because his (token) action was not *guided* by the belief that he was killing his uncle.[6]

Of course, the act of killing the man is free if the nephew did that, as he might have in the revised case, out of the desire to kill the man. The point is that the causal analysis of freedom requires that the content of the attitude and the description of the action under which it is intentional coincide.

DESIRE AND ABILITY

Since Davidson does not produce an analysis of freedom, contenting himself with the observation that the freedom to act may in any case be a causal power, he brushes aside Lehrer's general objection to hypothetical analyses of freedom as irrelevant to his, i.e., Davidson's project. But we have cast Davidson's views into the form of an analysis and cannot so easily brush aside this objection. Moreover, Lehrer's objection applies even to the claim that the analysis is just sufficient, not both necessary and sufficient, for freedom.

The objection, succinctly put, is that the freedom to do B cannot be constituted by the truth of 'If D, then B', no matter what D is, since, where D does not obtain, it may turn out to be a necessary condition of the very ability to do B. Applied to the analysis above, in the case where P fails to have an attitude that would rationalize the doing of B, we want to say that P is free to do B (assuming, of course, that C obtains); but this will not be so if the pro-attitude towards B is a necessary condition of the very ability to do B.

We said earlier that the absence of a desire to do A does not affect one's ability to do A. This is not true with respect to other necessary conditions of action. If this is right, we have a rebuttal of Lehrer and a defense of the use of the concept of desire in the analysis of freedom.

One obvious basis for a distinction between desire and an intact neuromusculature, for example, is that people occasionally raise their arms (intentionally) when they do not want to do so, but never raise their arms (intentionally) if, say, their muscles are (sufficiently) damaged.

But might I not be wrong as many philosophers suppose? Even if it is not conceptually necessary for the doing of A intentionally that I want to do A, could we not discover that it is empirically 'necessary'? All apparent cases of unmotivated action would be just that – apparent. There is always a law linking the act to an antecedent and independently ascertainable pro-attitude of some sort or another. On this proposal, if determinism is true, then all conditions of acting would also be conditions of the ability to act.

But the distinction between ability and its exercise is fundamental. Sartre is one of the few philosophers who has denied that a person's potentialities fail to be exhausted by his performances.[7] A person is the sum of his actions. He is not entitled to bemoan his fate by reflecting on all that he might have been. He was all that he might have been. What is so interesting is that Sartre's position is based on a radical anti-determinism. His rejection of unactualized potentiality is based on a rejection of human nature, i.e., a rejection of any structure beyond the sum of one's actions that would of necessity narrow the limits of human freedom.

Why should we give up such a fundamental distinction if, looking at things from a vantage point diametrically opposed to that of Sartre's, determinism is true? The argument must be that we lack the power to do what we do not do because it is necessary that we act in the way that we do. This key belief cannot be ignored by compatibilists; but it so often is. The compatibilist defense is necessarily incomplete if it fails to address this issue.

The difference between a failure to act because one is paralyzed and a failure to act because one does not want to appears to be so great that appeal to it is very powerful. If it turns out that there is both a law that people with damaged muscles do not raise their arms and that people who do not want to do A do not do A, we are not yet obliged to obliterate the distinction. But if finally it follows that in either case, the person must act in the way he does act and, therefore, that he cannot do otherwise, the difference between the two cases becomes minimal.[8]

But if the incompatibilist invokes this consideration, he would appear to be reverting to a primitive notion of necessity linking cause to effect or antecedent of law to consequent of law in some way we had hoped the concept of power might clarify.

Even if it is not possible to prove that desire in some relevant sense is not a condition of ability, it is clear that there is a concept of desire under which we sometimes act not from desire or, for that matter, any pro-attitude, including a sense of duty. Given that philosophers disagree about whether our *actual* concept of desire, assuming controversially that there is but one, requires the supposition that action is not possible without it, it is difficult to deny that we can formulate a viable and recognizable concept of desire, one which is not clearly at variance from ordinary usage, that accords with the principle that actions sometimes arise not from desire.

I would even go so far as to say that the concept of action intended in the preceding paragraph incorporates intentional as well as nonintentional instances. I have elsewhere defended the view that the concept of intentional action is essentially the concept of action guided by belief, a view which relegates the role of desire to the role of a state which is possibly an explanation of some (or all) intentional action.[9] But the plausibility of the view that *all* (intentional) action is action performed out of desire derives, I believe, from the idea that the concept of desire is in some way conceptually intertwined with that of intentional action. The severing of that connection renders the view a sweeping empirical hypothesis very unlikely to be true, especially when we have some leeway here in relation to the fine tuning of the concept.

So we have now forced the conclusion a compatibilist needs, to wit, that desire is not a condition of ability. And we can still insist that desire always issues in action under certain (unknown) conditions C. Moreover, we also have a response to the classical objection that a hypothetical analysis in terms of desire cannot be adequate because it may be impossible for the agent to acquire the pertinent desire. This possibility is not required because the agent can act in the required way without it.[10]

Specifically, Jones, who does not want to do A, is free (has the power) to do A if (but only if) Jones is in a type of state C such that if Jones were to desire to do A, then, in accordance with a law linking state C and the desire to do A, Jones would do A (intentionally). The absence of the desire to do A does not render Jones incapable of doing A, although it is a partial explanation of why he does not do A. The explanation is in fact partial just because he has done A-type actions in the past in spite of the absence of a desire to do so. Several clarificatory remarks are in order.

According to this analysis, state C combined with a desire to do A suffices for the action A. State C would be a composite state and one may wish to prune it down to the intrinsic state which may either be identified with the ability to do A or is at best a sufficient condition of that ability. For example, I may want to point to middle C on the piano, but am musically ignorant. If state C is everything but desire, it would have to include relevant true beliefs (or knowledge). But in *one* sense of 'ability' I can (am physically able to) point to middle C. A similar result obtains when we consider, as analogous to knowledge, opportunity. I may want to point to middle C on my Bechstein, but am prevented from so doing, not by musical ignorance, but rather by the unavailability of my Bechstein. A difference between knowledge and opportunity, however, is that, if C is supposed to be an intrinsic state of the person, it cannot include opportunity-conditions in spite of the fact that their absence renders a person incapable of performing the relevant action. We ought, therefore, to revise the analysis so that the sufficient condition of action A includes state C, the desire to do A, and opportunity-conditions.

In addition to physical capacity and knowledge, C would also contain various psychological states. The failure to do A may be due, not to a lack of physical capacity, knowledge, or opportunity, but rather to the presence of other desires, fear, moral reservations, memory lapses, beliefs of a certain sort, and the like.

With respect to the concept of ability as such, it is clear that different concepts are appropriate in different contexts. Sometimes, physical ability is the relevant notion. Sometimes, we include other elements of the C-state (as in 'That musical ignoramus cannot point to middle C') and sometimes we include features of the environment, i.e., opportunity-conditions (as in 'You can't play golf without clubs'). This much is beyond dispute.

We may wonder about the psychological components of the C-state. Evidently, we may be able to establish empirically that the presence of a fear is an obstacle the agent can overcome (he has, in similar circumstances, acted in spite of the presence of this fear in the same degree of severity). But, like desire, it may be difficult to ascertain whether a factor is causally relevant to the action or a necessary condition of the very ability to perform the action. It is sufficient for my purposes that the desire to do A can be shown not to be a necessary condition of A, regardless of whether or not similar demonstrations exist for other psychological factors.

A problem arises if we stipulate that the C-state be independent of the desire to do A. For counterexamples to the analysis can then be constructed in which a person cannot do A because he is in a state S he would not be in if he wanted to do A. A person who knows the Gettysburg Address may be unable to recite it now because he is asleep. But he would recite it if he wanted to because if he wanted to, he would not be asleep. If the C-state must be independent of desire, it cannot include the waking state, and a person sound asleep might consequently be in the C-state. Thus we have the unacceptable result that, on our account it could turn out that this person has the ability to recite the Gettysburg Address now.

Although the desire implies that the individual is not asleep, other such implications of desire are associated with different interpretations. I cannot raise my arm with this heavy stone resting on top of it. But I can raise my arm because, if I want to raise my arm, I will remove this stone and do so. So here too there is a barrier to an action which would not be present if the agent wanted to perform the action. But we affirm one person's ability *then* to raise his arm and deny the other person's ability *then* to recite the Gettysburg Address. Clearly the reason is that the desire to raise one's arm *causes* the agent to remove the barrier, whereas the desire to recite the Gettysburg Address *presupposes* that one is awake.

If the distinction between effects and presuppositions were clear, we could simply stipulate that the C-state contains all presuppositions of desire such as consciousness, adequate linguistic ability, and a sufficiently mature emotional system. Although I do not suppose that the distinction is clear, it strikes me as clear enough to suggest that a critic of conditional analyses of ability would be foolish to pin his hopes on its inherent unclarity. Wanting to recite the Gettysburg Address does not cause a person to be awake, a speaker of some natural language, and an individual familiar with anticipation and frustration. We will thus stipulate that the C-state incorporate relevant presuppositions of the desire in question.

Although the account may be criticized as vague, since the incompatibilist *we* are addressing is just as concerned about intentional theories of human behavior as he is about mechanistic theories, he would object to the basic project of formulating a hypothetical account of power along these lines.

To return to the notion of desire itself, we may render it more precise in several ways. We may, for example, consider all those cases in which in the past Jones did A because he was coerced, because he believed it to be his duty, or 'for no reason at all,' as instances in which Jones did not want to do A. So the complete explanation of why Jones did not in the present case do A might be that he did not desire to do A and that he did not believe it to be his duty and that he was not coerced into doing A and that he was not in the state he is in when he reports that he is doing A 'for no reason at all.'

Now, if determinism is true, there is a deterministic account of Jones' failure to do A. Suppose it is constituted roughly by the absence of any of these aforementioned factors, e.g., the desire to do A, the belief that A is his duty, etc. Call this conjunction of absences 'R'. Although Jones does A at times he does not want to do A, he never does A in the presence of R, i.e., in the absence of any possible cause of A. Yet the compatibilist wants to say that, given the opportunity, Jones can, in virtue of C, do A. If so, he must also say that R does not abolish the power to do A, but cannot appeal to the fact that A sometimes occurs in the absence of R. Thus, the fact that A sometimes occurs in the absence of a desire to do A is, according to the incompatibilist, inconclusive. He would want to argue that R, not the absence of desire, renders Jones impotent.

But this just brings us back to the familiar incompatibilist refrain. He wants to say that the absence of any empirically necessary condition of A renders a person incapable of doing A, whereas the compatibilist believes that there are some exceptions to this general principle, including even the case in which a person can do A in the presence of R, i.e., in the absence of any reason or motive, – any desire, sense of duty, or whim. Although we have not, therefore, refuted the incompatibilist, we have at least rebutted Lehrer's argument. The analysis of the ability to do A in terms of doing A if one desires to does not falter on the grounds that a desire to do A is a necessary condition of the very ability to do A.

POWER AND FREEDOM

A moral emerges. Why should a compatibilist be constrained to surrender his conviction that not all necessary conditions of action are necessary conditions of the power to perform that action? A thesis of this book is that only a necessitarian interpretation according to which any nomically sufficient condition of a certain outcome necessitates that outcome can serve as even a prima facie plausible premise of the anti-compatibilist conviction narrowing one's power over alternative outcomes to that determined one.

The term 'prima facie' is apt here for reasons provided earlier. How can the nature of necessitation matter unless it has a bearing on the nature of the induced impotence? For if 'power' is univocal, both the agent of a determined action as well as the agent of an undetermined (or self-determined) action working under the omniscient eye of a counterfactual intervener are, according to the incompatibilist, impotent in the same sense. But if the former person is not, and the latter is, morally responsible, impotence is irrelevant. Thus, the incompatibilist ought to rest his case on a 'direct' inference from deterministic necessitation to the absence of responsibility.

But is the compatibilist analysis of power given above, which permits us easily to absolve a person of responsibility for failing to reverse direction as he falls – the pertinent desire would be inefficacious – a cogent one? It is evident that the compatibilist faces a similar problem. An agent who acts out of the desire to do so may be acting freely. But if a counterfactual intervener is present, the agent is not free to act otherwise. If he had wanted to do otherwise, he would have been unable to do so. Yet if, again, this impotence is irrelevant to moral responsibility, the compatibilist should look upon his account as permitting a direct inference from acting freely to being morally responsible for the action. Power in the sense of control over outcomes turns out again not to play a crucial role. To be sure, the compatibilist is then obliged to produce an account of free action (as opposed to the freedom to do otherwise) according to which relevant distinctions, e.g., between compulsive or addictive or psychotic behaviors and their opposites, do not hinge on the determined or undetermined nature of the action. This project was partially undertaken in the preceding chapter (and will be continued in chapter 10). To be more specific, all he insists upon is that in a deterministic world, it does not follow that *every* action falls under one of these specific grounds of exoneration. The incompatibilist would fall back on a competing account of freedom resting on the principle that determination *per se* precludes freedom because determination implies necessity. But, as I have said, this issue must anyway be addressed.

POWER AND POSSIBILITY

Many philosophers have rejected what they regard as a simplistic conception of human freedom as indetermination.[11] They reject the idea that freedom is constituted by chance or randomness or, as it has historically been called, the liberty of indifference. The mere fact that my behavior has no sufficient condition, like perhaps certain behavior of electrons, cannot fully capture the idea of power or control that is implicit in the notion of freedom. Otherwise, why not say that an electron is as free as a human being who deliberately sets out to perform an action he has elected to perform?

This rejection of the analysis of human freedom in terms of the liberty of indifference lies behind the insistence, by Ayers[12] and others, upon the distinction between the possibility for a person to do something and the possibility that he will do it. But it is not too difficult to see what an incompatibilist would say here. He can concede the distinction and yet insist that the possibility for a person to do something depends upon its being possible that it be done. Of course, once the distinction is granted, this incompatibilist rebuttal would require defense, and he would then bring forth the familiar contention that the factual impossiblity of an action renders an agent impotent to perform it.

So the incompatibilist can certainly accommodate the distinction between 'possible that' and possible for'. We see also that he rests his case concerning powers on a link between determination and necessity. So even if he is induced to drop the concept of power from his formulation, we must address the formulation that moves from the presence of necessity directly to the absence of moral responsibility.

MORAL CONSIDERATIONS

Compatibilists have attempted to undermine the incompatibilist argument by charging it with a failure to acknowledge the relevance of moral considerations. Of course, the incompatibilist is clearly making a moral judgment by condemning the use of facets of a determined action in a reappraisal of someone's moral worth. But he fails to see, on the account now to be rendered, that his premise, say that the person could not have done otherwise or lacked the power to do otherwise, is itself value-laden in a way which permits it *sometimes* to be false in spite of the determined character of the action.

The idea, presented in a paper of Arnold Kaufman's,[13] is that usually, but certainly not always, when we say 'He could not have done otherwise', we are more or less saying something like 'It would be unreasonable to demand (retrospectively) the expenditure of energy (or the creation of fear or conflict or whatever) that would have been required for him to have done it'. Often, therefore, 'He could have done otherwise' expresses a proposition on which moral and valuational matters do bear. When a task becomes so difficult for someone, and there are no powerful reasons to insist that it be done, we allow the sentence 'He cannot do it' to pass unchallenged.

If this is right, we may expect to find cases of determined actions where valuational considerations permit us to say 'He could have done otherwise'. Compatibilism is vindicated.

Elsewhere, I argued that the incompatibilist can rebut this charge by denying the relevance of value considerations in this context.[14] The conclusion reached there is that the incompatibilist clearly intends and compatibilists must ultimately concede that the relevant sense of 'can' in these contexts is not moral or valuational and that in general value considerations do not bear on the premises of the incompatibilist argument.

If reflections on power will not advance the discussion, it behooves us to seek elsewhere for a handle which will help us to evaluate the incompatibilist point of view.

7

Contingent necessity

TYPES OF NECESSITY

A central assumption of this book is that the incompatibilist needs the assumption that a law of nature which subsumes a human action and which is the basis of the belief that the occurrence of that action is necessary is itself necessary. Although laws are not logically necessary, many regard them as stronger than statements of factual necessity. To accommodate the feeling that the factual necessity ($\boxed{f}$) of '(The moon is made of green cheese ⊃ Nothing travels faster than the speed of light)' does not suffice for counting this a law, systems of relative necessity or entailment, in both its logical and factual forms, have been developed.[1] The sentence does not express a law because its antecedent does not entail (in this case factually, symbolized from here on as '$\overrightarrow{f}$'), in a sense which requires explication, its consequent.

Now, in order for an action A to be determined, it must be the case that a sentence whose truth entails the existence of A^2 follows logically from a law or conjunction of laws L together with a conjunction of sentences S which state initial conditions.[3] Although S may include logically necessary sentences, the conjunction is logically contingent. An important feature of the incompatibilist's case is that S need not be factually necessary. Even if a person's heredity and environment are undetermined and, therefore, factually contingent, if they determine a certain outcome, say the possession of a certain character trait C, then C is necessitated.

Intuitive appeal for the latter is convincing. If having a mother with character trait B necessitates the development of character trait C in her child, how can it matter whether B was itself necessitated or, perhaps, a free choice of the mother? If the placement of sugar in water necessitates its dissolution, it matters not whether the person was constrained to place the sugar in water or did so freely.

The incompatibilist appears to accept, therefore, the following rule:

From p and $p\overrightarrow{f}q$, infer $\boxed{f}q$ (FNC)

Neither FNC nor the rule 'From p and $\boxed{f}(p \supset q)$, infer $\boxed{f}q$' are, however, acceptable on the conventional semantic interpretation of '$\boxed{f}$' as 'true in all factually possible worlds'. For even if p and $p\overrightarrow{f}q$ are true (in the actual world), q is false in those factually possible worlds in which p is false (and in which no other 'sufficient condition' of q is present). FNC must, therefore, be rejected.[4] Some believe that the incompatibilist has illicitly transferred the factual necessity of $p\supset q$ or the logical necessity of $(p \cdot p\supset q)\supset q$ to q. In other words, he has fallaciously argued that q is necessary because p (factually) necessitates q or because $(p \cdot p\supset q)$ logically necessitates q, transferring the necessity of a relation to an absolute necessity of one of the terms of that relation.

Two courses of action are open to the incompatibilist. The route taken by many recent advocates is the retention of a single notion of (nonlogical) necessity combined with the acknowledgement that both p and $(p\supset q)$ must be necessary in this sense. Once it is required that p, too, be true in all relevantly possible worlds, the inference succeeds.

Now the incompatibilist would appear to have no problems if determinism is true. For he is then guaranteed that the occurrence of the initial conditions is necessary and may accordingly proceed from there to draw the lamentable conclusion about human freedom. But an incompatibilist believes that a particular human action is necessary if it is determined regardless of whether determinism is true or not. One must here reiterate the irrelevance of the modal status of the initial conditions. What matters to the incompatibilist is their actuality for *that* determines and thereby necessitates the outcome.

UNALTERABILITY

A partial response to the objection that the incompatibilist has committed a modal fallacy can be discerned in the selection of the necessity operator by the advocates of this alternative, e.g., van Inwagen.[5] The basic idea is that the initial conditions are, at some point prior to the action, unalterable by the agent, i.e., such that no (possible) choice of the agent has a bearing on them. We can be assured that the initial conditions have this sort of necessity even if determinism is not true. In fact, we can be assured that they are necessary in this sense (call it 'NC') even if they are not determined! The past is unalterable even if it includes absolutely free acts (acts which were then free in an indeterministic sense).

Since laws of nature are also not alterable by human choice, they are necessary in the same sense as initial conditions, and we have a perfectly respectable scheme of inference in which 'NC' behaves in the relevant respects like other necessity operators.

$$\left[\begin{array}{l} \text{NC } p \\ \underline{\text{NC } (p \supset q)} \\ \text{NC } q \end{array} \right.$$

The position has interesting advantages. We are no longer saddled with a primitive notion of necessity whose links to freedom and moral responsibility are, in virtue of that very primitiveness, obscure. If necessity *is* unalterability by choice, further incompatibilist moves to exemption from responsibility and the like are not obviously untenable and at least open to rational explanation. The hope is that, even if laws of nature are physically necessary in a somewhat different sense, we can, from the perspective of the controversy between compatibilists and incompatibilists, ignore this sense. All we need to know about laws of nature is their immunity to change from human intervention.

Slote has taken issue with the new incompatibilism by challenging the validity of the argument.[6] His challenge is based on doubts concerning properties the operator must possess in order for the argument to succeed. 'NC', like logical and metaphysical necessity, must be both agglomerative (NC(p), NC(q), ∴ NC($p \cdot q$) and closed under logical implication (NC(p), $p \vdash q$, ∴ NC(q)). Citing examples of modalities which lack these properties, Slote raises the possibility that 'NC' lacks these properties as well. His most compelling illustration is nonaccidentality. Although it is nonaccidental that Jules is at the bank at 11 a.m. (his employer arranged it) and nonaccidental that Jim is at the bank at the same time (his employer also planned that he be there), it is an accident that these old friends are simultaneously present and renew their acquaintance in the bank (no one having planned their simultaneous presence). Nor is nonaccidentality closed under logical implication for it may be an accident that Jim is alive at 11 a.m. (he luckily and accidentally avoided being struck by a falling safe as he made his way to the bank), even though his being alive follows from his nonaccidental (living) presence in the bank at 11 a.m. If NC were like 'it is nonaccidental that' we would be able to move neither from 'NC(p)' and 'NC($p{\supset}q$)' to 'NC($p \cdot (p \supset q)$)', nor from there to 'NC(q)'.

So the question turns on the likelihood that 'NC' is like 'nonaccidentality'. Since Slote finds that the explanation that nonaccidentality and other operators lack the features of agglomeration and closure is in all cases based on a special sort of relativity he calls selectivity, his case would be strengthened greatly by the discovery that 'NC' is similarly selective. In the case of nonaccidentality the selected feature is a plan-requirement such that, although p and q are each planned, no one plans both, and although p entails r, r is not planned (even if it is presupposed by the plan that p). Finally, we do indeed find that 'NC' or 'unavoidability' is selective insofar as the remote initial conditions p are not alterable by our *current* desires and abilities. No ability or desire we now possess can have any bearing on the truth of p, can, that is, make p false. And even if the same limitation applies to us in relation to laws of nature, it does not follow that we are similarly impotent in regards to our future actions. Under nonfatalistic determinism, our future actions do vary as a function of our present desires and abilities. How I will behave tomorrow depends on my present desires and abilities, although changes in the latter will leave the past untouched.

The argument is ingenious and provocative, yet, as Slote is the first to note, inconclusive. It hinges on the assumption that 'NC' is selective in a way which requires the abandonment of agglomeration and closure and that assumption, apparently rendered plausible, is certainly open to challenge. Although I agree with Slote that the incompatibilist case is, in the end, weak, I believe that this particular onslaught can be repelled.

It is certainly true that my current desires and abilities are causally efficacious *only* in a forward direction and that I might bring it about that q, but not bring it about that p (or that $p \supset q$). We must, however, remember that 'NC' means 'it is *un*alterable by choice that' or 'no one has the power to *falsify*'. It would beg the question against incompatibilism to suppose that, just because my wanting to do A will bring it about that I do A that it is, therefore, in my power *not* to do A. The incompatibilist will claim that, in virtue of the existence of a deterministic account of A, it is not in my power to refrain from doing A and it would beg the question against this doctrine to suppose that the causal efficacy of my desire (or ability) in relation to the action A (the truth of q) entails '$-NC(q)$'. It may be that I make q true even if I cannot make it false. For the incompatibilist I make q true in the counterfactual sense that it would be false were my desires and abilities different (in the sense that a miraculous change now in my desires and abilities would leave the truth of p unaffected). But for the incompatibilist this counterfactual does not automatically provide me with a power to make q false because I may be unable to change my present desires and abilities accordingly.

In fact the incompatibilist can avoid an engagement with the opposition on this last point by restricting his example to a *clear* case of inability to change current desires and abilities. He need not argue that we never can make such a change under determinism. For even if a person has taken all steps in his power to change and has failed, it is still true that his actual desires are efficacious. We might *all* agree that the alcoholic who has wholeheartedly entered every form of therapy he has learned about, only to revert, cannot make false 'He seeks alcohol tomorrow' in spite of the fact that the truth of the sentence depends on his current desires.

To put it simply, Slote is talking about the wrong operator. What he says is true of 'I cause it to be the case (true) that', not 'I can falsify'.

Now it is still true that there is an asymmetry insofar as my inability to falsify p or $p \supset q$ rests on considerations inapplicable to q. I cannot falsify p because it has already been made true and I cannot falsify $p \supset q$ because it is a law of nature. Neither reason, of course, applies to q. But there would appear to be no special difficulty about the existence of different grounds of unalterability. It is not as if we are necessarily equivocating on 'unalterability' itself. The incompatibilist must believe that, just as pastness and the possession of a nomic status are sufficient grounds of unalterability in the case of the premises, so determination is a distinct ground of unalterability for the conclusion.

But are we not then supposing the necessity of laws? If unalterability is not grounded in necessity, what reason would we have to accept the conditional premise as unalterable?

On the other hand, is it not plausible to say that, necessity aside, a generalization cannot be a law if it is alterable by choice? Perhaps. But note first that the converse is not the case and that Slote is, therefore, right when he denies that unalterability implies necessity.[7] There are, for example, many cosmic accidents not within the power of human beings to alter. I do not choose that there be exactly 41 types of metals on earth; but it is not a law that there are this many in spite of (1) the fact that I cannot alter the situation and (2) the fact that I can do nothing about this is itself grounded in laws.

There would therefore, be valid instances of the incompatibilist's argument form (call them I-type arguments) which do not contain nomic-based premises (e.g., one whose conditional is 'If R is a rock 10 meters from the North Pole of the only planet of the star Rigel, R weighs exactly 1 ton') and the incompatibilist who thinks that it is crucial that I-type arguments contain or be grounded in laws would be shown to be wrong. What is disturbing about laws is a characteristic they share with non-laws, unalterability by human choice.

But then van Inwagen would appear to be wise to express laws in the incompatibilist argument as '$NC(p \supset q)$', for, even if he supposes that this implies or presupposes the factual necessity of the nomic conditional, if he is incorrect and the regularity theory is right, laws may still be unalterable and this will suffice if anything will to get out the incompatibilist result. The incompatibilist case will be more convincing if it does not rest on a debatable view about the analysis of laws. This new incompatibilist can be more radical than Hume on the metaphysics of necessity. Since there is prior agreement that laws are unalterable, that they set limits upon human capacities, determinism will have the same depressing consequences whether necessitarianism or the regularity theory provides the correct interpretation of laws. Determinism narrows human power to the domain of the actual, even in a world devoid of necessity.

Since this position strikes at the heart of a central thesis of mine, to wit, that the incompatibilist is basically worried about the necessity of laws, I have felt obliged to present it as attractively as I am able. A closer look at the unalterability operator, I believe, will reveal a serious flaw. Van Inwagen defines his operator 'Np' as: p 'and no one has, or ever had, any choice about whether'[8] p. He argues against compatibilist construals along conditional lines of 'Np' such as:

> p and, for every agent x, it is not the case that if x had ever chosen (or were ever to choose) to make it false that p, then x would have made (or would make) it false that p.[9]

A key merit of conditional analyses (for the compatibilist), van Inwagen himself notes, is that they render invalid I-type arguments. Although van Inwagen and I agree about this, its importance to my case makes it prudent for me to defend the point carefully.

Consider an upright contractor, Foster, who cannot deliberately bring himself to build a brothel.

(1) N(Foster does not try (choose) to build a brothel deliberately)

(2) N(Foster does not try (choose) to build a brothel deliberately ⊃ Foster does not build a brothel)

(3) N(Foster does not build a brothel)

A set of consistent assumptions can be found which would make premises true and conclusion false, thereby rendering the argument invalid, where 'N' is given the above conditional interpretation. Foster is so psychologically rigid that, were he to try to put himself in a position in which he is trying to build a brothel, he would fail. We may suppose he has expended enormous energy on psychoanalysis, lecture series on free sex, etc.; yet each time his services are requested, he finds that he cannot bring himself to begin work on a new brothel. Thus, (1) is true, although it might be false were the term 'deliberately' omitted. What I have in mind is a case in which Foster is sufficiently convinced of the desirability of brothel construction, perhaps because he is persuaded that his feelings of moral repugnance are irrational – a vestige of an outmoded world view he has not yet been able to discard on the emotional level, or perhaps because he is tempted by a huge fee. Foster might be able to take steps which will result in his trying to build a brothel, so long as he does not know what he is building. Thus, Foster commits himself to an undertaking which is likely to result in his building a brothel, although he will not know which project he embarks upon is of this nature. We might imagine him making some bizarre arrangements to be duped – he renders it likely that one of his next twenty clients is the town madam who needs larger facilities, but will not know which of his projects she may have contracted – so that, should he be contracted by her, he will build a brothel without trying to build one deliberately (in the relevant sense). In one sense, he has chosen to try to build a brothel, tries to build one, and does so. This is not the ordinary, nonextensional sense of 'tries' which presupposes deliberateness and, therefore, the failure of extensional substitutivity. (Although he is trying to complete the fourth project of the year, he is not trying to complete the brothel ordered by Mme Flora.) The inclusion of 'deliberately' underscores the ordinary reading of 'tries.' Thus (1) is true in spite of the possibility that Foster can try in the above special sense to build a brothel.

Since the antecedent and consequent of (2) are both true, so is the conditional. (2) itself is true on the assumption that Foster's powerful friends, guided by the belief that good and evil should be brought into the world only by agents fully aware of what they are doing, would sabotage any efforts he might expend on such a project, unless Foster was knowingly seeking as his goal the construction of a brothel. If Foster sets out to make the conditional false, he must try to make antecedent true and consequent false. On the basis of our original assumption that Foster cannot try to build a brothel (deliberately), there is no problem about the antecedent. Since it is true, what remains for Foster to do is to falsify the consequent. Now if Foster cannot try to build a brothel, he cannot set out (intentionally and deliberately) to falsify the consequent. But the truth of (2) does not yet follow for Foster can make the consequent false so long as he does *not* try to do so, as we saw above.

Although we must suppose that Foster can try to falsify (2) (for we want to see if his efforts will be successful), we need only suppose the bizarre arrangements described above to insure his failure. Foster's friends will sabotage his efforts at construction under ignorance just because he will not know precisely when he is engaged in this morally significant enterprise. Since Foster does not try deliberately, thereby rendering antecedent true, he cannot falsify the consequent and cannot, therefore, falsify (2).

(3), however, is false for, although Foster cannot try to falsify the contained proposition, if he were to try, he would succeed. His friends would not interfere once they see that Foster is bringing about the relevant result intentionally. Although Foster cannot try deliberately to build a brothel, he *would* succeed *were he to try* deliberately to do so.

A reasonable challenge against this conclusion may be mounted on the basis of the fact that the argument presupposes an arbitrary interpretation of one aspect of 'tries'. Suppose that Foster is not totally immobilized by his psychological state and is otherwise motivated to undertake the project. We suppose, as we have all along, that he possesses the necessary know-how and skills and that the environmental forces are entirely supportive. Thus, if he fails, the explanation is psychological. We imagine him embarking on the project and finding himself so preoccupied with his doubts and uncomfortable about his participation that he commits several key, and ultimately fatal, errors. He mistakenly engages an electrical contractor known for his incompetence; he fails to arrive in time to oversee a key stage in construction, etc. Since the project falls through, then, if our conclusions about (3) are right, it follows that Foster did not try to construct the brothel.

Now a psychological account of Foster's behavior may indeed support the conclusion that he was not 'really' trying, that he was unconsciously sabotaging the whole operation. But suppose instead that there is no support for this interpretation. Why can't we then say that Foster *was* trying to build a brothel, but his emotional state prevented him from succeeding? He may have been doing the best he can under the circumstances.

A failure to achieve one's aims admits of a variety of

explanations: ignorance, lack of relevant skills, a hostile environment, the physical impossibility of the goal, and emotional factors. Why should an explanation in terms of the last item actually imply that the agent was not trying in the first place?

All the above proves is that (3) *might* be true. All *we* have to prove in order to establish the invalidity of the argument is that (3) *might* be false. We may, therefore, safely concede the point about 'tries' and the conclusion that the Foster just described is trying and failing. But *our* Foster, the one who shows the argument to be invalid, is a stranger character. Though he is, in actuality, totally immobilized, he would discard *all* his psychological encumbrances were he to take *any* steps correctly described as 'trying deliberately to build a brothel'. Under these hypothetical circumstances, and in light of his own skills, a friendly environment (including the cooperation of those observant friends), he would forge ahead to success.

It is crucial to van Inwagen's case, then, that conditional analyses of 'N' be rejected and I do not want to take issue in general with his grounds for rejection. I do contend, however, that we are not entitled to suppose a stronger nonconditional (categorical) interpretation of 'N' for the laws (or the conditionals grounded in laws). Van Inwagen's case rests upon the plausible view that laws of nature are unalterable by choice, that they determine the limits of human ability. We are sympathetic with this position even if it is extended to psychological laws for, we suspect, they too are surely more than de facto true generalizations with the systemic features cited by regularity theorists as nomic-making.

Van Inwagen notes that the intuitive plausibility of the above rests on the conceptual link between laws and unalterability. But this link establishes only that no result of any human effort is the violation or alteration of a law of nature. But that we cannot alter a law of nature does not obviously imply that we cannot try to do so. The unalterability of laws is no restriction on our choices, only on the outcome of those choices. To be sure, we cannot describe what we are doing as choosing to violate a law. But we can choose to alter a state of affairs in ignorance of the fact that the state is grounded in the laws of nature. A deterministic account includes laws, not the concept of law, and for some particular law, I can choose to alter it, though I am bound to fail.

Notice that I am not now defending a general conditional analysis of ability. I am rather saying that, in the special context of laws or conditionals grounded thereon, we have no right to suppose that our inability with respect to their alteration is not fully analyzable conditionally. But on that analysis, the argument fails.

Van Inwagen might try to salvage the argument by adding the following disjunct to the definition of 'Np':

or no one can choose to make it false that p.

(Call the new operator 'N^2p'.)

Since 'N^1p' (the original operator) entails 'N^2p', premises (1) and (2) remain true. (3) is now true since Foster cannot choose (try) to build a brothel. (It seems clear that van Inwagen should relativize his operators to persons. *Someone* can try to build a brothel. I shall concede that the relativization can go through smoothly.)

'N^2p' is an odd operator to attach to laws. Whereas we may regard a person as incapacitated by the inability to try to do A, in spite of the fact that he would succeed were he to try, we would regard the analogous inability as peculiarly irrelevant in the case of the action type 'falsifying Snell's law'. No person can perform this action; hence, when Mabel and Martha each state an intention to do so, it matters little that Martha is bound and gagged – and, therefore, not trying to falsify Snell's law – whereas Mabel is desperately and futilely trying to interfere with the angle of the refracted ray to bring it about that: $n^a \sin \theta \neq n^b \sin \theta$. Neither Mabel nor Martha can violate Snell's law and Mabel's greater freedom to perform certain actions Martha cannot perform is utterly irrelevant in this context.

Yet, van Inwagen may insist, no challenge to the validity of I-type arguments with N^2 has been offered. True. But my contention, at this stage, has been, not that they are invalid, but that they rest upon the assumption that laws are necessary. In defense of that assumption, I would note first that the alleged validity of I-type arguments with non-laws rests upon ones *with* laws. Although it is not a law of nature that there are exactly 41 metals, my inability to create a new metal rests on laws of nature. Although it is not a law that the rock which happens to be 10 miles from the North Pole of the only planet of the star Rigel weighs exactly 1 ton, my inability to change that (together with the right equipment) rests on laws. The same goes for Martha's inability to try to falsify Snell's law. (In all these cases, the unalterability may not be genuine in that it may be relative to changing knowledge and technical facility. Van Inwagen makes clear that he is concerned only with 'metaphysical' unalterability, the sort that cannot change no matter how advanced our know-how.) And as we have seen, the unalterability of laws of nature is of a conditional sort, of a sort embodied in N^1, too weak to make the incompatibilist case.

The unalterability of laws of nature is grounded in the fact that the antecedent renders the consequent necessary and, *therefore*, immune from human intervention. According to the incompatibilist, whether or not something will submit to my efforts depends upon whether or not there are conditions co-present with my efforts which independently necessitate failure.

Another way of seeing the priority of necessity is to note that propositions would be necessary in a world devoid of people. If, in such a world, sugar happened to fall into water, it would have to dissolve (so long as we suppose this world obeys the same laws which govern our world and that laws are sentences which state factual entailments). It is more natural to suppose that this fact is a reason for the conclusion that no one can alter the matter by choice than to insist that the fact about this world we are reporting is a hypothetical one to the effect that, if there were people in it, none would be able to alter the state of affairs in question.

A shift to N^2 does not avoid necessity if 'she cannot choose' means 'it is necessary that she does not choose'. And what can this be grounded on except the presence of conditions which necessitate (determine by law) that she does not choose?

A de re reading of 'cannot choose' may then be preferred. But we argued at length in the preceding chapter that an incompatibilist believes that determinism drastically reduces our abilities or powers (to do only what we do) *only* because it presents a picture of causal chains, each link necessitating the next.

An essential premise for the incompatibilist, then, one which explains '$NC(p \supset q)$' is '$(p \overrightarrow{f} q)$' or at least '$\boxed{f}(p \supset q)$'. And the idea that the truth of $(p \overrightarrow{f} q)$ renders q necessary (hence unalterable), given only that p is true, suggests again the irrelevance of the modality of p.

The most powerful argument for the conclusion that the modality of p matters arises from reflection on cases in which p has not yet been made true by some event in the world. Suppose that e is an event whose occurrence is entirely under Foster's control such that his bringing it about or preventing it is an absolutely free act, whatever that means, and suppose that F is true if and only if e exists. Thus, Foster controls the truth of F. If it is now July 8, consider the following argument.

F: Foster places sugar in water on July 9 at 3 p.m.

F $\overrightarrow{f}$ D: Foster places sugar in water on July 9 at 3 p.m. $\overrightarrow{f}$ the sugar dissolves on July 9 at 3:01 p.m.

─────────────────────────────────

$\boxed{c}$ D: It is contingently necessary that the sugar dissolves on July 9 at 3:01 p.m.

We have replaced the notion of 'NC' with ' $\boxed{c}$ (it is contingently necessary that)' to reflect the same idea which led us to replace 'NC' with ' $\overrightarrow{f}$ ', namely, that the reason no one can alter the proposition is that it is, in some sense, necessary.

Another difference between contingent necessity and NC, we shall argue, is that all sentences made true by a past event are now (and forever more) NC, but may not be contingently necessary. If there is no deterministic account of the sentence, if the event which made it true was not necessitated, then the sentence is never contingently necessary.

Contingent necessity, like NC and unlike factual or logical necessity, is a function of time. Sentences become contingently necessary very roughly when an empirically sufficient condition of their truth is completed. At a point in time when no sufficient condition of e has yet been realized, and we are supposing this situation to prevail on July 8, F is not contingently necessary.

We may incorporate time into the system by simply adding a time variable to the sentential variable. If t_i = 3 p.m., July 9, we can recast the conclusion of the present argument as ' $\boxed{c} t_i$ D' and consider its validity now, prior to July 9. Notice, of course, that F is not now contingently necessary though, since e will occur, it is (timelessly) true.

Is F *ever* necessary? Once e has occurred and F has been made true, does not F become necessary in virtue of the unalterability of the past, even if it was not necessary prior to e?

We may try to characterize the necessity of F in terms of the same considerations which render any sentence contingently necessary. We have characterized these conditions roughly in terms of the time of completion of the sufficient condition. Thus, $\boxed{c}t_i$ P if there is a sentence O made true by an event completed by t_i such that $O\overrightarrow{f}P$ or at least $\boxed{f}(O{\supset}P)$. There is such a sentence, namely, P itself. For the following is a theorem of a system of contingent necessity.

$$\square(p{\supset}q){\supset}\boxed{f}(p{\supset}q)$$

This theorem follows from one of the modal ordering theorems:

(1) $(p\overrightarrow{f}q){\supset}\boxed{f}(p{\supset}q)$
(2) $\square p{\supset}\boxed{f}p$
(3) $\boxed{f}p{\supset}\boxed{c}p$
(4) $(\exists t)\boxed{c}_t\, p{\supset}p$

The premise which interests us at the moment, (2), along with (3), requires justification.

We certainly wish to expand the system of contingent necessity by introducing the various notions of possibility: logical possibility ('$\Diamond$'), factual possibility ('$\langle\!\!\!\Diamond$'), and contingent possibility ('$\diamondsuit\!\!\!\langle$').

(5) $\Diamond p \equiv -\square-p$
(6) $\langle\!\!\!\Diamond p \equiv -\boxed{f}-p$
(7) $\diamondsuit\!\!\!\langle p \equiv -\boxed{c}-p$

But, given these and their variants, we can derive (2) with the addition of an application of the principle that logical contradictions are not possible in any sense. Let K stand for any contradiction.

(a)	$\square p$	Premise
(b)	$\square-K$	From (a) by theorem of logic and deductive closure of logical necessity
(c)	$-\langle\!\!\!\Diamond K$	Principle
(d)	$\boxed{f}-K$	From (c) by variant of (6)
(e)	$\boxed{f}p$	From (d) by theorem of logic and deductive closure of logical necessity

As for (3), its contrary $\boxed{f}p{\supset}-\boxed{c}p$ is ruled out for the same reason.

(a)	$\boxed{f}T$	From (2) and fact that all tautologies (T) are logically necessary
(b)	$-\boxed{c}T$	Assumption
(c)	$\diamondsuit\!\!\!\langle-T$	From (b) by variant of (7)
(d)	$\diamondsuit\!\!\!\langle K$	From (c) by theorem of logic R. A. A.

But why should all factually necessary sentences, including the logically contingent ones, be regarded as contingently necessary?

Why not adopt $(\boxed{f}p \cdot -\Box p) \supset -\boxed{c}p$ instead of (3)?

First, a general semantical consideration. If necessity is characterized as truth in all worlds of a certain sort or appearance in all sets defined in a certain way, then logically necessary truths should be necessary in all weaker senses since sentences that are true in all logically possible words must be true in all subsets of such worlds, and logical truths are true in all factually and contingently possible worlds. Although this observation directly justifies (2), (3) is indirectly justified. For all factually necessary truths are similarly true in each contingently possible world and ought, therefore, to be counted as contingently necessary.

The argument is perhaps inconclusive. The modifiers 'contingently', 'factually', and 'logically' may not just represent increasing degrees of necessity. Thus, to characterize $(p \supset p)$ as factually necessary would mistakenly imply that its necessity is 'due' to factors that make natural laws necessarily true. Factually necessary sentences would be characterized as true in all and only factually possible worlds.

This proposal requires elaboration. We would, for example, have to be sure that the 'ways' represented by the modifiers are not just epistemological, i.e., ways of coming to know the strength of the necessity. In any case, there is a second argument against the proposal. Just as we do not want logical contradictions to be possible in any sense, so do we wish to avoid having to characterize factual impossibilities as contingently possible. But the adoption of $(\boxed{f}p \cdot -\Box p) \supset -\boxed{c}p$ would have this objectionable consequence.

(a) $\boxed{f}(p \supset q)$		Assumption
(b) $-\Box(p \supset q)$		Assumption
(c) $-\boxed{c}(p \supset q)$		From (a), (b) by proposal
(d) $\Diamond(p \cdot -q)$		From (c) by (7)

CONTINGENT NECESSITY AND THE NECESSITY OF THE PAST

Before proceeding with further details of the system, we must return to the current concern. In spite of the possibility of grounding the necessity of the past in this way, we reject the converse of (4):

A: $q \supset (\exists t)\boxed{c}_t q$

Q may be true although it is never necessary in the sense relevant to our purposes.

One may accept A without lapsing into fatalism, i.e., $q \supset (t)\boxed{c}_t q$(F). What follows from the truth of q is just that no one *will* do anything that will result in the falsity of q. I can make q false if it is early enough, although I will not if q is true. The argument for A, on the other hand, depends rather on the fact that the event that makes q true is past, has happened. If Jones drank carrot juice on June 7, 1986, I *cannot* prevent him from doing so on June 8, 1986, although I could have (perhaps) prevented him from doing so on June 6, 1986, although I did not then perform the act of prevention. The past cannot be altered.

Although a case for A exists, therefore, we can skirt the issue because, if we were to include A in our system, we would have a sense of contingent necessity that is too weak for our purposes. For if all true sentences are contingently necessary after they have been made true, and if necessity is responsibility absolving, no one is responsible for any action he performs even if the action fulfills the libertarian's wildest dreams, i.e., if it flows from the true self in a manner the omniscient psychologist would never have expected. Even if it turns out that necessity alone is not responsibility absolving, the necessity attributable to a sentence in virtue of just some event having already made it true has nothing to do with the question of the responsibility of the author of the event. Although the past cannot now be altered, when we ask if it was necessary that Jones perform a certain past action, in order to pass judgment on his responsibility, we are obviously not asking about the

99

presence of a characteristic which follows from the fact that he already performed the action.

More precisely, if we were to adopt A on the grounds being considered, we should have to conclude that the state of affairs ⌊Jones shoots Ripley at t_1⌋ is contingently necessary at t_2 ($>t_1$). If this is supposed to have some relevance to Jones' moral responsibility, then we should conclude, perhaps with the help of additional premises, that Jones is *not* morally responsible for this state of affairs at t_2. But this is absurd even if Jones has done everything in his power to rectify the situation. That he has made amends *presupposes* his moral responsibility. A fortiori, he is surely morally responsible for shooting Ripley if he has taken no morally appropriate steps. The only sensible conclusion is that, whatever contingent necessity means, it is not the necessity of the past and since the necessity of the past is the basis of A, we reject A.

Our conception of moral responsibility accords with this finding. The relevance of an action to the moral evaluation of an individual is a timeless matter. Making amends 'cancels' an action by the addition of a countervailing consideration, not by the literal obliteration of the original fact.

Thus, no matter what time it is, it may be that p is true, but not contingently necessary. Moreover, if q is contingently necessary (contingent on p), it is almost certainly not factually necessary. We, therefore, suspect that an incompatibilist will have to permit more than one nonlogical modality to permit the inference he wishes to make. An approximation, ultimately defective of this rule, is: From p and $\boxed{f}(p \supset q)$, infer $\boxed{c}q$ or $(\exists t)\boxed{c}_t q$: R_1.

Not only does R_1 represent the abandonment of the single modality approach; it also embodies the idea, commonly regarded as incoherent, but defended here, that, in such an inference, we need not suppose that p is, in any sense, necessary.

In reply, a critic might cite what appears to be a reference by incompatibilists to the necessity of the past. When hard determinists cite early environment and heredity as excusing factors, they typically describe these states of affairs as ones over which we have no control. They seem often to be invoking as a premise something like 'NCS' where S is made true by a past event g at t_1. Suppose as well 'S $\overrightarrow{f}$ Jones kills Brown at t_2 (T)'. If our earlier argument is sound, the necessity of T which interests an incompatibilist is not a mode which, like NC, adheres to the principles of the necessity of pastness. In other words, if T is not governed by $(S\overrightarrow{f}T)$, but is rather utterly free, then at $t_3>t_2$, although NCT, T is *not* necessary in a different sense, one we have labelled contingent necessity. What $(S\overrightarrow{f}T)$ in particular makes true, therefore, is $\boxed{c}$T.

At best, therefore, this critic would have to propose, as an alternative to R_1, a rule which involves *three* nonlogical modalities: From NCp and $\boxed{f}(p{\supset}q)$, infer $\boxed{c}q$ (or $(\exists t)\boxed{c}_tq$): R_2.

The evaluation of R_2 as an alternative to R_1 brings results if we consider, as in the case of Foster and the sugar, a time prior to the time the event which makes the first premise true has occurred. Suppose, then, it is now t_0 and g has not yet occurred. Since g will occur, S will be (is) true, though let us also suppose that neither $\boxed{c}_{t_0}$ S nor NC$_{t_0}$ S. These latter suppositions are different for if g is an undetermined event which happens to pop into existence at t_1 in an utterly uncontrollable and random manner, we have $-\boxed{c}_{t_0}$ S, yet NC$_{t_0}$ S.

Suppose in fact that g is entirely under the control of Jones. So that $(t)_{t<1}-$NCS, although Jones loses this power at t_1 in virtue of the unalterability of the past. Yet as long as there is a time gap between g and the killing, we will always have a case of NCS prior to the killing. The irrelevance of NCS may, however, be revealed whether or not the killing is later than g. (Simultaneous causation is usually conceded to be a respectable notion by philosophers who delve into issues of causation.)

The assumption of simultaneity does not affect $\boxed{c}_{t_1}$ T for, though Jones controls g, and, therefore, the killing, once g has been completed at t_1, then in virtue of the incompatibilist assumption that $S\overrightarrow{f}T$, it follows that $\boxed{c}_{t_1}$ T. The incompatibilist believes that the killing becomes contingently necessary whenever an empirically sufficient condition of it has been completed. Since in this special case, the condition and the killing are simultaneously completed, $\boxed{c}_{t_1}$ T but no earlier. The important consideration is that the following arguments each contain a first premise that is unnecessarily strong.

I: NC$_{t_1}$ S (S: g occurs at t_1)

(S f T) (T: Jones kills Brown at t_1)

$\overline{\boxed{c}_{t_1}\ \text{T}}$

II: NC_{t_1} S

(S$\boxed{f}$T') (T': Jones kills Brown at t_2)

$\boxed{c}_{t_1}$ T'

Each remains valid if the first premises are changed to 'S'. For in I, even if $-NC_{t_n}$ S (for any $n < t_1$), all this implies is that $-\boxed{c}T_{t_n < 1}$. But $\boxed{c}_{t_1}$ T! Of course, the simplest reason for the sufficiency of S is that S implies NC_{t_1} S. Since S is 'g occurs at t_1', it follows that, at t_1, no one can alter the truth of S (in a sense in which its 'truth' could have been altered prior to t_1.) In II, also, even if Jones can affect the truth of S up to t_1, at t_1, he can affect neither S nor T (on the incompatibilist's assumptions).

None of this is affected by the assumption that it is now t_0. In either case T is not now contingently necessary if Jones has control over S. But why should an incompatibilist who does not automatically assume determinism believe otherwise? An incompatibilist who is not also a logical determinist believes only that the effect is necessitated by the cause and is not committed to believe, therefore, that the effect is necessitated at a time the cause has not yet come into being or been completed.

CONTINGENT NECESSITY AND MORAL RESPONSIBILITY

Although we would expect bizarre consequences from the assumption of reverse causation, we seem to be permitting an odd consequence from an assumption not commonly regarded as implausible. If g is the simultaneous cause of the killing, then, even if Jones retains control over g and can, therefore, inhibit its occurring at any time prior to its completion, rule R_1 permits us to say that the killing is contingently necessary. Thus, Jones can exercise indirect control over his killing of Brown insofar as he can take steps to prevent this act at any time prior to its completion. To be sure, if Jones permits g to happen, he will not be able to prevent the killing. Yet Jones exercises as much control over the killing as he does over whether or not he signals a left turn, given that he has complete control over whether or not he holds his left arm straight out the window.

The above becomes paradoxical only on the assumption that contingent necessity absolves, i.e., on the assumption that a person is not morally responsible for a state of affairs S which is contingently necessary. For we do want to hold Jones responsible for the killing or the signalling in such cases.

We may be disposed to use this case against the incompatibilist for it is one in which the demonstration that a sentence is contingently necessary is compatible with an agent's moral responsibility for the designated state of affairs. But the reason we feel this way is the same as the reason we hold people derivatively responsible in the more common cases in which there is a temporal gap between the action the agent is clearly responsible for and the resultant state arising necessarily from that action. We blame Jones for the killing if he freely instituted g in the knowledge that he would as a consequence have to kill Brown, just as we blame a person for a failure to appear at a meeting because that person rendered his appearance impossible by a prior, willful action. The fact that g is simultaneous with the killing, whereas the willful action is earlier than the failure to appear at the meeting, is irrelevant to the assignment of responsibility.

We, therefore, do not have a counterexample to R_1 for nothing here suggests that either $-\boxed{c}_{t_1} T$ or $-\boxed{c}_{t_1} T'$. There may be problems proceeding to conclusions concerning Jones' moral responsibility for T or T', but those are the general problems associated with derivative responsibility.

THE USE OF CONTINGENT NECESSITY IN REASONING

If then we opt for R_1, we commit ourselves to the coherence of cases of $-\boxed{c}p \cdot \boxed{c}q$, the second conjunct being based on $p \cdot \boxed{f}(p \supset q)$. Although it may be difficult to provide a coherent interpretation of the modalities to render R_1 a possible rule (or $[(p \cdot \boxed{f}(p \supset q)) \supset \boxed{c}q]$ a possible theorem), it is reasonable to believe that such a rule is employed in ordinary reasoning. If so, we have a responsibility, in light of the role of logic as a codifier of reasoning, at least to attempt to provide a plausible interpretation.

It is, first of all, evident that *if* necessity is detached in accordance with R_1, the necessity in question is not logical or factual, and must be something like contingent necessity. Consider the following inference:

Jones is thrown out of the window (T)

$\boxed{f}$(Jones is thrown out of the window $\supset$ Jones falls)

∴It is necessary that Jones falls (It is necessary that F)

We often argue in such a way that the above is a prima facie reconstruction of our reasoning. The intended necessity in the conclusion is obviously not logical for we would deny '$\Box$F'. It is also evident, although not as blatantly so, that we would reject '$\boxed{f}$F' as the intended interpretation. For we either believe $\boxed{f}$T or $-\boxed{f}$T. Even if we believe the former, we do not believe that the inference rests on $\boxed{f}$T. In other words, we would respond negatively to the question 'Given T, do you believe that the fall would not have been necessary had T not been true in some other factually possible world?' In other words if Jones is thrown out the window, he has to fall. Period. It does not matter whether he had to be thrown out. Thus if we believe $-\boxed{f}$T, we do not question the inference.

There is undoubtedly a wealth of linguistic evidence that we do the detachment, that we categorically assert that Jones' fall is necessary, although this truth, like the categorical truths about our world, depends on other contingent facts. The opponent of R_1 is forced, therefore, constantly to reinterpret categorical utterances as disguised hypothetical ones like 'It is necessary that if T, then F'. Unless fatal failures of formalization force this result, I would deny that the necessity of F is constituted by the necessity of some proposition P such that P⊃F. Bleach whitens clothes. Hence, the whiteness of certain clothes depends on their being whitened by bleach. But the clothes are white. Their whiteness is not constituted by a relation between them and the bleach. (It does not follow that no relational analysis of 'is white' is correct. The position that color predicates are to be analyzed in terms of relations between objects and standards is not ruled out.) Thus the burden is upon those who adhere to a relational interpretation of necessity.

A SYSTEM OF CONTINGENT NECESSITY

Let us then attempt to delineate the principal syntactic and semantic features of a system of contingent necessity (SCN), some theorems of which have already been specified.

A theorem we have alluded to earlier is:

(8) $(\boxed{f}(p \supset q) \cdot \boxed{f}p) \supset \boxed{f}q$

Since no sentence can be both contingently possible, and factually impossible, the following, but not its converse, holds:

(9) $\langle\!\!\!\!\Diamond\rangle_c\, p \supset \langle\!\!\!\!\Diamond\rangle_f\, p$

Similarly,

(10) $\langle\!\!\!\!\Diamond\rangle_f\, p \supset \Diamond p$

Clearly,

(11) $p \supset (\Diamond p \cdot \langle\!\!\!\!\Diamond\rangle_f\, p \cdot \langle\!\!\!\!\Diamond\rangle_c\, p)$

Although we allow all factually necessary sentences to be contingently necessary, we have not yet formulated the rule that allows us to characterize some factually contingent sentences as contingently necessary. Aune has shown that the following simple theorem (our R_1 without the temporal designation) will not do.[10]

(12) $(\boxed{f}(p \supset q) \cdot p) \supset \boxed{c} q$

For, since $\boxed{f}(p \supset p)$, p alone warrants $\boxed{c} p$, and the result is (contingent) modal collapse, a result we have rejected, preferring instead $\Diamond(p \cdot -\boxed{c} p)$. Although Aune's remarks are directed against a simple position in which only one nonlogical modality is used, they obviously work against (12). This conclusion is important because a person familiar with the fact that the standard semantic interpretation renders $(\boxed{f} p \supset q \cdot p) \supset \boxed{f} q$ invalid anyway, as we noted earlier, may wrongly suspect that (12) is acceptable since it employs two nonlogical modalities and the system in which it appears does not contain the objectionable $(\boxed{f} p \supset q \cdot p) \supset \boxed{f} q$.

Guleserian has defended the libertarian's use of a concept of factual necessity against the charge of modal fallacy.[11] But his use of a single concept of factual necessity leaves his position open to attack in a way that the system under construction here is immune from.

Or at least that is the hope. Recognizing the falsity of $(\boxed{f} p \supset q \cdot p) \supset \boxed{f} q$, we thought (12) would do the trick. But our commitment to (2) renders Aune's attack successful. Failing to see that the issue goes deeper than the factual status of logically necessary truths, Guleserian rejects (2), arguing that factually necessary propositions are logically contingent. In this way, Aune's attack on $(\boxed{f}(p \supset q) \cdot p) \supset \boxed{f} q$ is repelled.

But Guleserian does not consider the arguments for (2) described above, contenting himself with an observation I do not find compelling, to wit, that we do not count or call logically necessary propositions factually necessary. I think we should.

Note also that, even if Guleserian is right in thinking that $\boxed{f}(p \supset p)$ is false, we need contingent necessity anyway. The inference to $\boxed{f} q$ from p and $\boxed{f}(p \supset q)$ is independently fallacious.

DE DICTO VERSUS DE RE NECESSITY

Before we attempt to revise (12), the theorem justified by R_1, we must note that the theorems involving contingent necessity have not incorporated the relativity to time we have argued for. We must render the system more complex by adding variables for times. But we can do this in two different ways, depending on whether we choose a de dicto or de re construal of necessity. Our construal up to this point has been de dicto. But we must consider the possibility that events are literally necessary (rather than the sentences made true by the events).

The de re construal is metaphysically appealing. For it at least provides an intelligible answer to the question: What makes necessary truths true? If events have the property of necessity or occurring necessarily, we at least have a model for thinking of the way the world makes assertions of necessity true (even if we do not grasp the nature of this particular property). If, on the other hand, necessity is an operator on sentences and truth conditions are given by possible world semantics, some would regard as obscure the way the actual world makes these assertions true. They are true of or at the actual world; but their truth-conditions are partially given by their status in non-actual worlds. There is a resistance (although the forces seem to be rapidly diminishing) to the appeal to non-actual worlds in this context if such propositions are confirmed or disconfirmed by what goes on in the real world.[12]

Although this uncomfortable feeling about possible world semantics is one I share, in this case the move to a de re interpretation as a solution will not do.

First, it will be difficult or impossible to interpret operations on a de re reading. For example, it is reasonable to believe that contingent necessity is agglomerative, i.e., if $\boxed{c}p$ and $\boxed{c}q$, then $\boxed{c}(p \cdot q)$. If however, events, say e_1 and e_2, are each contingently necessary, we cannot conclude that $\boxed{c}$ $(e_1 \cdot e_2)$, for, since '$\boxed{c}$' would have to be read as a predicate, '$e_1 \cdot e_2$' should be a name. But it is rather meaningless for only names of truth bearers can

107

flank sentential connectives. For similar reasons, we cannot employ other sentential transformations involving connectives such as negation, disjunction, etc.

The advocate of the de re interpretation may try to concoct interpretations of the connectives; but he would end up with sum events, negative events, disjunctive events, and the like and would face an uphill battle making sense of all this.

Another argument against the de re reading rests on the need to construe some events as contingently necessary before they occur. An event in a deterministic chain would be contingently necessary at a time it has not yet occurred. Moreover, if its cause is undetermined, it becomes contingently necessary at a time it has not yet occurred. Moreover, if its cause is undetermined, it becomes contingently necessary although it does not yet exist. Clearly, though, entities must exist in order to have and acquire properties.

DETERMINISTIC ACCOUNTS AND EVENTS

There are advantages to the position we are adopting. If events are contingently necessary, they are so according to the incompatibilist because they are determined. Since deterministic accounts show that events are determined, we must establish a connection between events and deterministic accounts.[13] The difficulty, perhaps impossibility, of doing this is an advantage of and argument for the view that contingent necessity is not a property of events.

The most promising approach would define 'D is a deterministic account of event a_{t_n}' as 'D is a deterministic account whose conclusion is a sentence which entails a sentence of the form '$(\exists e)(Fe_{t_n})$' and 'Fa_{t_n}' is true'. ('e_1', 'e_2', 'e_3', etcetera are event variables and 'a', 'b', 'c', etcetera are event names.) If the conclusion of a deterministic account is 'Brutus stabs Caesar on March 15, 44 B.C.', we may infer '$(\exists e)(e$ is a stabbing of Caesar by Brutus on March 15, 44 B.C.)'. (The rules governing this inference are linguistic rules and rules governing the logic of events.) A problem with this account is provided by examples in which two events satisfy one sentence of the form '$(\exists e)(Fe_{t_n})$'.[14] For example, suppose Brutus stabs Caesar twice, once at 3:00 p.m. and again at 3:01 p.m. If a is the first stabbing and b the second, it may be that a alone is determined. But on this account, since a and b are both stabbings of Caesar by Brutus on March 15, 44 B.C., both a and b are determined.

In certain cases uniqueness is not a problem. Since a man cannot be killed twice in one day, then there cannot be more than one killing of Caesar by Brutus on March 15, 44 B.C. In other cases, the law plus the initial conditions will determine that the event occur at a precise time. So that, since the act of stabbing takes time, if it is determined that an act occur at 3:00 p.m., a, not b, is the determined act.

But suppose at 3:00 p.m., Brutus had stabbed Caesar with each hand. If we call this a case of two simultaneous stabbings, a_1 and a_2, might not only one be determined? We may have a deterministic account whose conclusion is 'Brutus stabs Caesar with his left hand at 3:00 p.m. on March 15, 44 B.C.' But we may not. And even if we do, the above account (in which the conclusion of the deterministic account was applicable to two stabbings) still constrains us to say that both a_1 and a_2 are determined.

If determinism is true, the problem we face now is academic. For deterministic accounts will be as precise as language allows. Hence, there will be a distinct deterministic account for each event. This follows from the fact that if $e_1 \neq e_2$, there is a property F that e_1 has and e_2 does not. Since determinism is true, there will be a deterministic account that ends in a sentence whose conversion into a sentence asserting the existence of some event will be such that e_1 does and e_2 does not satisfy the sentence. For example, the conclusion of one deterministic account is 'Brutus stabs Caesar with his left hand at 3:00 p.m. on March 15, 44 B.C.' and the conclusion of another is 'Brutus stabs Caesar with his right hand at 3:00 p.m. on March 15, 44 B.C.' Hence, the two simultaneous stabbings, a_1 and a_2, have distinct deterministic accounts. Even if events differ only spatially, there will be separate deterministic accounts for them because the initial conditions will differ spatially.

But we cannot assume that determinism is true. Recall again that incompatibilists are not committed to determinism. There may, therefore, be no account more specific than 'Brutus stabs Caesar on March 15, 44 B.C.' And if both a_1 and a_2 exist, there is no basis for deciding whether both or just one is determined. And if we say only one is determined, which is it?

Since we have concluded that contingent necessity is not a property of events, we are free to adopt the position that 'is determined' does not apply to events.[15] (If events are contingently necessary, they are so because they are determined.) An independent argument for the position that events are not determined is that if events (and only events) are determined, determinism should be true if all events are determined. But if there is no deterministic account more specific than 'Brutus stabs Caesar on March 15, 44 B.C.', determinism is not true. There would be, however, no event that is not determined if a_1 had been the only stabbing. For a_1 is a stabbing of Caesar by Brutus with Brutus' left hand at 3:00 p.m. on March 15, 44 B.C. Hence, a_1 is determined even if we have no deterministic account of 'Brutus stabs Caesar with his left hand at 3:00 p.m. on March 15, 44 B.C.' So all events are determined although determinism is not true. Events are not, therefore, the subject of the predicate 'is determined'.

The example is a poor one, however. For the more precise characterization, although introducing no additional stabbing, does introduce an additional event, to wit, a movement of Brutus' left hand. Call this movement 'm_1' and suppose that it, along with a_1 is determined. Now, although it may be difficult to imagine how this can be so unless, in addition, there is a deterministic account of 'Brutus stabs Caesar with his left hand at 3:00 p.m. on March 15, 44 B.C.', better examples can be found. Certain event modifications, e.g., speed, do not involve additional events. So if a movement is determined, but not that it is a slow movement, we will have a case in which the failure of determinism is not reflected in some event's not being determined.

I propose that we treat this problem of duplication in exactly the same way we treat other cases of incomplete determination. If

a_1 alone occurs, but we only have a deterministic account of 'Brutus stabs Caesar at 3:00 p.m. on March 15, 44 B.C.', we say simply that there is no deterministic account of 'Brutus stabs Caesar with his left hand at 3:00 p.m. on March 15, 44 B.C.' and we can say the same sort of thing about the case of duplicate events.

Suppose again that a_1 and a_2 both occur, yet, although it is determined that Brutus stabs Caesar when he did, it is not determined that he do it with his right or left hand, or, as actually happened, with both. If we characterize a stabbing in such a way as to say that Brutus stabbed Caesar twice, or dually-stabbed Caesar once, each stabbing being a part of the dual-stabbing, then it is not determined that Brutus dually-stabs Caesar. Just as a movement may be determined, though not all its qualities, so a stabbing may be determined, though not its number. This simple suggestion does not yield a determinate answer to the question of which events are determined, a_1, a_2, or the sum-event composed of the two; but it is a question we are not forced to address in light of our insistence that the locution we should adopt is 'S_1 has a deterministic account' rather than 'e_1 is determined'. This insistence coheres with our earlier defense of the view that states of affairs rather than events are the entities we are morally responsible for. Although not all true sentences identify states of affairs, the sentences which would replace 'S_1 has a deterministic acount' may be regarded as picking out states of affairs, i.e., entities agents may or may not be morally responsible for.

An attempt to save the view that events are determined may be based on a rejection of the necessity to link event determination with deterministic accounts. I may be accused of conflating ontological and epistemological questions. Determination (or causation) is a relation between events and the provision of a deterministic account tells us which events stand in this relation.

I cannot here defend adequately the view that the analysis of determination must make reference to deterministic acounts. There are views to the contrary, for example, modal accounts of determinism according to which, roughly, the past narrows logically possible futures to one metaphysically possible one.[16] Elsewhere, I have defended the view to which I still subscribe, although I believe that that defense is incomplete and in need of other revisions.[17]

Accordingly, we may introduce the sentential operator 'It is determined that' and the compatibilist-incompatibilist controversy could then be characterized in terms of the dispute over whether 'It is determined that S' implies '$\boxed{c}$S'.

Many of the problems which must be faced in formulating truth-conditions for 'It is determined that S' (or '$\boxed{c}$S') concern issues separate from the complex issue of characterizing natural laws. What are the constraints on initial conditions? What are the admissible substitutions on sentences reporting initial conditions? What are the a priori restrictions on the kinds of sentences which can be determined? (Can law-sentences be determined? Or evaluative sentences? Or sentences about sets?) These questions will not be taken up here.

NECESSITY AS AN OPERATOR

We must, therefore, view contingent necessity as a sentential operator. It is then easy to produce analogues to the basic theorems of alethic modality:

(1) $(\exists t)\boxed{c}_t p \supset p$

(2) $p \supset (t)\diamondsuit_t p$

(3) $-p \supset (t) - \boxed{c}_t p$

(4) $(t) - \diamondsuit_t p \supset -p$

(5) $(t)(\diamondsuit_t - p \equiv -\boxed{c}_t p)$

(6) $(t)(\diamondsuit_t p \lor \boxed{c}_t - p)$

(7) $(t) - (\boxed{c}_t p \cdot \boxed{c}_t - p)$

In addition, we have:

(8) $\Box p \supset \boxed{f} p$

(9) $\boxed{f} p \supset (t)\boxed{c}_t p$

(10) $(\boxed{f}(p \supset q) \cdot p) \supset (\exists t)\boxed{c}_t q$

(11) $(\exists t)\diamondsuit_t p \supset \diamondsuit p$

(12) $p \supset (\diamondsuit p \cdot \diamondsuit p \cdot (t)\diamondsuit_t p)$

(13) $(t)[(\boxed{c}_t p \cdot \Box(p \supset q)) \supset \boxed{c}_t q]$

112

(14) $(\exists t_1)\ (\exists t_2)(\boxed{c}_{t_1} p \cdot \boxed{c}_{t_2} q) \supset (\exists t_3)(\boxed{c}_{t_3}(p \cdot q))$

(10) is now the theorem justified by R_1. Not only does it require revision, as we have indicated. It also should be supplemented by rules determining the time at which q becomes contingently necessary, intuitively understood as the time when the 'cause' of the event which makes q true occurs. (We shall not in this work formulate those rules since this project has no real bearing on the issues which concern us.)

If the problem with (10) is that $(p \supset q)$ might be logically necessary, we might try:

(10′) $(\boxed{f}(p \supset q) \cdot -\square(p \supset q) \cdot p) \supset (\exists t)\boxed{c}_t q$

This revision should be perfectly acceptable to all parties since, if contingent necessity is a legitimate notion at all, we do not countenance an *atomic* sentence p being made contingently necessary by some sentence that logically entails p. (Although $\square p$ entails p and makes it contingently necessary, the only true substitution instances of p are molecular.)

(10′) does not render (9) redundant. For reasons mentioned above, we wish to countenance logically necessary truths as contingently necessary and (10′) will not enable us to achieve that result. For if t is some tautology, so is $p \supset t$, where p is any sentence. Thus, $\square(p \supset t)$ and t will not be detachable via (10′) since the second conjunct of the antecedent is violated. (8) and (9) must then be invoked to derive $\boxed{c}t$.

We are not out of the woods yet for (10′) will not prevent modal collapse. If q is an arbitrary true, but not logically necessary sentence and p any factually but not logically necessary sentence, itself logically independent of q, then $\boxed{f}[(p \supset q) \supset q]$ (since p entails $(p \supset q) \supset q$ and any logical consequence of a factually necessary sentence is factually necessary). We then have:

(a) q — Premise
(b) $p \supset q$ — From (a) by theorem of logic
(c) $\boxed{f}[(p \supset q) \supset q]$ — Premise
(d) $-\square[(p \supset q) \supset q]$ — Logically demonstrable
(e) $(\exists t)\boxed{c}_t q$ — From (b), (c), (d), by (10′)

Since $\square(q \supset (p \supset q))$, and since it is reasonable to require of the factually necessary sentences that ground inferences to conclusions of the form $\boxed{c}q$ that antecedent and consequent be logically independent of one another, the following revision suggests itself:

(10″) $(\boxed{f}(p \supset q) \cdot -\square(p \supset q) \cdot -\square(q \supset p) \cdot p) \supset (\exists t)\boxed{c}_t q$

Again, however, we need something stronger, given that contingent necessity is closed under entailment (15) and agglomerative (14).

(15) $[(\exists t)\boxed{c}_t p \cdot \Box(p \supset q)] \supset (\exists t)\boxed{c}_t q$

On the assumption that we can find an appropriate r, we can construct, for any arbitrary true sentence q, two factually necessary sentences in the following way. For any factually but not logically necessary sentence p, since p logically entails both

$$((p \cdot q) \lor -p) \supset ((p \cdot q) \lor r)$$

and

$$((p \cdot q) \lor -p) \supset ((p \cdot q) \lor -r),$$

we have

$$\boxed{f}((p \cdot q) \lor -p) \supset ((p \cdot q) \lor r)$$

and

$$\boxed{f}((p \cdot q) \lor -p) \supset ((p \cdot q) \lor -r).$$

The following argument demonstrates again the fact of modal collapse:

(a)	q	Premise
(b)	$(p \cdot q) \lor -p$	From (a) by theorem of logic
(c)	$\boxed{f}[((p \cdot q) \lor -p) \supset ((p \cdot q) \lor r)]$	Premise
(d)	$-\Box[((p \cdot q) \lor -p) \supset ((p \cdot q) \lor r)]$	Logically demonstrable
(e)	$-\Box[((p \cdot q) \lor r) \supset ((p \cdot q) \lor -p)]$	Logically demonstrable
(f)	$(\exists t)\boxed{c}_t((p \cdot q) \lor r)$	From (b), (c), (d), (e) by (10″)
(g)	$\boxed{f}[((p \cdot q) \lor -p) \supset ((p \cdot q) \lor -r)]$	Premise
(h)	$-\Box[((p \cdot q) \lor -p) \supset ((p \cdot q) \lor -r)]$	Logically demonstrable
(i)	$-\Box[((p \cdot q) \lor -r) \supset ((p \cdot q) \lor -p)]$	Logically demonstrable
(j)	$(\exists t)\boxed{c}_t((p \cdot q) \lor -r)$	From (b), (g), (h), (i) by (10″)
(k)	$(\exists t)\boxed{c}_t((p \cdot q) \lor r) \cdot (\exists t)\boxed{c}_t((p \cdot q) \lor -r)$	From (f), (j) by conjunction
(l)	$(\exists t)\boxed{c}_t[((p \cdot q) \lor r) \cdot ((p \cdot q) \lor -r)]$	From (k) by (14)
(m)	$\Box\{[((p \cdot q) \lor r) \cdot ((p \cdot q) \lor -r)] \supset q\}$	Logically demonstrable
(n)	$(\exists t)\boxed{c}_t q$	From (1), (m) by (15)

114

The issue is still logical independence because the objectionable feature of cases like this is the logical dependence of the antecedent of the factually necessary conditional on the very sentence determined in part by that conditional to be contingently necessary.

But we can tamper with neither (14) nor (15), as we can see by an informal appeal to possible world considerations. If we reject (14), there is a sentence s that is contingently necessary and a sentence t entailed by s that is not contingently necessary. Since $\boxed{c}s$, then, via the theorems, $-\Diamond-s$. Consider *any* contingently possible world w_1. Since $-s$ cannot appear there, s must appear there. Since w_1 is also a logically possible world, t would have to be true in it, too. T appears, therefore, in each contingently possible world. $-T$, therefore, appears in no contingently possible world. But $-\Diamond-t$ is equivalent to $\boxed{c}t$ and the latter contradicts our assumption. Hence, we are committed to (14) and, by an analogous demonstration, to (15). Contingent necessity is closed under logical consequence.

Thus, the acceptance of both $(\exists t)\boxed{c}_t((p \cdot q)\lor r)$ and $(\exists t)\boxed{c}_t ((p \cdot q)\lor -r)$ leads inexorably to modal collapse. The fault must, therefore, lie with the factually necessary premises used in the derivation of these two sentences. But in each case, the sentence is clearly factually necessary and antecedent and consequent are clearly logically independent of one another. From what point of view, therefore, can a negative judgment be rendered?

Intuitively, the kind of independence we are looking for is one in which the possible ways in which the consequent of a factually necessary conditional can be true do not all logically presuppose each way in which the antecedent can be true. Accordingly, I propose the following definition:

(The definition is provided for the simple case of sentential logic without variables for time. We use the notion of a factually necessary material conditional since we are not anyway providing a definition of such a notion.)

A factually necessary sentence s displays strong logical independence (SLI) if s is factually necessary and derivable from a member f of the set of factually necessary conditionals in the following way:

1. The antecedent (a) and the consequent (c) of f are both converted into a normal form in which each disjunct of the antecedent, if there are any, is a conjunction of atomic sentences and negations of atomic sentences and contains at least each

atomic sentence or its negation which appears somewhere in the antecedent and in which each disjunct of the consequent, if there are any, contains at least each atomic sentence or its negation which appears somewhere in the consequent. Call the result $a' \supset c'$.

2. Each disjunct which is factually impossible in either a' or c' is eliminated. Call the result $a'' \supset c''$.

3. Each disjunct d of c'' such that $-\Diamond(a'' \supset d)$ is eliminated. Call the result $a'' \supset c''$.

4. Each atomic sentence (or its negation) which appears in each disjunct of c''' which is also a logical consequence of each disjunct of a'' or, if a'' is just a conjunction, a logical consequence of a'', is eliminated. Call the result $a'' \supset c''''$.

Here are sample transformations (assuming still that p and t are factually necessary):

Original

   (a) $((p \cdot q) \lor -p) \supset ((p \cdot q) \lor r)$
   (b) $((p \cdot q) \lor -p) \supset ((p \cdot q) \lor -r)$
   (c) $((p \cdot q) \lor -p) \supset [((p \cdot q) \lor r) \cdot ((p \cdot q) \lor -r)$
   (d) $(s \cdot u) \supset (t \cdot u)$
   (e) $(p \supset q) \supset q$

Result

   (a) $(p \cdot q) \supset (r \lor -r)$
   (b) $(p \cdot q) \supset (-r \lor r)$
   (c) $(p \cdot q) \supset (r \cdot s) \lor (-r \cdot s) \lor (r \cdot -s) \lor (-r \cdot -s)$
   (d) $(s \cdot u) \supset t$
   (e) none

The results, where there are any, are harmless because all consequents are contingently necessary independent of their respective antecedents. The consequents of (a), (b), and (c) are logically necessary and the consequent of (d) is factually necessary. Since each step must have a result, no SLI-conditional is derived from (e).

A conditional may be SLI, although a logically equivalent sentence is not. $p \supset q$ is SLI; but $p \supset (p \cdot q)$ is not. (The fact that this property is not closed under logical consequence is, of course, irrelevant to the fact that contingent neccessity is.)

Since a requirement to the effect that a factually necessary sentence be SLI eliminates the necessity for the weaker logical independence requirement, we may replace $(10'')$ with $(10''')$: $(\boxed{f}(p \supset q) \cdot p) \supset (\exists t) \boxed{c}_t q$, provided $(p \supset q)$ is SLI.

CAUSAL NECESSITY AGAIN

Even if we have avoided modal collapse, $(10''')$ is still too weak. The idea of one sentence p making another q contingently necessary is, we know, not captured by the factual necessity of $p \supset q$ and the truth of p. Guaranteeing that p and q are independent of one another in a sufficiently strong sense is not the only additional task. We must also rule out those cases in which the event e_2 that makes p true is an effect of the event e_1 that makes q true. For if e_1 is the only possible cause of e_2, it may also be the case that e_1 is undetermined. Thus, although $(p \supset q)$ is SLI and p is true, $-q$ is contingently possible. Requiring that e_1 not precede e_2 will not help if e_1 and e_2 can be simultaneous and yet stand in a cause-effect relation. The case for simultaneous causation has often been made in the philosophical literature and I do not intend to question its merits.

Many proposals regarding the direction of causation have also appeared in the literature and mine may be found among them.[18] Later, after my conception of laws has been formulated, I shall briefly reconsider the question of which term in the law does the accounting and which is accounted for. We suppose at this stage, therefore, without argument, that appropriate syntactic restrictions on SLI-conditionals can be formulated and that revisions in the semantics of contingent necessity can be incorporated without difficulty.

SEMANTICAL CONSIDERATIONS

In order to defend the viability of SCN, we must suppose that modal systems incorporating an operator for contingent necessity can be given semantic sense, including, of course, the provision of truth conditions for sentences of the form '$\boxed{c}p$'. We suppose that this defense can be provided by considering a simplified context of sentential logic without time variables. Moreover, the standard disputes among opponents of competing sentential modal systems may similarly be put to one side as they have no bearing on the question that interests us.

We suppose, then, some standard system providing truth conditions for $\boxed{}p$ at a world w_1 (in a model m) in terms of the truth of p at every world possible relative to w_1, the relativity being provided by a suitable (accessibility) relation r of m, and the truth of p at some world w_n being given by the value assignment v of m. We designate as U the set of all worlds k in m accessible to w_1, i.e., such that $w_1 r k$.

We must then define a subset of U, F, representing intuitively the set of worlds nomically possible relative to w_1, i.e., the set of factually possible worlds (where w_1 is understood as the actual world). (Since we are only concerned with the semantical development of SCN, we need not confront here the enormously difficult task of specifying a plausible definition of F.)

$\boxed{c}q$ is true if $\boxed{}q$ is true (and if $\boxed{f}q$).

The other truth condition of $\boxed{c}q$ (at w_1 in m relative to value assignment v) is: There is a sentence of the form $p \supset q$ such that, on v, 'p' is t at w_1 and '$p \supset q$' is t at every world in F (including w_1) and such that p and q each take the following form (an account designed to reflect their strict logical independence):

It is either an atomic sentence or its negation, a conjunction of atomic sentences or their negations, or a disjunction each disjunct of which is a conjunction of atomic sentences or their negations where, if s or $-s$ appears in p, s or $-s$ appears in each disjunct of the disjunction.

118

Each disjunct in p or q, if either is a disjunction, is t (on v) in some member of F.

If q is a disjunction, for each disjunct d of q, $p \supset d$ is t (on v) in some member of F.

If q is a disjunction, and if each disjunct of q contains a common atomic element or its negation d_i, then for each such d_i, $p \supset d_i$ is not t (on v) in some member of U.

If $\boxed{c}p$ and $\boxed{c}q$, then $\boxed{c}(p \cdot q)$.

If $\boxed{c}p$ and $p \supset r$ is a member of each member of U, then $\boxed{c}r$.

If a sentence p cannot be shown to be contingently necessary in the above ways, $-\boxed{c}p$.

The fundamental difference between contingent necessity and the other alethic modalities is the dependence of the truth of sentences of the form '$\boxed{c}q$' on the truth of logically independent sentences which might be atomic. This reflects the distinctive feature of contingent necessity, to wit, that atomic sentences may be 'made' contingently necessary by the truth of other atomic sentences. Yet, insofar as similar modal operators have been suggested in the literature, the idea is not that strange. There is an obvious kinship, for example, between contingent necessity and Chellas' historical necessity ('$\boxed{\cdot}$'), defined in such a way that $\boxed{\cdot}\,a$ in a world, say w_1, at time t when a is true at every world in the model identical to a up to t. In a similar way, therefore, the truth of $\boxed{\cdot}\,a$ in w_1 depends upon contingent features of w_1. For example, had some event e failed to occur shortly before f, w_1 would have failed to be historically identical to the other worlds in which a is true. Moreover, a may fail to be true in some worlds historically identical to w_1, on the assumption e did not occur.[19]

8

Laws as necessary truths

THE SIGNIFICANCE OF THE NECESSITY-REGULARITY CONTROVERSY

A major thesis of this book is that incompatibilists are committed to the position that laws of nature are (factually) necessary. They are not alone in this belief. Indeed, they may take great comfort in the fact that ' ... nowadays it is a matter of widespread agreement that some characteristic mode of nomic necessity is involved in lawfulness, although writers differ as to just how the factor of nomic necessity is to be explicated'.[1] Rescher goes on to quote the relevant article in the most recent philosophical encyclopedia. R. S. Walters says that the current point of dispute 'is not about the propriety of using such terms as "nomic necessity"; rather it is about the interpretation of these terms or the justification of their use'.[2]

We begin with some elementary remarks about necessity. Logical necessity ('$\square$') is a monadic operator which forms sentences (or propositions) when attached to sentences (or propositions).[3] If q is logically necessary, then so is $p \supset q$, where p is any sentence. Some philosophers have attempted to formulate a notion of logical entailment ('$\rightarrow$') such that p entails q only when the logical necessity of $p \supset q$ is grounded in a 'genuine relation' between p and q. So $\square$(The moon is made of green cheese$\supset r \lor -r$); but the antecedent does not entail the consequent. And $\square(r \cdot -r \supset$The moon is made of green cheese); but $-(r \cdot -r \rightarrow$The moon is made of green cheese). The burden of clarifying the conditions under which cases of logical necessity are also cases of entailment is not an easy one to bear and my argument in this chapter does not really hinge on the successful explanation of this notion.[4]

The other two concepts are the analogues in the factual realm of the above two notions. If nothing can travel faster than the speed of light, then $\boxed{f}$ (Nothing travels faster than the speed of light). Although $\boxed{f}$ (The moon is made of green cheese⊃Nothing travels faster than the speed of light), the antecedent does not factually entail ('$\vec{f}$') the consequent.

The structure of the semantics of weaker forms of necessity such as factual necessity or entailment is based on the structure of the semantics of logical necessity. If we can define the truth conditions of sentences of the form '$\boxed{}p$' in terms of the appearance of p in all the model sets of a system where the sole restriction on membership in the system is adherence to logical laws, then we can easily define the truth conditions of sentences of the form '$\boxed{f}(p⊃q)$' in terms of the appearance of $p⊃q$ in all the model sets of a subsystem of the first where the subsystem has been created by eliminating all sets containing sentences which are inconsistent with the conjunction of natural laws.[5]

But what is a natural law? Suppose the conditions a sentence must meet to be a natural law, including those which determine the difference between factual necessity and factual entailment, can be entirely stated in a truthfunctional language. No recourse to modal notions is required in order to make the distinction between laws and non-laws. It is of the utmost importance to notice that, under these circumstances, an antinecessitarian (call him a 'regularity theorist') cannot be disturbed about, of all things, nomic necessity. How can he be? The notion has been defused. Even though '$\vec{f}$' is primitive in the object language, a regularity theorist can consistently use the language. He has no metaphysical objection to the language because the notions in its truth-definition can be defined without appeal to modal ideas.

Thus, there is a sense in which Walters' observation is harmless. No one should object to a system of nomic necessity so long as the syntax and the semantics have been clearly specified and the system has some application. A necessitarian must believe, therefore, that the predicate 'is a natural law' cannot be defined without using modal notions or else his position is uninteresting. If this metalinguistic notion, crucial to the interpretation of the object language, can be defined in a truthfunctional metalanguage, it is a relatively trivial matter to construct an object language with '$\overrightarrow{f}$' as primitive. Thus, the issue is not whether or not there is a bona fide modal system in which nomic necessity or entailment is primitive.

It is a serious matter for the incompatibilist, therefore, if a truthfunctional definition of 'natural law' can be provided. It is first of all evident that if '$(x)(Tx \supset Ux)$' is accidentally true, then the fact about Jones that he is T does not necessitate the fact that he is U or, a fortiori, any moral consequences alleged to rest on necessitation. Hence, the difference between accidental generaliz-ations and bona fide laws must be sufficient to warrant the difference in the inferences we make. Since the incompatibilist draws the conclusion that the occurrence of a human action is necessitated in a sense which absolves the agent of moral responsibility for having performed it only if the occurrence is subsumed under a law, the conditions which convert a true generalization into a law must suffice to ground such an inference. But it is a simple matter to show that a regularity interpretation of laws removes the underpinnings of the incompatibilist contention.

There are, of course, different regularity accounts. Although reasonable differences exist concerning the conditions of accept-ability of the predicates in laws, reasonable restrictions on predicates alone will not narrow the class sufficiently. We will be left with an indefinitely large number of true generalizations which happen to subsume human actions, but do not render them necessary in any interesting sense.

Now regularity theorists do not all agree on the other conditions a generalization must meet to be a law. But the important point is that the kinds of conditions traditionally postulated, e.g., scope, non-locality, comprehensiveness, cannot ground the difference between an action's simply obtaining and its necessarily obtaining (assuming solutions to the other nontrivial problems associated with this inference). Nor would that conclusion be warranted on the basis of the additional piece of information that the pertinent generalization belongs to a comprehensive and relatively simple system of general-izations. But these sorts of features are precisely what constitute the nomic status of certain generalizations according to regularity theorists. Hence, the truth of the regularity theory would block the inference desired by the incompatibilist. At least, the burden of proof would fall upon the shoulders of the incompatibilist.[6]

THE SIGNIFICANCE OF ALTERNATIVE
SEMANTIC ACCOUNTS

A central question, then, concerns the possibility of defending a nonmodal definition of the predicate 'is a natural law'. The centrality of this question can be highlighted by the relative unimportance to the issue before us of the construction of a system of necessity, and a possible world semantics for such a system.

Smith is afflicted with agoraphobia. Let 'Ps' describe the collective sufficient condition of the state which makes As true where 'As' means 'Smith flees from an open space'. If Ps f As is a law (or an instance of a law), we may detach As and, in system SCN, infer 'It is contingently necessary that As'.[7]

Now one apparent merit of the possible worlds interpretation is that it seems intuitively to capture a notion of inevitability. For the idea of As's inevitability can be explained by noting that As obtains not just in the actual world, but also in other worlds where Ps obtains, no matter what the other conditions are. We may imagine Smith trying to tamper with other conditions and, as the model system would show him, being doomed to frustration. All model sets containing Ps also contain As even if they vary from Smith's world in all the ways Smith might try to prevent As. One might even say, therefore, that the possible worlds account captures the idea of necessity that forms the basis for exempting Smith from responsibility. We cannot justly hold Smith responsible if, given that Ps is fixed, he is only allowed to change conditions that will leave As unaffected.

The argument fails. The possible worlds interpretation does not capture the inevitability of As; it rather presupposes it. If we begin with a model system for logical necessity, there will be a world with Ps and $-$As. Ps$\supset$As is not a logical truth. So Ps $\cdot$ $-$As is logically possible. If we say that As is inevitable given Ps, we do not mean 'logically inevitable'. So, in the above paragraph the alternatives to the actual world or fixed model set must be limited to those which are physically possible. That is, the possible worlds interpretation says that the contingent necessity or inevitability of As given Ps is constituted by the appearance of As in all model sets which both contain Ps *and* – this is crucial – do not violate natural law. So Smith is doomed to frustration because he does not succeed in any *nomically* possible world. But why those worlds? Why don't we regard Smith as responsible for As given that there is a logically possible world in which Ps obtains and As does not? Conversely, why do we not exempt Smith from responsibility for some action, say B, if there is some truth Cs such that Cs⊃Bs is true in many other possible worlds, but not *all* nomically possible ones. For example, 'All the coins in my pocket on V-E day are dimes' is, let us suppose, a true accidental generalization. I cannot claim that the removal of a certain nickel from my pocket a week before V-E day is inevitable just because there is a model system containing no set which violates this generalization. For the model system is now too narrow. It can have been arbitrarily obtained from the system of nomically possible worlds. Just as the system of logically possible model sets is too large; so this set is too small. Only the model system of all nomically possible worlds is, to quote Baby Bear, just right. But why?

Not only are we not provided with an answer to this question, but we know that the question can be rejected if the regularity theory is true. For reasons given earlier, the inference that As is necessary is not justified if the regularity theory can be defended.

One might wonder if an incompatibilist can construct a semantic interpretation which would be immune to the above rejection, that is, one a regularity theorist cannot accept. We know that the shift to a de re interpretation of necessity is fraught with difficulty.[8] Yet even if necessity were treated as a feature of events, it is difficult to formulate precisely a semantic approach which would be rejected by the compatibilist and embraced by the incompatibilist. Assuming no objections to events as such, we may have them in the domain of the interpretation. The predicate 'is necessary', then, would typically be interpreted via its extension, i.e., a set of events. This extensional interpretation cannot upset the compatibilist unless he is also an extreme nominalist. He not only would not object to this set; but he, too, regards it as a natural set to identify, i.e., the set of law-governed events. One is inclined to say then that he objects to the intension of this predicate. But if the intension of a predicate is given, for example, by a function which maps possible worlds into extensions, it is clear from earlier remarks that the notion of intension is also acceptable to a compatibilist.

Continuing our search for a semantic interpretation which will permit the debate between compatibilist and incompatibilist to be joined, we consider now the construal, not prima facie implausible, of 'necessary' as a predicate modifier. The attractiveness of this proposal is grounded in part on the frequency with which the adverbial form 'necessarily' is found in ordinary discourse, relative to other grammatical constructions. Rather than saying that a law and initial conditions establish that the assumption of a property by an individual is necessary, we say rather that the property was shown to be assumed necessarily. The adverbial form becomes paradigmatic – properties and relations are acquired necessarily or contingently. The predicate modifier 'necessarily' appears as an operator, forming new predicates out of old ones. Clark and others have explored the semantical possibilities of systems incorporating this approach and the results are again neutral from the perspective of the compatibilist-incompatibilist controversy.[9] Briefly, according to Clark, the complications produced by predicate modifiers require the introduction of the notion of a state of affairs, i.e., the exemplification of some n-tuple of an attribute whose extension is some subset of all n-tuples construct-ible from the domain.[10] Rather than having the interpretation just assign extensions to predicates, instead it assigns states of affairs. Core predicates, i.e., ones which have not been constructed from simpler predicates, will be assigned the set of states of affairs which actually obtain, i.e., the facts, when the predicate is truly ascribed to individuals, relative to the interpretation.

The next stage involves the formulation of rules for determining how a modifier changes the set of states of affairs assigned to the original predicate by the interpretation. Modifiers vary here. For example, the set of things rapidly done by John is a subset of the set of things done by John. But the set of things nearly done by John is not a subset of the set of things done by John. A standard modifier like 'rapidly' determines a subset of the set of states of affairs assigned to the core predicate. 'Necessarily', of course, is a standard modifier and so, it, too, determines a subset of the set assigned originally to its core predicate. And that ends the story, a story which does not have an unhappy ending for a compatibilist.

For he has no objection to the identification of those truths about the world that are so in virtue of laws and initial conditions from the larger class of truths. For him, too, this is a natural class to form because there is a real distinction between natural laws and other true generalizations.

The moral is the same if we reflect upon van Fraassen's treatment of predicate modifiers.[11] This theory, a variant of Clark's, regards the intension of 'necessarily Φ' as simply a proper subclass of the intension of 'Φ'. So we again have the harmless result that acts done necessarily are a subclass of acts which are done. The results are harmless for the familiar reason that the compatibilist has no objection to the identification of a bona fide subclass of human actions, namely, the law-governed ones. Moreover, the manner by which the compatibilist identifies this subclass does not preclude his using van Fraassen's semantics in all its detail.

In fact a radical regularity theorist can treat 'necessarily' the way van Fraassen treats 'brightly' when applied to 'hard', that is, as having the null set as its intension. To be sure, 'brightly' modifies some predicates, e.g., 'is colored', so as to determine a nonempty intension. But nothing van Fraassen says precludes treating 'necessarily' as a modifier of predicates which reduces the intension of the original to the null set.

But it is again more illuminating for the compatibilist to allow 'necessarily Φ' to have a nonempty intension and a nonempty extension. The point again is that the semantic characterization of necessity is in no way objectionable to the compatibilist. So we do not yet know why the attribution of necessity to an action (in any of the various logical forms considered) is cause for concern, i.e., why it is the basis of a longstanding philosophical dispute.

The moral, though not unfamiliar, is worth stressing. The semanticist's concern with interpretations which enable him to define validity and consequence within some theory also enable him to ignore vital components of the meaning of terms within the theory.

This conclusion survives an examination of a system constructed in order to express a novel, yet substantive view about the meaning of modal terms. Morton, who explicitly recognizes that a semantics designed for a modal language cannot capture the important components of meaning, even if it can impose constraints on a theory of meaning, replaces possible worlds with partial worlds.[12] These vary in terms of the amount of detail they contain and their proximity to the maximal detail of the total world, and represent the intuition that modal words are used to indicate features of the world we cannot or do not want to describe explicitly.

In this system 'A→B' represents the subjunctive conditional. But since Morton's truth conditions have as a consequence that A→B in the total world if A and B are both true, this connective requires no necessary (or any other) connection between A and B. A similar result accrues to the monadic operator 'it is necessary that'. It turns out that it is weaker than we require, failing, for example, to distinguish de facto empty sets from necessarily empty sets. Morton had warned us that we might look for too much in semantics.

Compatibilists, we conclude, ought not to be disturbed by systems of necessity, but rather by philosophical claims about such systems. Each provides *some* way of distinguishing de facto from de jure truths, but does not preclude the eventual reduction of this distinction to a more complex distinction within the de facto domain. The use of any of these theories, therefore, to characterize modal talk and the resultant characterization of the truth of some sentences of the form 'It is necessary that Jones do A' will not, according to the regularity theorist, entitle one to draw the conclusion that Jones is absolved from moral responsibility for having done A.

Is it then impossible to construct a semantics for factual necessity which would be unacceptable to a compatibilist? Let us try. Suppose that it is a law that all P is Q. Consider now a simple world with two objects a and b in which the following is true: Pa, Qa, −Pb, −Qb. Since the compatibilist-incompatibilist controversy is independent of general ontological questions, we shall simplify issues by allowing ourselves a liberal ontology. An atomic sentence S is true if and only if the state of affairs |S| is a member of the set of facts. Since 'All P is Q' is a law, it tells us that if Pb were true, Qb would be true, i.e., that Pb subjunctively implies Qb. A sentence S_1 subjunctively implies another S_2 if and only if the ordered pair $\langle |S_1|, |S_2| \rangle$ is a member of the set of ordered pairs $\{\langle |Pa|, |Qa| \rangle, \langle |Pb|, |Qb| \rangle\}$. (Call this set SL.) Suppose now that, for some predicates V and W, Va, Wa, −Vb, −Wb. So it is also true

127

that all V is W. But since neither ordered pair $\langle |Va|, |Wa| \rangle$ nor $\langle |Vb|, |Wb| \rangle$ is a member of SL, it is neither true that Va subjunctively implies Wa nor that Vb subjunctively implies Wb.[13] 'All V is W' is then accidentally true. Consider now the converse domain of SL, namely $\{ |Qa|, |Qb| \}$. The intersection of this set and the set of atomic facts is $\{ |Qa| \}$, the set of contingently necessary facts. We may now easily characterize 'S_1 factually entails S_2'. This sentence is true if the ordered pair $\langle |S_1|, |S_2| \rangle$ is a member of SL and each element of the pair is also a member of the set of facts.

Without considering more detail, is there anything in this account that is unacceptable to a regularity theorist? Factual entailment or necessity and contingent necessity are defined in terms of subjunctive implication. But the extension of subjunctive implication is just given. 'SL', thus, is introduced as a primitive predicate. For example, $\langle |Pb|, |Qb| \rangle$ is, but $\langle |Vb|, |Wb| \rangle$ is not included in its extension. Nothing accounts for this difference. Or, if it rests on something, we will in any case have to reinvoke, at a deeper level perhaps, this primitive and unexplained distinction. Qua regularity theorist, therefore, he is not bothered by the relation in extension of subjunctive implication or factual entailment or by the very liberal ontology herein involved. He is disturbed rather by the word 'primitive'. He believes that 'SL' need not appear in a list of primitive predicates. A description of the world can be complete even if it does not identify this extension. 'SL' is like 'fatherhood'. There is a set of ordered pairs constituting the extension of 'is a father of'; but we need not identify it to say all we want to say. There is no primitive property (relation) denoted by 'SL'.

This is not to say that 'SL' cannot be (logically) primitive. We earlier noted the acceptability to an opponent of necessitarianism of a syntax which contains a modal primitive. For the issue can be defused by a nonmodal account of 'natural law'. The issue, then, can be formulated in terms of the necessity of having a system in which 'SL' is primitive. If the regularity theorist is right, we don't need such a system. A nonmodal definition of 'natural law' or 'SL' would enable one to bypass such systems, even though simplicity would have to be sacrificed, and the inclination to treat subjunctive implication as ultimately more than a relation in extension, as a primitive feature of facts, may disappear.

Am I then contending that the classical freewill debate between compatibilist and incompatibilist is nothing other than the classical debate in the philosophy of science between necessitarians and regularity theorists? Not quite. If the regularity theory is not defensible and the incompatibilist argument cannot in this way be blocked, we are left with something like the primitive relation of necessitation between facts and the related contingent necessity of some of those facts. Now the incompatibilist believes that a fact's being contingently necessary implies the absence of responsibility for that fact. Can this belief be justified or must he rest upon an appeal to intuition? Granted that normative conclusions must ultimately rest upon descriptions, why does this normative conclusion rest upon the presence or absence of this property, namely, contingent necessity? An attempt to answer this question may be doomed to failure; but if not, we will be delving into aspects of the meaning of necessity left untouched by accounts we have considered or alluded to. So the burden upon an incompatibilist is constituted by the dilemma: Either I appeal to intuition to establish the link between the metaphysical and the moral or I explain the link. If I appeal to intuition, I am subject to the typical responses to any such appeal. If I try to explain the link, I must have something to say; but what?

The burden on the compatibilist, even if he establishes the regularity theory, is one he has borne, but not with distinction. If we cannot say of the man falling out of the window that he is absolved from responsibility for failing to reverse direction because he literally must fall, why then is he absolved? Or given that we say that he cannot go up, what nonmodal fact is the basis of this judgment? We all know many inadequate proposals, like the fact that he would not reverse direction if he tried to do so. Anti-compatibilist writers like Campbell, Chisholm, and Anscombe have documented numerous failures. If the compatibilist is right, there must be a nonmodal grounding of freedom and responsibility. But no proposal so far advanced is free from difficulty though we advanced some suggestions on this score in chapter 6.

So there are real issues that survive a resolution of the necessitarian-regularity debate. But the centrality of this debate is worth emphasizing and that is one of my aims.

DIRECT EVIDENCE FOR NECESSITARIANISM

Most of the evidence for the view that laws are necessary is indirect. But a case might be constructed on direct empirical grounds. The claim has been advanced that we actually perceive instances of nomic or causal necessity. Suppose that '$(x)(Fx \supset Gx)$' is a law whose instances, e.g., '$Fa \cdot Ga$', are alleged to be perceived as necessary. That is, '$Fa \overrightarrow{f} Ga$' is allegedly known to be true on the basis of perception.

This position is untenable for several reasons. First, laws in which there is a large temporal gap between instances of the antecedent and corresponding instances of the consequent would have to be excluded. No one can literally observe the necessitation of Smith's agoraphobia by his constitution and some early childhood experiences. Second, A. Michotte found in his important work on *The Perception of Causality* that we do not perceive causal necessity.[14] This conclusion is especially interesting in light of Michotte's bias against the regularity theory. He does contend that we perceive causal *activity*. But I have argued elsewhere that this conclusion is not warranted by the evidence he cites.[15]

Third, although it is true that we form causal beliefs and, perhaps, have impressions that one event is causing or necessitating another, it does not follow that we perceive (causal) necessity. To show this, we need only establish that the beliefs and impressions in question, e.g., the belief that $Fa \overrightarrow{f} Ga$, are partially caused by psychological and/or neurological facts about the perceiver which are not also facts that are causally relevant to evaluating the sentence '$Fa \overrightarrow{f} Ga$'. Elsewhere, I argued that these considerations justify the conclusion that causal impressions are subjective or nonveridical.[16]

The phenomenon of unsuccessful effort may give rise to the belief that necessity is experienced, either the necessity of failure or the necessity that one must try harder. But if one does not know that one's efforts are maximal, one does not know that failure is necessary. For if one can try harder, either one is uncertain that one will fail or the certainty of failure is the result of inference, not perception. I know that even if I were to try harder, as hard as I can, I would not lift the World Trade Center. But I do not *experience* the necessity of failure; I know it prior to any effort, by inference.

Suppose that, even if I am not certain that an effort is supreme, I believe strongly that it is. Might I not have experienced a necessary fact? The fact that I might be wrong about an object's color does not mean I don't perceive the color.

A compatibilist may well accept this possibility and the consequence that I am absolved from responsibility for the failure. But the belief that laws are generally necessarily true must be based on stronger considerations. For if it is necessary that I do not try harder, then '(P⊃it is necessary that I do not try harder)' is a law regardless of what we substitute for 'P'. But the core laws are those whose consequents are not intrinsically necessary, whose necessity is grounded in a relation between antecedent and consequent.

The necessitarian may note that such necessity is not intrinsic, that it depends, for example, on facts about one's musculature. If we represent these facts by M, then the law is: M⊃I fail to try harder to do A. Given M, and certain conditions, I have an experience (of 'maximal' effort) which grounds an inference to the conclusion that the failure is necessary. And why not call this necessity, depending as it does on M, contingent necessity?

An advantage of distinguishing the maximal effort from the contingent necessity to which one is entitled to infer is that one may then inductively infer the necessity in cases in which one does not have the experience of maximal effort, so long as conditions are relevantly similar.

The necessitarian case ultimately fails, however, for suppose I am not making a maximal effort to do A and would do A if I tried harder. There may be laws governing my minimal efforts which cannot be grounded in the experience of maximal effort for, if it were expended, I would do A.

If the incompatibilist is right and the world is deterministic, there is a sense in which *all* effort is maximal. Since nothing can be different, no one can ever try harder than he in fact tries. But such views, I believe, *rest* on the belief in the necessity of laws and cannot be advanced, therefore, in *defense* of necessitarianism. If there is something special in the experience of maximal effort, an argument which generalizes to all laws on its account cannot bear the required weight. No independent reasons to believe that the law explaining my expenditure of 'minimal' effort is necessary has been provided.

INDIRECT EVIDENCE FOR NECESSITARIANISM

A recourse with greater prospects for success is the grounding of the necessity of laws in considerations less direct than the alleged perception of a necessary connection.

The general form of indirect arguments for the necessity of laws is that a certain fact can only be or is better accounted for on the assumption that laws are necessary.

Laws are, of course, used for prediction. But the fact that laws are used successfully for this purpose cannot be a basis for the conclusion that they are necessary for predictions based on true accidental generalizations will also be successful. It may be pointed out that predictions from accidental generalizations are not legitimate because their instances do not confirm them and do not, therefore, ground inferences. But the class of generalizations which are confirmed by their instances is larger than the class of laws and includes generalizations that are clearly not necessarily true. A generalization is confirmed by its instances if we believe that the existence of exclusively positive instances is no accident or has an explanation that warrants a generalization of the instances. For example, if the first 30 men I observe in a room are over 7 feet tall, I am entitled to infer that the next man I observe in the room is over 7 feet tall. For it is more plausible to suppose this than it is to suppose that it is just an accident that all the men I have observed are so tall. Perhaps it is a special group, e.g., tryouts for the position of center on a professional basketball team. But 'All the men in this room are over 7 feet tall' is neither a law nor necessarily true.

The reason this generalization is not a law is that if Jones, who is 6 feet tall, were in the room, not all the men in the room would be over 7 feet tall. The fact that laws sustain counterfactuals is a very persuasive reason for believing that laws are necessary. The argument is as follows.

If laws are formulated nonmodally, they take the form '$(x)(Px \supset Qx)$'. But the acceptance of a generalization of this form does not warrant 'If c were P, c would be Q'. In nontruthfunctional terms, all one can say is '$Pc \supset Qc$'. This is obviously too weak since the falsity of the antecedent also renders true '$Pc \supset -Qc$'.

The response of the regularity theorist is that 'If c were P, c would be Q' is warranted not by the truth of '$(x)(Px \supset Qx)$', but rather by the stronger claim that the sentence is a law. (Obviously there are true sentences of this form that do not sustain counterfactuals.) But this rebuttal succeeds only if the law-making characteristic the regularity theorist has in mind enables a grounding of the inference to the counterfactual. According to the necessitarian, a characteristic that does this perfectly is necessity. If the law is necessarily true then instances of the law would take the form '$Px \vec{f} Qx$'. Most, but not all, necessitarians would say that any instance of this form entails '$(x)(Pf \vec{f} Qx)$' and, therefore, '$Pc \vec{f} Qc$'. We can read '$Px \vec{f} Qx$' so that it does not entail 'Px', in which case '$Pc \vec{f} Qc$' can be used counterfactually. (It can be read subjunctively because it does not entail '$-Pc$'; but this can be conjoined to make explicit the counterfactual feature.) This direct grounding of the counterfactual is made possible by reading '$Pa \vec{f} Qa$' as a's being P would render necessary a's being Q'. The sentence is not about properties or their realizations. But the necessitarian grounds the sentence in such a fact, viz., the fact that the appearance anywhere of some property requires the appearance there of some other property. Hence, a knowledge of a single instance is a knowledge of all instances, even possible and counterfactual ones.

But if we mere mortals are entitled only to instantial knowledge of the form '$Px \cdot Qx$', what good are these speculations? The necessitarian's point is that our acceptance of counterfactuals belies a rejection of the stronger sentence, whether or not we have direct empirical evidence for it.

Although it may be true that a necessitarian interpretation would explain the truth of counterfactuals, we do not have sufficient reasons to accept that explanation.

If we had sufficient reasons to accept the necessitarian account, we would have to conclude that inductive inferences grounded in laws presuppose necessitarianism and that regularity theorists cannot, therefore, consistently argue inductively. I do not deny the categorial difference between the actual and the merely possible. But inferences about the character of the possible have the same basis as do inferences about the as yet unobserved. My reason for believing that the next crow I see will be black is the same as my reason for believing that a handkerchief would be black if it were a crow. The basis for my belief remains unaffected whether or not my handkerchief turns into a crow. And if I report that the bird is black because it is a crow, and then learn that in fact it is a European blackbird, I can say that it would still have been black had it been a crow for the same reasons I originally applied (mistakenly) my information. But then if I have to suppose that laws are necessary to make counterfactual judgments, I shall have to suppose them necessary to make predictions about the future. To put it simply, the necessitarian says that one has no right to suppose that the possible conforms to the actual if the actual is comprised of mere regularities. But the regularity theorist presses the case by saying that, if the necessitarian is right, we have no right to suppose that the actual unobserved conforms to the actual observed if the regularity theory is true.

I cannot show here that this argument constitutes a reductio ad absurdum of the necessitarian position since such a demonstration would take us far afield. The literature on the question of the justification of induction is vast and all we can do here is note the prominence of many positions that are consistent with the regularity theory. There are the practicalists,[17] the inductivists,[18] the dissolutionists,[19] and the ordinary language proponents,[20] to name a few. If they are all wrong, then, perhaps, the necessitarian is right.

9

The regularity theory of laws

DEFENSE OF THE REGULARITY THEORY

The regularity theorist is obliged to do two related things. Since he believes laws are not distinguished from other true generalizations by their necessity, he must say how they differ and he must show how his account helps to explain the truth-values assigned to counterfactuals. Consider the latter first.

When we examine the implications of a false proposition, we wonder how *our* world would have been had the proposition been true. We do not, therefore, adopt other false assumptions gratuitously. To quote Pollock, 'what is involved in counterfactuals is the notion of a minimal change being made to the actual world in order to accommodate the counterfactual supposition. We must change the world in some way in order to make the antecedent true, but we are constrained to make the change as small as possible'.[1] If we imagine that Jones lives on Elm Street, we do not as a consequence imagine that he is a pacifist, even if in fact all people living on Elm Street are pacifists (E), because (1) the rejection of E does not reverberate through the rest of our knowledge, i.e., the fall of E leaves the rest of our knowledge pretty much intact, and (2) any necessary conditions of pacifism not possessed by Jones would, as a consequence of considering him a pacifist, no longer be regarded as necessary conditions of pacifism and this supposition would have more or less serious implications for our knowledge, but in any case more serious than the rejection of E. According to the regularity theorist, what makes a true generalization a law is this very systemic importance and it remains for us now to formulate this idea more precisely.

To wonder how *our* world would have been had some proposition been true is *not* to wonder how our actual beliefs are affected by the addition to our knowledge of this proposition. As Lewis says, if a Warrenite comes to believe 'Oswald did not kill Kennedy', then since he retains 'Kennedy was killed', on the view that the relevant matter is the effect on our beliefs, he should affirm

(1) If Oswald had not killed Kennedy, someone else did.[2]

Instead, he affirms

(2) If Oswald had not killed Kennedy, Kennedy would not have been killed.

In our world, Kennedy would not have been killed had Oswald not killed him beause there was in fact no other potential killer or conspiracy, or so we believe, and because of the laws by which our world operates. Although we continue to believe Kennedy was killed in spite of the supposition that Oswald did not kill him, we do not permit 'Kennedy was killed' to be a background assumption along with 'Oswald did not kill Kennedy' to draw further inferences. For the two assumptions combined with other admissible assumptions such as 'There were no other potential killers' are nomically inconsistent or worse. Any conclusions would then follow about a world quite remote from ours.

I do not here suppose that I have made any advance on the famous issue of the definition of this class of admissible assumptions, i.e., the issue of cotenability. I am saying that the resistance to nomically impossible worlds derives from the systemic importance of laws which explains why such worlds are far removed from ours in a way worlds in which true nonnomic generalizations are denied are not. Thus, learning that Jones, the man I had always believed to be a warmonger, lives on Elm Street, I readily surrender E for very little else is at stake. A non-E world is quite close to ours; so that 'Jones is not a pacifist' is judged cotenable with 'Jones lives on Elm Street'. Since my concern is to change as little as possible besides the counterfactual assumption, the systematic isolation of E permits its rejection over the belief in Jones' non-pacifism.

Suppose the following propositions form a nomically inconsistent set:

(1) The sun is in position P_1 (true)

(2) I am in position P_2 (true)

(3) I am seven feet tall (false)

(4) My shadow is other than fourteen feet long (true)

Suppose as well that the conjuction of (1) and (2) is cotenable with (3) and with (4). We would all agree that if (3) were true then (4) would be false. Similarly, (1), (2), $-(3)$, $-(4)$ are a nomically inconsistent set and the conjunction of (1) and (2) is cotenable with $-(3)$ and with $-(4)$. But why on my account would we *not* say that if $-(4)$ were true, $-(3)$ would be false, i.e., if my shadow were fourteen feet long, I would be seven feet tall?

First of all, we do say such things. Counterfactuals are not always causal in character. They sometimes can be interpreted as affirming what it would be reasonable to infer, and that is not always an effect. (If he looks gloomy, he lost.)

Second, although we shall soon take up the issue of the direction of causation, here we need only remind ourselves that I am not arguing that an understanding of the role of laws *suffices* to account for the truth conditions of all varieties of counterfactuals. That would be absurd. Many other factors play a role.[3]

Elsewhere, I defended a conception according to which laws are those true generalizations that appear in systems that account in an economical way for at least as many facts (sentences) of a given type as any other system.[4] This conception highlights the systemic importance of laws and the consequent seriousness of rejecting a sentence hitherto believed to be a law. For a law combines the virtues of strength and economy. But the details turned out to be unduly complex and appeared to have an ad hoc quality. I believe the basic feature of that account can be preserved without these deficiencies.[5]

DETERMINISTIC ACCOUNTS

A deterministic system of laws or a deterministic theory will be regarded in an admittedly idealized and oversimplified manner as a deductive system whose axioms are true generalizations, most or all of which are logically contingent and display strong logical independence (SLI) formulated in a first-order language rich enough to accommodate the scientific vocabulary of a natural language like English combined with required mathematics and extended in whatever ways deemed essential by scientists. Certain predicates are ruled out of axioms by a set of admissibility requirements. We require as a minimum that predicates not be self-contradictory, closed (applies *by virtue of meaning* to a finite number of instances) and positional. (Positionality is, of course, a problematic notion. Accordingly, I would not want to preclude the manner of rejection. We can all agree that the basic laws of nature should not contain 'grue' even if we disagree about the weapon to use and even if 'grue' is eliminated without invoking the concept of positionality at all, e.g., by noting that 'green' is better entrenched than 'grue'.)

There is in this language a set of true sentences $\{R\}$ such that determinism is true only if each number of $\{R\}$ has a deterministic account.[6] Sentence R_1 has a deterministic account if it is deducible from a true theory T conjoined with a state description legitimate relative to that theory and R_1.

Given the transitivity of deducibility, it follows that a deterministic account of S is an account of all logical consequences of S. There are problems here. By advancing the reasonable stipulation that T be required for the deduction, one of Kim's objections is overcome. He notes that 'one logical consequence of x is the disjunction $x \lor y$, where y is the state description used in the given deterministic account of x'.[7] Since T is not required to derive $x \lor y$ from y, we are not saddled with the unacceptable result that y is a deterministic account of x or y. The more serious and familiar problem, also pointed out by Kim, is that the Frege-Gödel argument would permit one deterministic account to be the

138

account of all truths if we allow unrestricted referential substitutivity. Reams have been written on the problem for it is relevant to a number of philosophical issues, including one closely related to my concern, namely, the construction of an account of deductive explanation. Although I have no original insights to offer here, I believe that an approach which would bar referential substitutivity, or permit it in such a way as to preserve distinctions of scope,[8] should block the Frege-Gödel argument.

A state description is a conjunction C of true sentences some conjuncts of which may be mathematical or linguistic sentences; but C as a whole, through describing a particular state of the system at a moment or during an interval to which T applies, has empirical content. Moreover, C is logically and criterially independent of R, a consideration which renders T nonredundant. There will also be characteristics a system must possess in order to have T apply to it.

For each sentence in {R}, there may or may not be a deterministic account for it, known or not. Suppose we collect the sentences into groups, depending on the theory embodied in the deterministic account. So, for each theory T_n, there is the set of sentences {S_n} accounted for by it (plus state descriptions). {S_n} determines all the facts T_n *can* account for.

The above is a highly minimal sketch, abstractly rendered. For our purposes, the important deficiency is the absence of a criterion for ruling out theories (or laws) which are only de facto true, which merely record accidental relations among properties.

There are difficulties in this account which pertain to a more precise account of the thesis of determinism. If {$S_1, S_2, \ldots S_n$} is the set of sentences accounted for by all true theories, the set constituted by the deductive closure of the conjunction of all the members of this set should include {R} if determinism is true. But there are problems moving from the idealized realm to which theories apply fairly neatly to the real world of human behavior where events, described in a nontechnical vocabulary, are the products of a variety of distinct forces. It has frequently been pointed out, for example, that the occurrence of any mundane event depends not just on the causal factors which may be alluded to in a nomic account which is the most obviously relevant one, but also on the failure of an indefinitely large number of intervening factors to take place, any one of which would have prevented that event from occurring. This sort of situation is far more common than the one in which we are able to produce a law without a ceteris paribus clause, a clause which requires us to acknowledge that a bona fide sufficient condition of the predicted event includes the nonexistence of all possible interferences, a set we can only loosely characterize. The determinist is forced, the charge continues, to broaden the characterization of the state description to include the entire universe, either at an instant or during a brief interval, so as to be sure that there is nothing outside the system which might interfere with the expected effect. Correlatively, he would then have to form a supertheory by conjoining all true theories. What emerges is quite remote from standard scientific accounts of explanation by appeal to laws.

Remoteness is not the only issue. Events depend on a variety of factors studied by different sciences. My behavior may depend on a combination of psychological facts (a cheery disposition), meteorological facts (the persistent rain), physiological facts (kidney stones), chemical facts (my failure to create gold from iron ore), and other (?) facts (my sister's winning a great deal of money in Atlantic City). The determinist must suppose, not only that each science can produce deterministic theories for its own domains, but that theories can be formulated which would demonstrate that *any* combination of forces can be described as a determinate function of the individual ones. These theories would not be theories of any known science; yet the determinist is committed to a belief in their existence (and, a fortiori, truth).

Other issues pertaining to determinism concern the desirability of a formulation, as we have presented, in terms of sentences rather than propositions. Appealing to sentences, we have had to specify the language in which theories are to be formulated and have done that quite loosely ('a first-order language rich enough to accommodate the scientific vocabulary of a natural language like English combined with required mathematics and extended in whatever ways deemed essential by scientists'). We could have avoided the vague allusion to language extension by relativizing determinism to a specific language. But the price, which some are prepared to pay, is the impossibility of defining a general thesis of determinism, the sort of doctrine which plays a role in free will debates. (Libertarians in 1984 are not worried about determinism-in-English$_{1984}$. A new scientific concept formulated in 1985 may permit the construction of theories which the libertarian would be rightly concerned about.)

But our concern is not determinism. As stated before, we can study the issues of interest to us by understanding what a deterministic account is. There are such, whether determinism is true or not. This is not to say that all these problems may be ignored. We are obliged to give a general characterization of a deterministic account and have had, therefore, to specify a language in the vague way presented. (The alternative, an account in terms of propositions, suffers from the familiar vice of offering a word in place of hard work.) But we, unlike the determinist, are not committed to those super-theories which belong to no science, although the existence of deterministic accounts for most of the interesting ones, bits of real human behavior, require something like super-theories.

Another thesis seriously narrowing the scope of deterministic accounts, but not within the scope of our concerns, should at least be identified. Instrumentalists and fictionalists of various ilks would object to the assumption that theories, deterministic or otherwise, should be characterized as true. Although the more familiar version of this doctrine would preclude the characterization of theories as true or false, some versions, e.g., Cartwright's, proclaim that theories contain false propositions, in particular, the fundamental equations of advanced physical theories.[9] The generalizations which have the best chance of being true are the lower level phenomenological ones, the ones formulated in terms of observation concepts and possessing, for that reason, quite narrow scope. On Cartwright's view, then, if a deterministic account must contain only truths, they are few in relation even to the phenomena 'covered' by nonstatistical scientific theories. Moreover, given the nature of scientific theorizing, there is no hope that future scientific progress will provide greater support for determinism even if more phenomena are captured by scientific accounts. If we embrace her point of view as well as the other objections to super-theories, we will be left with very little human behavior falling within the scope of determination, and we will have achieved this result independently of purely empirical doubts, many of which are, it seems to me, well-grounded, pertaining to the scope of psychological determination.

CAUSAL PRIORITY

There is, in addition, another serious deficiency, to wit, the absence of a criterion to determine whether C and R_1 are causally related and if so, whether indeed C is causally prior to R_1. Since the account is deterministic only if C is causally prior to R_1, the fact that T contains only bona fide laws is not sufficient for describing the account as causal.

It is clear that virtually all proposed solutions to the problem of the nature of causal priority are compatible with the denial that laws are necessarily true. One can, that is, supplement a regularity account with those features claimed by some to be the ground of causal priority. I shall suppose that adequate defense of this statement could be provided for such candidates as temporal priority, fixity, identity or transference,[10] manipulatibility, various asymmetries of the condition relation, and the view I advanced in *Determinism*. (Obviously, the regularity theory is also compatible with the denial of causal priority.)

The picture is not that clear for those positions which deny that the causal relation is constituted by two separate features, one which establishes that two events are causally connected and the other which tells you how to distinguish cause from effect. In fact, there are three possible stages. Two states or events may be linked by a noncausal law such as Kepler's laws or any of the taxonomic ones of biology. If a necessitarian wishes to regard all laws as necessary, he would thus engage the regularity theorist at a stage prior to the introduction even of the notion of causal connectedness. Assuming that the regularity theorist is successful, he would then tackle causation by insisting that states or events which are causally connected are so related by virtue of a feature, either of the sequence or the law subsuming the sequence, which implies neither that the sequence nor the law is necessary. If this feature is dubbed the causal connectedness feature (CCF), it may be distinguished, conceptually at least, from the causal priority feature (CPF), the characteristic which determines the distinction between cause and effect. Again, if the regularity theorist has survived up until this point, he would still have to determine whether CPF involves necessity.

But suppose there is no coherent notion of symmetric causal connection, or CCF. Causal priority would nontrivially imply causation (CPF would imply CCF) in that whatever condition establishes causal direction would ipso facto establish causation. Those who defend the primitiveness of the concept of causation have at least this in mind.[11]

This conception of causation is typically advanced by singularists, i.e., those who believe that the causal relation does not involve, except perhaps epistemically (and perhaps only in some cases), laws linking causally related events. One identifies causal relations directly, independently of nomic relations between event types (though nomic knowledge is useful and, in certain cases, essential), and in such a way as to close the question of causal priority. One notes that *a* causes *b*, not that *a* and *b* are causally connected *and* that *a* is prior to *b*.

I have criticized the singularity view elsewhere.[12] I would but add the observation that, if it were sound, it would have nothing to say about the analysis of laws per se. In denying the importance of laws to causation, it does not bar any particular conception of laws, including a regularity conception. Moreover, the conception of determinism we are working with is essentially nomic, one which does not permit causal *determination* between events which is not constituted by a nomic relation.[13]

Idealist analyses of causal priority in terms of causal activity or agency are embedded in a necessitarian outlook. But, unlike the singularists above, idealists advance causal activity as an *addition* to causal necessity, even were causal necessity to be explicated nonnomically.[14]

Now, if the regularity theory is construed narrowly as just a view about laws, an advocate can ignore the idealist position regarding causal activity and address just the view that laws are necessary truths. (A critique of idealist arguments may be found in *Determinism*.[15]) If, on the other hand, the regularity theorist incorporates an anti-singular stance, he would be obliged to defend it against idealist critics. But the important question for us at this point is whether the regularity theorist can again divide and conquer. Can he, in other words, do again what the primitive conception would bar him from doing, namely, separate the question of connectedness (CCF) from that of priority (CPF), taking his stand on the former (namely, regularity, together with the characteristic, different from necessity, which makes the generalization causal[16]) and an indifferent attitude on the latter? Or does this account of priority in terms of agency preclude or at least render implausible the regularity account of connectedness? To put it simply, does activity itself imply necessity?

Finding the notion of causal activity too obscure and probably ill equipped, due to its source in a narrow range of cases involving human intervention, to provide a general account of causal transactions, I conclude that the regularity theory need not be perturbed by unclarities which persist in the area of causal priority.

We shall at this stage then suppose that, if some law is necessarily true, it does not possess this feature because of the CP-feature which might be present. As we noted earlier, the candidates for CPF in the literature pose no problems for anti-necessitarians.

I have spoken of the CP-feature as if it is a property of the law itself. But this is misleading. Suppose we first attempt to put to one side noncausal laws such as taxonomic, perhaps even developmental ones. (The laws of foetal development do not state that the earlier stages of development *cause* the later ones, although they 'imply' that a causal mechanism explaining the development is operative.)

Where now should we place the laws formulated as, or embodying, differential equations? It is a familiar observation that the symmetrical character of such laws requires us to provide the direction of causation, when the laws are applied to causal processes, from sources extrinsic to the equations. The equations do not have CPF. The temporal symmetry of Maxwell's equations, for example, permits spherical electromagnetic radiation to proceed outward from a point *or* inward from infinity. The decision to regard certain mathematically possible solutions as physically impossible, say, ones permitting radiation to proceed inward, is not derived from the equations, but supplied from independent considerations.[17]

Notice that causal processes are described by laws which do not dictate the causal order because the direction of the process is otherwise ascertained. One can make an even stronger claim.

Differential equations may be used to formulate noncausal laws in the sense that the magnitudes related by the law are not related causally at all. Examples would be the law of the (average) rate of radioactive decay or statistical theories of stochastic chains.[18] (Obviously, these processes may be causal in the sense that other laws may cover *and* explain the processes 'causally.')

Thus the knowledge that a law applies to process P in itself tells you neither that P is causal nor, if it is, what the direction of the process is. Even if P is causal and, unlike the example of spherical radiation above, all the relevant information regarding CPF is contained in the law or theory, although theorists differ as to which information is relevant, CPF is a feature of the process, not the law. This is the trivial observation that if, say, causal priority just is temporal priority, even if the law relates magnitude M_1 at t_1 to M_2 at t_2, the law states an objective feature of the process, namely, that the assumption of some value of M_1 is temporally (causally) prior to the assumption of some value of M_2. Thus, CPF, unlike necessity (interpreted as an operator) is a feature of the process. Nor need we be disturbed about laws not formulated with the help of sophisticated mathematical symbolism, and containing causal language ('Removal of reinforcement *causes* extinction of response', 'Water deprivation *leads* to death'). These state that CPF is present *in* certain processes, without telling us what it is. (But I already said that this sense of the claim is trivial. We do learn that CPF is not an operation.)

Let us then return to the regularity-necessity issue as it pertains to the laws in deterministic theories, putting to one side problems which may arise from the fact that the relation between C (state description) and R_1 (determined state) embodies, not just the nomic connection, but CCF and CPF as well, where the presence of these latter features may or may not follow from the theory itself.

SUPERFLUITY AND AXIOM ECONOMY
REQUIREMENTS ON LAWS

We shall begin to tackle the problem of distinguishing laws from de facto truths by imposing as a requirement on theories that they account for some facts (sentences) not accounted for by a distinct theory (or theories). (Call this the superfluity requirement (S).[19])

Thus, T_1 is eliminated if T_2 accounts for all the facts T_1 accounts for and more. In order to prevent the trivial realization of this condition by conjoining arbitrary axioms to T_1 to form a 'richer' theory which may then be invoked to eliminate T_1, we impose an axiom economy requirement (AE). It is plausible independently of our concerns to require that a theory not be a mere concatenation of assumptions, that a conjunction of two axioms accounts for some facts not accounted for by the axioms considered separately.

A proviso must be introduced, however, in order to prevent the elimination by application of the S-requirement of a bona fide law, e.g., 'All emeralds are green' via replacement by two generalizations, 'All emeralds in China are green' and 'All emeralds outside China are green', the conjunction of which is equivalent in accounting power to the original. If we compare this relationship to that which obtains between a sentence such as '$-(B_1\lor -B_2)$' and two generalizations totally irrelevant to each other, B_1 and B_2, whose conjunction is equivalent to that sentence, we can identify a genuine advance in the formulation 'All emeralds are green' inapplicable to '$-(-B_2\lor -B_2)$'. The former tells us that location, e.g., 'in China', 'outside China', is irrelevant to 'is green'. Thus, the initial conditions or state of the system is significantly altered relative to the accounts of facts of the form 'x is green'. Such is not the case for '$-(-B_1\lor -B_2)$'. 'All emeralds are green' is not just a concatenation of the two lower-order generalizations in virtue of the fact that we learn that 'being an emerald' identifies, in itself, a sufficient condition of being green. In fact, then, there is an inconsistency between 'All emeralds are green' and each lower-order generalization. The inconsistency is not formal, but derives

146

rather from the assumption that only relevant properties may be mentioned in laws. Thus, a theory T_1 is not eliminated even if it is equivalent to a conjunction whose conjuncts collectively account for the same set of facts T_1 accounts for, so long as T_1 has all the merits of the conjunction and is simpler.

The concept of simplicity is a notoriously difficult one and I avail myself of it here only because its specific character in this context is clear and unproblematic. The adoption of 'All emeralds are green' explains all the facts explained by each subtheory by reference to a state description that is simpler than each insofar as location-facts are omitted, while everything else remains the same.

The AE-requirement does not eliminate 'All metals conduct electricity' in favor of distinct T's for each distinct metal for the reason that 'metal' is not equivalent to 'copper or brass or zinc or . . . '. Thus, the higher-order generalization is not equivalent to the conjunction of all the lower-order ones and subsumption of the lower-order ones under the higher-order generalization is genuine. Even if we have all the metals, therefore, and even if we suppose that 'All metals conduct electricity' accounts for no fact not accounted for by the more specific generalization, the AE-requirement does not rule out 'All metals conduct electricity' for, although it may be equivalent in accounting power to the conjunction concerning specific metals (in truth it is not), it is not logically equivalent to that conjunction.

T_1 may also be eliminated by incorporation. T_1 may be reduced to or explained by or in some way or another incorporated into a more comprehensive theory T_2. Many so-called accidental generalizations are easily explainable by reference to a bona fide theory. We know, for example, that the workers in London always go to lunch when the factory hooter in Manchester hoots (LM) because that hooting is simultaneous with the hooting of the London factory hooter, a signal the London workers conventionally accept as the initiation of the lunch hour.

We may attempt to block the derivation of LM as a derived law by noting that the deduction itself requires at least one non-nomic generalization such as the information that the London hooter hoots at the same time as the Manchester hooter hoots. But such a restriction, perhaps on state descriptions, may be judged too strong if we consider other illustrations of the derivation of one set of laws from another set, where instantial, non-nomic information about the system is required. The most famous illustration is, perhaps, the derivation of Kepler's from Newton's laws. The derivation requires the factual assumption that the masses of the planets in our solar system are small in comparison to the mass of the sun, thereby rendering negligible the gravitational attraction of the planets. From our point of view, it does not matter whether a generalization is eliminated (as merely 'accidental') or accounted for (and called a 'derived' or 'mixed' law) so long as the acceptability of the theory which accomplishes this is not based on considerations unacceptable to regularity theorists. The issue is joined at the level of basic laws.

At this level, the regularity theory confronts a classic difficulty, to wit, the mode by which he may successfully eliminate generalizations ascertained by enumeration. The elementary illustration concerning metals will do. If it is known that there are but forty-one metals, M_1 to M_{41}, we may derive the bona fide law that all metals conduct electricity from the objectionable theory that each specific M_i conducts electricity plus 'All metal is M_1 (copper) or M_2 (silver) or . . . M_{41}'. The theory is objectionable because it may be an uninteresting contingent fact, not a law, that the world happens to contain no more metals.

Critics of the regularity theory, e.g., Mackie, identify this issue as a serious one. After formulating the core regularity position, to wit, that a law is a part of a system of laws with 'very wide application',[20] Mackie renders the doctrine more precise, but also highly vulnerable, by characterizing width spatiotemporally. Thus, the regularity theorist is placed in the embarrassing position of having to deny that generalizations about living organisms are laws if it turns out that life occurs only on the earth, a closed and limited space-time region. To be sure, some of these generalizations are derivable from physico-chemical laws whose application is as wide as possible; but might there not be biological laws not reducible in this way to generalizations of wide application?

As we shall soon see, a different interpretation of 'width', one which takes into account the fact that such basic biological laws, in spite of the narrow spatiotemporal range of their confirming instances, would account for a set of facts no other theory is capable of providing, can deal with this sort of case. But Mackie notes here that, however this issue is resolved, a distinction between such basic laws and mere 'cosmic accidents' would have to be preserved. The type of example of the latter he considers is an occurrence unique in the history of the universe. He selects this type because it illustrates that a generalization can be accidentally true even if it is made true by the global fact that the predicate in the generalization applies nowhere else in the universe. 'Not being made true only by what is locally the case is therefore neither necessary nor sufficient for a contingent universal's having what we intuitively recognize as the status of a law'.[21]

Since we do not adopt the criterion of laws Mackie here criticizes, our concern is not that expressed in the above quotation, but simply that of the manner of making this distinction. Mackie's generalization of the type 'Nothing of exactly such and such a sort ever occurs anywhere (or anywhere other than spacetime region r)', as an example of a possible cosmic accident, is similar to 'All metals are copper or gold or . . . ' in the crucial respect that confirming instances do not increase the probability that unexamined instances will similarly confirm the generalizations, i.e., that the generalizations are not projectible. Only exhaustive enumeration is a sound basis for accepting these generalizations – the discovery of a disconfirming instance is not ruled out by their repeated confirmation.

Yet even if the notion of projectibility were clear, it would not distinguish laws from non-laws, as we earlier noted. Non-laws, such as 'All the men in this room are taller than 7 feet' are confirmed by their instances, at least after several confirming and no contrary instances. If nonprojectibility is the mark of the accidental, 'accidental' is not the contradictory of 'lawful'. Some generalizations are projectible in virtue of the fact that the most plausible explanation of the confirmation of several instances is one suggesting that the relationship of properties specified in the generalization is not coincidental. If the generalization is a law, the relationship is not coincidental, but not conversely. Laws may enter into the full explanation of the fact that all those men are over 7 feet tall; but we would not want to count 'All the men in this room are taller than 7 feet' as even a mixed or derived law.

A response for dealing with enumerative generalizations, coherent with the regularity approach, is based upon their systemic isolability. We are considering two theories, T_1 and T_2.

T_1: (A_1) All metals conduct electricity

(A$_3$) All copper (M$_1$) is metallic (Copper is a metal)

$\vdots$

(A$_{43}$) All silver (M$_{41}$) is metallic

T$_2$: (A$_2$) All metals are copper (M$_1$) or . . . or silver (M$_{41}$)

(A$_{13}$) All copper (M$_1$) conducts electricity

$\vdots$

(A$_{53}$) All silver (M$_{41}$) conducts electricity

(A$_1$) is a theorem of T$_2$, whereas (A$_{13}$) to (A$_{53}$) are theorems of T$_1$. In fact, since (A$_2$) is clearly to be read as '$(x)(x$ is metallic iff x is M$_1$ or . . . or M$_{41}$)', T$_1$ follows from T$_2$, although, since T$_1$ does not contain (A$_2$) as a theorem, the converse is not true. This fact would eliminate T$_1$ on the S-requirement *if* T$_2$ were satisfactory. But T$_2$ fails to satisfy the AE-requirement. Although (A$_1$) is derivable only if all of the axioms of T$_2$ are retained, AE imposes the stronger requirement that T$_2$ account for a fact not capable of being accounted for if the theory is broken up. Since T$_2$ fails here, we need only consider (A$_2$) alone as a theory to see how its isolation counts against it.

We have not even had to take into account a fact which would permit us to recognize another deficiency in T$_2$, namely, the possibility of explaining (A$_1$) in a way superior to that provided by T$_2$, in a way, in fact, which involves the incorporation of T$_1$ into a more comprehensive theory. The genuine explanation of the conductivity of metals in terms of the relation between the wave nature of electrons and the lattice structure of metals permits, along with other principles, the derivation of a great deal of information and, ultimately, facts not at all accounted for by T$_2$. We shall later see how this consideration, the comprehensive character of scientific theories, plays a crucial role in the definition of the distinction between laws and accidental generalizations.

Yet the regularity theorist must still indicate why (A$_2$) *alone* is but a cosmic accident. It does permit numerous derivations, e.g., that a substance is gold, from the information that it is a metal, but not one of the forty specific metals, or that a handkerchief is not metallic from the fact that it is neither M$_1$ nor M$_2$ . . . nor M$_{41}$.

CAUSAL CONSIDERATIONS

The fact that A_2 is not a causal generalization might be useful information in this context. But the distinction between laws and accidental generalizations applies to generalizations of coexistence as well as those of succession or causation.

From an epistemic point of view, we can grade generalizations of coexistence from nomological at one end of a scale to purely accidental at the other. Thus, some generalizations, perhaps 'All dogs are carnivores', do not fall clearly into either group. Although it is not an accidental generalization, the claim to have discovered a species of herbivorous canines would be met with surprise, but not with the degree of incredulity with which the discovery of some ordinary, pure copper which failed to conduct electricity would be met.

A regularity theorist would explain these differential responses in terms of the extent of reverberation through our knowledge resulting from the surrender of the generalization required by the new information. Cosmic accidents are so called because counter-instances would have minimal impact on our theories, whereas the rejection of a proposition treated hitherto as a law would seriously upset our doctrines. This does not mean that a law cannot be relatively isolated from the rest of our knowledge. For we can be upset about surrendering such a generalization if we have no better candidate to account for the facts formerly accounted for by that generalization. Thus, we accord a generalization the status of a law basically because it belongs to a theory (including the extreme case where the law is more or less the sole axiom) which accounts for a set of facts not all of which are accounted for by any other bona fide theory. This condition, shortly to be characterized more precisely as a comprehensiveness requirement, explains why disconfirmation of generalizations believed to be laws is disturbing.

The surrender of A_2 is not disturbing for that amounts simply to the discovery of a new metal. The important consideration for our purposes is that A_2 fails to account for facts not accounted for by different theories for the simple reason that the derivation via A_2 of sentences like 'x is copper' from premises which include 'x is metallic' or the derivation of 'x is nonmetallic' from 'x is neither copper nor zinc . . . nor silver' do not constitute accounts of the appropriate sort. For example, the instantial sentences are not criterially independent of the ones purportedly being accounted for. A_2, in other words, does not provide us with a deterministic account. We must seek elsewhere for the story of the origin of metals and that story does not preclude the existence of metals beyond the ones known to exist. Thus, if the consideration of comprehensiveness fails to effect elimination, we may appeal to these causal matters.

We are not presupposing here that all noncausal generalizations are accidental because they fail to account for instances. That absurd presupposition is not foisted upon us because laws of coexistence do appear as parts of theories which provide deterministic accounts. We must be reminded, however, that the contribution to the theory must be genuine in a sense, captured by the S- and AE-requirements, A_2's contribution to T_2 is not. It is the sense in which, for example, the noncausal law that nothing exceeds the velocity of light contributes to relativity theory.

Are we not then supposing that all noncausal generalizations 'covering' a set of facts better than any other theory become laws only if they are part of a deterministic theory (and 'cover' the facts by the theory's accounting for them)? There would be no ultimate classificatory law, for example, 'All carnivorous animals are mammals' (CM). My contention is indeed that our recognition that a noncausal generalization's truth is not just a cosmic accident is based in part on its failure to play a role in any causal theory. It may be, for example, that a genetic theory accounts for all instances of the predicate 'is a mammal' and fails to contain CM as a theorem. CM would be eliminated then unless it were part of a different biological theory. Since our belief that it should be retained as a law rests on information regarding *causal* relationships between the properties mentioned in CM and properties such as the possession of canine teeth (and other dental characteristics) and speed, CM might indeed be part of a theory which accounts for facts of the form 'x is a carnivore'. If we believe that a generalization like CM plays no role in any causal theory, we treat it like an accidental generalization.

There is a third possibility in which CM is treated like LM, i.e., a generalization derivable from a theory supplemented by instantial, non-nomic information, e.g., facts about various environmental contingencies such as the relative availability of plants and animals for food. We saw earlier that it matters little for our purposes whether we regard such generalizations as accidental generalizations or derived laws. It is not an accident that animals eat only edible matter in their environment. But if they would easily accommodate a major dietary change necessitated by environmental disruption, e.g., from a carnivorous to an omnivorous diet, we would not think of their carnivorous condition as biologically deep (although it may have evolutionary significance).

A charge of circularity threatens the account. The current effort is directed towards the characterization of the difference between universal laws and other true generalizations without invoking modal concepts. We have identified as a separate issue, pertinent to the definition of determinism, the statement of additional conditions for a law's being causal or, should causal information be provided from without, a law's being used to describe a causal process (CCF) or for ascertaining in a causal process which term is cause and which is effect (CPF). We have not maintained, however, that one of the conditions which makes a generalization a law is its use in some causal theory. But, according to our own assumptions, we would be unable to identify a bona fide causal theory (as opposed to an accidental generalization of succession) unless we could tell that its generalizations were laws and, to do that, we would have to have a handle on the causal-noncausal distinction. How can 'causal' be a qualification of 'nomic' if the latter presupposes 'causal'? Is there a way to break into this circle?

First of all, 'nomic' presupposes 'causal' in a weak sense, according to which laws, which may appear in noncausal theories, simply must appear (essentially) in some causal theory as well. The laws appearing in that causal theory automatically satisfy this proviso (and must, of course, satisfy all other conditions on laws).

An accidental generalization of succession will have to be eliminated from the class of laws by means of other stipulations on laws since there may be no other way of establishing that the generalization is a pseudocausal account. Herein lies the solution to our dilemma. If L_1 is a law only if it appears in some causal theory C_1, and C_1 is a causal theory only if L_1 (or C_1) is a law, there are two possibilities: (1) L_1 is the sole generalization of C_1; (2) L_2 is (at least) another generalization of C_1.

(1) If C_1 satisfies the conditions for being a presumptive causal theory, either by designating CCF and CPF, or by there existing appropriate additions to the formalism, then if L_1 satisfies all (other) conditions on laws (some of which have not yet been stated), then L_1 automatically satisfies the condition that it appear in a bona fide causal theory and is thereby a bona fide law.

(2) Assuming again that C_1 is a presumptive causal theory and that L_1 satisfies all other conditions on laws, the conclusion that L_1 is a law hinges on the assumption that L_2 is a law. But the same tests L_1 had to pass can be applied to L_2. (We assume that L_2 is a candidate for nomic status rather than a stipulation or statement of a boundary condition or some other role-occupier.) Of course, if L_2 is a generalization of succession and passes muster on all other counts, it is a law for the same reason L_1 is a law when it is the sole generalization of a theory. A worry may arise from the specter of a string of accidental generalizations advanced as a bona fide causal theory. But the theory would have to satisfy our requirements and, if we are right, it will not. For example, it will fail the AE-requirement if the 'string' does not do accounting work not done by segments of the string.

I think, then, that the circularity charge can be vitiated along these lines.

COMPREHENSIVENESS REQUIREMENT

There are, of course, accidental generalizations of succession which are 'superior' to ones of coexistence by virtue of their ability to provide a pseudodeterministic account of their instances. The initial conditions would, in these cases, be criterially and logically independent of the fact being accounted for. LM is a case in point since the behavior of the workers in London is accounted for in terms of the distinct and prior episode of the hooter in Manchester hooting.

Elimination of LM ought to be effected by a requirement we have invoked, but without a precise formulation. The comprehensiveness (C) requirement stipulates that a theory achieve comprehensiveness of the following nature. Among the singular sentences accounted for by theory T, many will be substitution instances of a single sentential function. That is, they will be the attribution of a specific property to an object at a time ('Px, t') or the attribution of a specific relation to several objects at a time ('$Rx_1, x_2. \ldots x_n, t$'). If these are collected into sets, the comprehensiveness requirement (C) demands that at least one of these sets be such that no other theory exists which accounts for all its members plus other instances of the function that determines the set.

Thus, if Harry throws ten pieces of wood into the water, the theory whose sole axiom is 'All objects thrown into the water by Harry float' accounts for ten instances of the function 'x floats on water'. This theory is eliminated because 'Wood floats on water' accounts for those ten plus others. There may be no single theory that accounts for all structurally identical sentences. Suppose a certain type of ulcers (U_1) can be caused by a psychological condition (PS) or a physiological condition (Y). '$(x)(PSx \supset U_1x)$' is nonetheless a law so long as its cases are not all accounted for by a more comprehensive theory. If there is a more comprehensive theory, the theory whose sole axiom is '$(x)(PSx \supset U_1x)$' is eliminated; but it does not follow that this axiom is not a law. For it will be a law if it is a theorem of that more comprehensive theory.

LM is easily eliminated since we believe there is a theory linking human behavior to the acceptance of certain conventions, e.g., pre-arranged signals, for the initiation of instances of that behavior which would be far more comprehensive than LM. (Again, it is of little consequence whether LM is 'eliminated' or treated as a mixed law by dint of its derivation from the theory combined with instantial information.) We cannot, to be sure, produce that theory now or even in the foreseeable future; but our belief that LM is not a law rests on our belief that such a theory would be formulated given enough time, effort, etc.

A deficiency in the account now being developed is that it presupposes determinism. Since our definition of an account is really that of a deterministic account, we are unable to make room for accounts of phenomena by statistical theories, thereby permitting counterexamples such as the following. If the world is not deterministic, there is an event type, perhaps the passage of an atom from one energy level to another, which lacks any deterministic account. If, then, an accidental generalization is concocted by finding an irrelevant antecedent event type for every case or specified subset of cases of the passage of an atom from one to another energy level, we will not be able to rule it out by reference to a theory providing a deterministic account of such a phenomenon. Any difficulty we might have finding an appropriate antecedent for the generalization can be surmounted by creating one from a suitable disjunctive predicate formed out of disjuncts describing events which are unique and spatiotemporally proximate to an instance of atomic passage.

There are two ways of dealing with this issue. We may try to define the notion of a statistical theory's accounting for or explaining an individual event and then appeal to quantum theory as the basis of elimination of the above unwanted generalization. The feasibility of such a notion is debatable, however, and an exploration of these issues would take us far afield. An alternative proposal with strong intuitive backing would rule out many of these accidental generalizations on the grounds that they postulate connections which conflict with principles of causal irrelevance implied by theoretical knowledge. Given our theories, in other words, principles of the form 'Property P is causally irrelevant to property Q' are 'implied' or at least suggested and can serve to eliminate some generalizations. This approach confronts several difficulties. Even if we could formulate the idea so that it is not relative to knowledge, the relation between theories and principles of causal irrelevance is unclear. In what sense does a theory imply a principle as opposed to rendering it likely? Would it just be very surprising that P causes Q in light of theory T or does T really render that impossible? Also, a cleverly concocted generalization may designate as cause event types not *so* implausibly selected in relation to the rest of the truth.

Yet where there is a relevant statistical theory, a more powerful case against the causal relevance of some property may be constructed by noting restrictions implicit in the statistical theory itself. It is also worth recalling that these generalizations would suffer from the same isolation which permitted us to eliminate via the C-requirement other accidental generalizations.

Thus, although certain generalizations resist elimination by reference to devices specifically defined herein, the tools for dealing with these have, I believe, been identified for those who are jittery about a definition of the distinction between laws and accidental generalizations which is relative to the assumption of determinism.

Another difficulty pertaining to the C-requirement emerges when we reflect on the possibility of constructing sets of bizarre fact-types and pseudo-theories 'accounting' for those fact-types better than any other theories. If 'D' is an arbitrarily concocted predicate extensionally equivalent with 'gold', and if 'E' is an arbitrarily concocted predicate extensionally equivalent with 'red litmus paper', the C-requirement (or the AE-requirement) may establish the superiority of 'All gold is soluble in aqua regia' to 'All objects which are D are soluble in aqua regia' and the superiority of 'All red litmus paper becomes blue in acid' to 'All objects which are E become blue in acid'. But what if we now demand a theory for the various truthfunctional compounds of the predicates of this generalization, 'is soluble in aqua regia' and 'becomes blue in acid'?

Disjunctions pose no problem for either bona fide theory accounts for sentences of the form 'x is soluble in aqua regia or becomes blue in acid'. (Deterministic accounts have been characterized as closed under entailment.[22]) Conjunctions are a more serious problem because the AE-requirement prevents us from arbitrarily conjoining axioms of distinct theories. The (illicit) result in this context would be useful insofar as it would permit us to rule out bizarre cases in which the conjunction is 'accounted for' by concocted predicates. For example, if we cannot account for the fact that a is falling at the rate of 32 ft. sec/sec and can conduct electricity by reference to the fact that a is a piece of copper near the surface of the earth, and resort instead to a predicate (CS) concocted to be extensionally equivalent to 'is a piece of copper near the surface of the earth', we shall have a generalization (All CS falls at the rate of 32 ft. sec/sec and conducts electricity) certified by the C-requirement as a law.

If we call this generalization G_1, we may note that it is, in a sense, superfluous. On the assumption that the two bona fide laws are not bumped by G_1, an assumption made plausible by the fact that each genuine law is part of a more comprehensive theory accounting for facts far beyond G_1's scope, we may, by looking at the matter serially, find a way to rule out G_1.

Although the AE-requirement prevents us from arbitrarily conjoining theories, we are still free to form the set accounted for by each bona fide theory along with its deductive closure. The latter set, the set of determined facts, includes all facts of the form 'x falls at the rate of 32 ft. sec/sec and conducts electricity' even if G_1 is omitted from the class of theories. Let us accordingly revise the S-requirement to insist that a theory account for some facts in the set of determined facts not accounted for by a distinct theory or by any collection of distinct theories, where the latter is expanded by its deductive closure. In other words, a theory is ruled out if its elimination does not reduce the set of determined facts.

This strategy succeeds on the assumption that the bona fide laws such as the law of falling bodies are certified as such by the C-requirement. But no matter how sweeping we may suppose a genuine theory to be, can we not concoct even more sweeping generalizations by suitable gerrymandering of primitive predicates?

For example, if we have two basic, distinct laws, 'All A is B' and 'All C is D', we can construct a generalization 'All E is B and D', where 'E' is an arbitrarily created predicate extensionally equivalent with 'A and C'. But this pseudo-law fails to have all the 'accounting' power of the two bona fide ones and can, therefore, be eliminated. The pseudo-law cannot account for cases of 'B' (or 'D') which are not cases of 'E', but only of 'A' (or 'C').

Perhaps we should attempt the gerrymandering at the level of the primitive predicates themselves. The C-requirement tells us roughly that a theory must account for one type of fact at least as well as any other theory. In the absence of any constraints on primitive predicates, however, what happens if we choose perverse examples? To use an earlier example, if we now suppose incredibly that human beings are incapable of recognizing 'falls at the rate of 32 ft. sec/sec and can conduct electricity' as a conjunction and demand *a* theory to account for this type of fact, then we will not be able to eliminate 'All copper falling near the surface of the earth falls at the rate of 32 ft. sec/sec and can conduct electricity' in the wildly implausible event that people with such a serious disadvantage could discover this truth (or, for that matter, do science at all). I see nothing problematic for us in this. The C-requirement *is* relative to primitive predicates in that the generalizations a group counts as laws is partly a function of that group's primitive predicates and can change over time as the set of primitive predicates does.

It may be objected that I am here diverging from a purely ontological account of laws. In rebuttal, I would say, first of all, that I am not advancing an epistemic conception of laws as some have. More directly, however, since I treat laws as sentences anyway, the sort of relativity I am here conceding is already implicit in that sentential treatment. If laws are sentences, they are in some language or other. Hence, the laws of L_1 may *not* be expressible in L_2 if L_2 is not as rich a language as L_1. Perhaps regularities are ontological; but laws are sentences, i.e., language-bound entities, which state regularities. It is not surprising, therefore, that the laws of L_1 are a function of the primitive predicates of L_1. There is no comfort for necessitarianism in any of this.

Similar remarks would be made for the somewhat more plausible case of primitive predicates in L_2 we count as disjunctive in our L_1. Since speakers of L_2 cannot distinguish emeralds from sapphires (they call them 'emerires'), or green from blue (they say 'grue'),[23] their law 'All emerires are grue' is not eliminable by their AE-requirement, although we speakers of L_1 can effect the elimination.

We conclude that an explication of laws and, derivatively, deterministic accounts, can be provided in a nonmodal language. The laws in deterministic accounts will be those true generalizations containing only admissible predicates and satisfying the Superfluity Requirement (suitably modified), the Axiom Economy Requirement, and the Comprehensiveness Requirement.

10
Autonomy

FREEDOM AND EFFORT

If we have been successful in removing the underpinnings of the incompatibilist's case by disallowing the necessitarian premise which grounds the conclusion that it is contingently necessary that an agent perform a certain action, we must seek an alternative way of delineating the conditions of moral responsibility. If nomic subsumption of an action does not per se obliterate responsibility, what does?

We have also suggested, in qualified agreement with Frankfurt, that powerlessness per se is not sufficient for exemption from moral responsibility. We noted in chapter 6 that free action is relevant to responsibility in a way that freedom to do otherwise (power) may not be. At that point, we were still worried about the specter of universal necessity. If we are now permitted to cast aside this worry, we might render this notion more precise. What is it to act freely and what is the connection between this and moral responsibility?

Another matter that bears on these questions concerns the role of effort, a notion we have placed at the core of the idea of moral responsibility. In this context, too, we may forge ahead now that the specter of universal necessity is dissolved. We are free to say that an agent is prima facie morally responsible (blameworthy) for A, a heinous action – even under determinism – if and only if he failed to exert maximal effort to refrain from doing A, where he is uncertain the effort would be futile. The 'prima facie' may be dropped after a complete examination of the context reveals relevant facts such as (1) that the failure is not due to a belief that

A is morally preferable to the only other alternatives open to the agent and (2) that it is not unreasonable, considering the circumstances, that the agent be expected to expend the required effort. If, for example, the agent tried quite hard to refrain from A, he would perhaps be exonerated unless (2) obtains.

Under necessitarianism, the agent's failure to be morally responsible for A follows from its being necessary that he not take steps to prevent A, a necessity the incompatibilist would posit under conditions of determination for A. Of course, if the incompatibilist is, as we think, wrong, we may turn to the question: What are the conditions of the ability to try (maximally) to refrain from doing A? This question is crucial to the dispensation of praise and blame for actions agents in fact do not take (maximal) steps to prevent, as an answer is relevant to the determination of the reasonableness of an expectation that the agent would have expended the required effort.

Does this preoccupation with effort render irrelevant the earlier concern with free action if free action is roughly action which results from the agent's uncoerced, healthy, non-addictive, autonomously generated desires? Our critique of Frankfurt rested in fact on the observation that Frankfurt placed too much attention on concepts like desire and character and failed as a consequence to give adequate due to notions such as will, intention, and effort. Where they diverged, we argued, one must attend, if moral responsibility is the issue, with the *direction* (in the sense of 'directing') of behavior rather than its *motivation*.

The importance of character and related concepts may be seen by noting an asymmetry in the account of moral responsibility. 'Prima facie' is needed there only for one direction. If an agent tries as hard as he can not to do A, but does A anyway, he is absolved. Period. The discovery that he was forced against his will to undertake these efforts may, as we saw earlier, affect our estimate of him as a person, but will not incline us *in addition* to count the action he was maximally trying to prevent against him. But if an agent fails to exert maximal effort, not because he is morally misguided, i.e., not because he erroneously believes A is the best action (in the possibly dismal circumstances), we may still doubt that he is morally responsible. Our doubts *now* will not be based on necessitarian premises, but rather on a diverse set of possible worries we must try to characterize.

The worries are of two general types. Some lead us back to effort for their presence constitutes reason to believe the agent lacks the capacity to exert the required effort. Thus, we may be disposed to exonerate an agent if his failure to take steps to prevent himself from acting is due to external coercion, internal compulsion, or addiction. Alternatively, his excuse may be that he is in possession of a character he did not create or does not identify with or is in some appropriate sense 'heteronomous.' (So notions like character appear in this light as relevant again.) Thus the new problem of free will arises – the problem of defining both sets of distinctions within a broadly compatibilist framework. Preliminary work on this problem was carried out in chapter 4, where we characterized several sorts of defective behavior: impotence, compulsion, and addiction.

There are other types of 'unfreedom', e.g., coercion by others. Since this notion has been the subject of much recent discussion, I shall concentrate my attention on the other sort of ground of exculpation involving the appeal to the elusive idea of autonomy. An understanding of this and related notions will put us in a better position to see whether we have a right to judge an individual morally responsible if he permitted himself to perform an action he knew was morally objectionable. For we will be able to judge the merits of the excuse that his failure was not really 'his.'

IDENTIFICATION

In order to focus on the issue of autonomy, we shall designate as free actions which are not deficient in a variety of respects. A free action has the following features:

(1) The agent performs it intentionally, deliberately, and with knowledge of its morally relevant consequences.

(2) The action is not, as specified in chapter 5, that of an addict, a compulsive, or an impotent.

(3) The agent is not being coerced by another to perform it.

(4) The agent does not mind doing it, that is, he possesses neither a desire that he not do it nor a desire that the desire moving him to act be ineffective.

(I make no claim that these conditions are necessary or sufficient for freedom in some 'ordinary' sense of the term. From here on, 'free' has the stipulated meaning it is now being assigned.)

The problem may now be characterized in the following way. An agent, Wilton, performs a free and terrible act. He has no moral reason which would excuse him, that is, there was a morally preferable alternative known to Wilton and recognized by him as morally preferable such that, had Wilton tried as hard as he can to perform the alternative, he would have succeeded. Moreover, even if determinism is true, Wilton could have exercised the required effort and his motivation is not so strong that it is on that basis unreasonable to expect him to expend the required effort.[1]

Let us characterize Wilton in these circumstances as 'prima facie responsible'. Could we yet discover grounds for absolving Wilton of moral responsibility based on an examination of the springs of action, that is, the genesis and/or circumstances of the psychological states explaining the action or Wilton's failure to perform the morally preferable action?

The view of Frankfurt that concern about the genesis of a person's motivational structure is misplaced as long as he has a stable character of some sort is based upon his belief in the all-importance of identification with one's volitional nature. 'To the extent that a person identifies himself with the springs of his actions, he takes responsibility for those actions and acquires moral responsibility for them; moreover, the questions of how the actions and his identifications with their springs are caused is irrelevant to the questions of whether he performs the actions freely or is morally responsible for performing them'.[2]

Since Frankfurt insists that the key question in the determination of moral responsibility concerns the features of the explanation of an action, he concedes the importance of genesis in ascertaining moral responsibility for actions, but shifts his position when he considers moral responsibility for wills. The libertarian may rightly be puzzled. If action A may be charged against Wilton's account because he did it out of a desire to do that sort of thing, why do we not ask why he had that desire in order to determine his moral responsibility for that psychological state?

The agent, on Frankfurt's account, becomes morally responsible for a desire not necessarily by creating it, but simply by identifying with it, regardless of source. This position has a ring of plausibility, I think, because Frankfurt is really invoking a different conception of responsibility on the higher level. He is telling us that, on the level of springs of action, an agent may *take* responsibility for his character. But, on any level, that is different from and compatible with the absence of moral responsibility. One can take responsibility for many things one is not morally responsible for, e.g., the actions of a child or employee, though one then becomes morally responsible for possible failures to discharge the assumed liabilities.

If Frankfurt denies that he intends to shift to this different concept, the libertarian may reiterate his puzzlement. Why does explanation matter on the level of action, but not on the level of springs?

In siding with the libertarian and, thereby, endorsing our intuitions that, at least in *some* cases, identification does not totally nullify the relevance to moral responsibility of the genetic story, I am not endorsing a central tenet of the libertarian that often motivates the acceptance of antilibertarian accounts like Frankfurt's. The tenet in question, call it 'MRE', is: The class of entities an agent is morally responsible for is closed under the relation of explanation. That is, if Wilton is responsible for an act, he is responsible for the desire that explains the act, and whatever explains the desire, and so on. So, under determinism, since this chain will break at some point, we can be responsible for nothing, whereas under libertarianism, we are responsible for those desires – and, therefore, the actions they explain – that are not explained by any prior states.

I reject MRE. If a desire D_1 is induced to arise in me by OD, an omnipotent demon, I am not responsible for it whether I identify with it or not. But unless D_1 is compulsive, I would be responsible for whatever I (*choose to*) do, even if, in fact, I choose to satisfy D_1. To rebut this, a libertarian would have to suppose both that an action that satisfies D_1 is determined (in part by D_1) and that its being so precludes the agent's being morally responsible for it (incompatibilism). We have attempted in this work to refute at least the second of these grand assumptions.

Thus, some resistance to libertarian skepticism regarding the responsibility of an agent for his volitional nature in case certain conditions pertaining to genesis are met is undermined once we reject the implications he draws from his skepticism. We may agree that an agent does not bear (full) responsibility for his nature without necessarily having to deny that he is morally responsible for his actions.

Our position on moral responsibility is also closer to Frankfurt's now insofar as he is primarily concerned with moral responsibility for actions. That is, we do concede that facts concerning the genesis of our wills are inherently limited in their power to affect, by themselves, moral responsibility for actions.

MANIPULATION AND OWNERSHIP

In order to see more clearly the relevance of genetic considerations, we will suppose that OD implants in Wilton the desire he eventually acts upon. Recall, though, that we do not suppose that Wilton performs this action, A, unfreely (in the specified sense).

Of course, OD creates desires in an unusual way and an exploration of this difference looks promising. At one extreme, OD's influence might work entirely through Wilton's rational and appetitive nature. His autonomy is respected insofar as his desiring nature as given is accommodated and the method of influence is restricted to the techniques of rational persuasion.

Although non-rational methods, e.g., coercion and bribery, also appeal to the present desires of Wilton, they do not respect his desire not to be moved in these ways and are, therefore, precluded by our definition of 'free action'. And should Wilton desire to be moved by coercion or bribery, his autonomy is intact so long as the desire is a part of a system of desires independent of OD. (An utterly content slave lacks autonomy if his system of desires is so completely malleable that there is no possible course of action for the master which would fail to please the slave.)[3]

Now manipulation can take two forms. We may either employ non-rational methods to create desires, where a knowledge of the actual desires of the person are taken into account, e.g., we appeal to a person's vanity, ego, or fears, or we create desires without regard to the present desires of the person. We either do not demand his rational assent to the course of behavior we are inducing him to perform or coherence with his desiring nature. In essence, we bypass the self or crucial elements thereof.

We may here be inclined to argue that, since OD is a manipulator, that is, he does not work through Wilton as constituted, then Wilton's moral responsibility is diminished because the act does not really represent him.

I would express suspicion concerning extrusion from self.[4] More importantly, however, we must, first of all, see that manipulation is not anyway the issue, since the process initiated by OD and terminating in the creation of a desire can be imagined to have come about naturally. I am no less morally responsible for a murderous impulse that arises in virtue of mysterious processes that begin with the appearance of the full moon than I am for that same sort of impulse as transmitted by OD.[5] For that matter, nature provides us with desires, e.g., to drink, that do not depend on our rational faculty and, in a sense, do not have to mesh with our other desires. Surely we 'own' the desire to drink as well as the murderous impulse, as initiated by the appearance of the full moon, especially since we have no other agent to whom to assign these desires.

In an attempt to formulate the conditions of moral responsibility or autonomy for our wills or desiring natures, the concept of ownership appears to be unhelpful. We earlier found the notion of identification inadequate, and have just rejected as well the idea of manipulation (but not yet the idea that genesis has *some* role to play here).

AUTONOMY AND MORAL RESPONSIBILITY

Suppose we can isolate facets of character and personality that can be charged to the agent in virtue of past acts and omissions of his that had a causal bearing on genesis. For the libertarian, we have isolated all that can rightfully be attributed to the agent (as well as a great deal – in particular those desires whose ancestry is traceable through a past act to elements outside the self – that the agent is not responsible for).

I do not wish to take issue with the libertarian here partly because his position does not have two unattractive consequences one may erroneously infer from it. We have already pointed out that the rejection of MRE permits us to regard agents sometimes as morally responsible for actions explained by natures the agent is not responsible for. Secondly, we shall come to grips with the problem before us by separating two notions we have hitherto taken as identical, moral responsibility and autonomy, and the libertarian view may then be more plausibly cast in such a way as not to deny *autonomy* even in a deterministic world.

We can see the necessity for this divorce most clearly in the case of a person who finds himself attracted to an activity or vocation, organizes his life in order to pursue it, and proceeds willingly and steadfastly in this direction, never regretting his decision, and continually finding that his pursuit is deeply satisfying.

The only ground we can have for holding this person morally responsible for this trait, if the libertarian is right, would be based upon (tacit) decisions he may have made at various stages to continue this pursuit or not to inhibit its development. Even if he is a Frankfurt-wanton and never considered a course contrary to his desires, it may be reasonable to hold him responsible for failures to question the direction in which his life is going when circumstances suggest that a reappraisal is in order. Under a liberal interpretation, then, the libertarian will always be able to find people morally responsible for their character and personality traits.

But even if we decide that this person is not morally responsible for having this interest, either because we are impressed with the influence of the attractiveness of the pursuit – perhaps he cannot be held responsible for that – or because we agree with the libertarian that those causally relevant reinforcing decisions whose causal ancestry can themselves be traced to heredity and/or environment do not confer moral responsibility upon the agent, we cannot deny that this agent is autonomous. The concept of autonomy involves the idea of self-generation and we cannot deny that occurrences of the impulse to pursue this activity, by a certain stage in his life, are generated from within.

The libertarian may part ways here since he will concede autonomy only on his own metaphysical terms, i.e., only if an efficacious decision to support this activity can be found *and* if it emanates from the agent as an absolute source outside the causal scheme of things.

Although the metaphysics of libertarianism may not be viable, I am not familiar with serious attempts to provide an alternative in the compatibilist literature.

The idea that an agent is autonomous with respect to a certain desire involves the indecently vague idea that the external stimuli which are partly responsible for the appearance of desire-tokens must work through a complex psychological structure, especially the rational or deliberative components together with the interests and desires that are already a part of that structure. Thus, whether it be the moon or a hypnotist that explains my impulse to murder, that impulse arises heteronomously because its source does not filter either through my deliberations or my interests. The daily urge to pursue my philosophical project, on the other hand, is clearly dependent upon various intellectual desires and, perhaps, decisions regarding the best way to satisfy my philosophical interests.

On this account, a paranoid schizophrenic may be quite autonomous when he forms a desire to avoid the man he takes to be a serious threat since that man's behavior is unimportant relative to the role played by the paranoid's complex delusion and associated pattern of cognitive processes. A normal person, however, is not typically autonomous with respect to his appetites. They may be aroused by external stimuli or physical deprivation in a manner independent of the structure of his personality.

In light of this account, we can understand the appeal of Frankfurt's ideas about identification. Insofar as an agent identifies with a second-order desire, he has taken a step toward the integration of this element into his psyche so that, eventually, future token-desires of this type will arise autonomously. A decision to support certain desires can obviously contribute to their subsequent internalization. But this achievement is the result of an integrative process and is not independent of genesis. Consider Charlie, the mischievous chair puller. On the first occasion this impulse arises, he may experience mild regret even if it never recurs. This, I contend, is due to the suspicion that the desire is linked to other facets of his self. Though vague, the idea has a meaningful opposite insofar as personal regret will disappear once Charlie discovers his suspicion is ill-founded. He finds out, let us suppose, that OD has produced this impulse in an utterly capricious manner. Moreover, should OD continue to induce these desires in Charlie in ways that have no other pervasive effects on his personality, Charlie may continue to be disappointed; but the object of his disappointment will not be himself, but rather his fortune. He may legitimately be asked to be absolved from moral responsibility, of course; but *further*, he lacks autonomy, not because he refuses to identify with these desires, but rather because they arise independently of his personality structure.

Have we not, however, depicted an agent as possessing a far greater degree of unity than obtains in fact? If autonomy requires coherence of all our propensities, desires, and attractions, we would lack autonomy in relation to many psychological episodes, including not just passing whims, but recurrent, yet apparently isolated episodes. Why should it be supposed that a structure must exhibit a level of integration in which each desire is linked with every other desire?

If unrelated interests are permitted, it is not a large step to the admissibility of conflicting interests. Disharmony, in other words, can be internal in spite of the hierarchical theorist's view that freedom of will is constituted by a lack of dissonance across levels of desire.[6] If freedom is denied us when we lack the will we want, the explanation may be that two impulses, embedded deep in our personalities, have surfaced in a context that displays their conflicting natures. And I am not talking just of inabilities, due to circumstances, to satisfy two desires that are, in themselves, perfectly acceptable to the agent, but also of those deeper conflicts in which one part of us wants to condemn another, although the latter has, perhaps, the upper hand in terms of control over action. The woman who has suppressed powerful desires in order to devote her energies to the rearing of her children *may* be dishonest if she identifies herself with those suppressed desires to the exclusion of her maternal ones. The satisfaction of her maternal desires may be deeply satisfying and may become 'self-generated,' so that dissonance persists indefinitely as an internal phenomenon. Her attraction to an ideal represented by a woman who satisfies desires she has suppressed incorporates elements of self-deception, so that the resultant identification is not an entirely honest one. Frankfurt's 'either-or' picture of identification fails to take these crucial dimensions into account. Identifications can be thoughtful or rash; honest or inauthentic; firm or wavering.[7]

If freedom is the absence of dissonance across volitional levels, as the hierarchical theorist says, then autonomy is different from freedom because autonomy permits reservations about first-order volitional structures. How arbitrary it can sometimes be to cast out a level for the sake of a forced harmony. And if our earlier conclusion is sound, an agent may be autonomous without moral responsibility for his will. From the point of view of freedom and moral responsibility, therefore, our failure to characterize autonomy carefully may not be a serious deficiency. There is a difference between a man who develops murderous impulses as the result of the appearance of the full moon (where the moon's efficacy is contingent only on physiological features, say the shape of the man's head) and one whose impulses develop out of the paranoid structure of his own personality; but it matters little to his moral responsibility.

Note then that autonomy is *doubly* remote from moral responsibility for actions. An autonomous agent may lack responsibility for his will, where it remains yet an open question as to his responsibility for an action explained by that will.

MENTAL HEALTH

The severing of autonomy from responsibility in the area of will might be restored with an account of autonomy which linked it more intimately with mental health by distinguishing developmental patterns which result in neurotic/psychotic individuals through a distortion of the self in its thrust for personal integration from patterns which produce healthy and integrated persons. In other words, a disturbed individual lacks autonomy just because the self has not been permitted to develop fully or naturally. There is, in the total structure of the schizophrenic, a vestige of a self in conflict with the diseased portions. The assumption of an integrated structure is naive by dint of its failure to locate in the hidden recesses of the mind a normal self, distorted by an abnormal physiological or psychological condition. Relative to this deepest layer, the bizarre impulses of the mentally ill may be regarded as heteronomous. The natural development of an individual would promote what is unfortunately suppressed in the disturbed person.

It is important to see that this account embodies at least two elements. It is not enough to note that a person's desires or attitudes are in conflict. Unless some are judged extrinsic to the person, the most plausible response, as claimed earlier, is to treat each as part of the self – a self in conflict. It is, therefore, crucial to the position under examination that a value judgment be rendered so that the 'sick' elements of personality represent an 'unnatural' distortion of a self which is tacitly rejecting those elements. Through this rejection, heteronomy is established. The healthy 'me' is in there, yearning to break through.

We are certainly inclined in some cases to describe ourselves in this way. Psychotherapy, when successful, occasionally induces people to say that they are once again in touch with their 'true selves.' They regard themselves not just as happy and conflict-free, but autonomous as well.

In making these moves, we are tacitly deemphasizing the core component of the concept of autonomy – independence – in favor of the distinct notion of health or naturalness. The extent to which the idea of independence plays an important role in the explication of the concept of mental health (or natural development) is an open matter. Let us look at the details.

Naturalness would appear to be preferable to independence if the latter is grounded in identification. In addition to our earlier criticisms we may add an observation of Dworkin's, quoted by Thalberg: '"A person's . . . identification with his motivations . . . may have been produced by manipulation, the withholding of relevant information," and in general "influenced by others in such a fashion that we are not to think of it as his own choice."'[8]

To see the difficulties in making sense of natural development, however, we can look at Thalberg's efforts to use this notion to clarify the idea that many women lack autonomy because they have been socially conditioned to accept a submissive status.[9] If we accept the malleability thesis, the dictum that personality traits are not genetically linked to sex, then cultural conditioning is the sole determinant of these traits. Thus, submissiveness is neither more nor less natural than assertiveness.

We can, however, 'say that if females were not singled out for special conditioning, what would "naturally" occur is the kind of socialization that goes on otherwise, the kind that males have hitherto generally monopolized'.[10] Since all forms of social conditioning are conventional, the appropriate use of 'natural' here is as a contrast with 'freakish' or 'chance'.

There is a confusion here between an account of autonomy in terms of naturalness and an explanation of the development of autonomy, conceived as a trait *not* defined in terms of naturalness. Thalberg's original project is the development of an account of autonomy which would provide us with the element in freedom beyond action from desire. It would tell us what makes some desires 'alien.' But he implicitly adopts an account of autonomy as self-directedness or independence and replaces his question with the distinct question: Is autonomy, i.e., self-directedness, natural?

With respect to the latter question, we may note the crucial role played by the charge that women are singled out for a submissive status. Without this assumption, we would have the absurd result that submissiveness is the natural state for men! For that is their contrast state. In fact, in one sense, it is just as true of men as it is of women, that they would have been socialized in the way the members of the other group are had they not been 'singled out' for special treatment. So the absurd result remains unless we distinguish the way one group is singled out from the way the other group is.

I do not challenge Thalberg's charge; but I do not see how the idea can be generalized into an account of naturalness. Surely not all self-conscious, directed efforts to develop traits result in unnatural ones. Where does that leave the profession Thalberg and I are members of – the teaching profession? Thus, Thalberg is guilty of more than just a 'moral bias in favor of individual self-determination';[11] he has permitted this bias to infiltrate what he claims is a purely 'conceptual problem'.[12] 'Unnatural' has not been given a value-free meaning. What is unnatural about submissiveness is that a group has been selected for the development of this trait and *it is an undesirable trait*.

What about Thalberg's account of autonomy in terms of independence? This notion is closely related to the working notion of autonomy we have until recently been using. Insofar as an independent person does not rely more than is necessary on the opinions of others and is relatively uninfluenced by their attitudes and values, he seeks a way of life in which his actions depend as much as possible on his own cognitive and affective states. Each impulse and opinion not obviously self-generated is submitted to careful scrutiny to insure that it receives his own personal stamp of approval, thereby *becoming* self-generated. (The confusion between Thalberg's two projects is evident when he *rejects* the above account as an account of autonomy on the grounds that an independent person might choose slavery. But it is not a criticism of this account that one can make an autonomous decision to reject autonomy – many people do.)

I have no serious objections to this conception of autonomy. But it does not help me. For it remains true that a paranoid schizophrenic is autonomous since input is filtered through a vast hierarchy of beliefs and attitudes before issuing in action. This person is independent, even more so than the rest of us who rely on conventional modes of thinking and response. I want to know why we are inclined to regard this independent individual as lacking in moral responsibility. One purpose of the current discussion has been to seek out an alternative account of autonomy to evade this difficulty. If we return in a circle to that original idea, we are not advancing the discussion. We shall later return to the idea of naturalness to see if it can yet play any useful role. On this point, we shall seek grounds of exoneration other than ones linked to the concept of autonomy.

OTHER ACCOUNTS OF RESPONSIBILITY FOR WILL

Some philosophers have stressed the insensitivity to reason of disturbed individuals; but others have pointed to serious deficiencies in such an explanation.[13] Obstinacy, even obtuseness, does not automatically absolve.[14] Geniuses are *praiseworthy* (when they succeed) for their 'irrational' dedication to a goal. A more plausible attempt along these lines, therefore, would require the agent to be sensitive to reasons the *agent judges* as relevant.

Now it may be, as Shatz has indicated, that sensitivity to reasons is not sufficient for freedom, or, we might add, moral responsibility. A compulsive or addict might be responsive to therapy or life threatening reasons.[15] But it does not follow that sensitivity to reasons is not a necessary condition of (freedom and) moral responsibility. An agent who does not respond to reasons he regards as relevant ought perhaps not to be judged a responsible agent.

First of all, since there are usually reasons for not doing many things we end up doing, we shall have to strengthen the last sentence by changing 'relevant' to 'decisive'. Second, although the stipulation may be plausible if restricted to actual reasons, advocates of this view surely want to extend absolution to those who are not aware of some fact F_1 which they would regard as decisive against an envisaged course of action A, but which would not, anyway, upon discovering F_1, inhibit them from doing A.[16] Even if this account succeeds, it fails to explain the exemption from responsibility of all cases of mental illness. The problem in serious cases of cognitive malfunctioning is the extent of discrepancy between the subjective and the objective. Information processing is so distorted that facts any rational individual would regard as decisive against A are filtered through a mechanism which converts them into support for A. So even if the counterfactual condition embodied in the account is sustained, the individual fails to be responsible. He would not do A if he saw F_1 as decisive against A. The problem is that any rational person should see this; but he does not.

A suggestion that emerges then is that there are at least two sufficient conditions of nonresponsibility: the agent must be sufficiently irrational or, failing that, he must be reason-insensitive.

There is surely something to be said on behalf of the limitation of moral responsibility to agents who satisfy minimal conditions of rationality, as many philosophers have noted.[17] How far that will take us depends, of course, on delicate issues pertaining to the analysis of rationality. Unfortunately the other condition is not helpful as we have already taken it into account under the requirement (on freedom) that an agent not be an addict, a compulsive, an impotent, or under coercion. For, as I have once before noted,[18] a rational person who fails to respond to a consideration he deems decisive against a contemplated course of action is incapable of doing otherwise in one of the ways designated as sufficient for unfreedom.

Another candidate deserving of attention is counterfactual control. Here, again, our concern is not the formulation of a sufficient condition of freedom or moral responsibility, but rather a necessary condition. Is an agent excused because he would have done the action even if he had wanted not to? Our qualified agreement with Frankfurt that a counterfactual intervener does not per se obliterate responsibility does not permit us to answer this question affirmatively.

Feinberg has argued that a crucial factor in the mentally ill person's exculpation from blame is the sufferer's ignorance, specifically of motivational factors.[19] Now our conception of freedom requires that the agent act intentionally, with knowledge of relevant moral consequences, but does not insist upon knowledge of motivational factors. One reason for this exclusion is that we are often ignorant of motivation, except for the most obvious and immediately relevant factors, e.g., the attractiveness of the object of desire. Yet we certainly do not exonerate a pickpocket because he can provide only the most shallow etiology of his behavior. Clearly, Feinberg is alluding to a special sort of ignorance suffered by the mentally ill person, but owes us a more careful account of its special character than he provides. It may, for example, be just as difficult for the healthy pickpocket to learn the causes of his proclivities as it is for the neurotic/psychotic. A different and possibly crucial factor is the dependence of the appeal of the action on etiological ignorance only in the case of the disturbed person. The defense of this contention depends upon the elaboration of a distinction between types of knowledge. For it will not be regarded as a difficulty for this suggestion that, say, a neurotic continues to find satisfaction in self-destructive displays of overly demanding behavior, upon learning of the etiology of his condition. The crucial consideration is that his knowledge is only 'intellectual.' He must 'really accept' or 'see' the truth of the information he now assents to in a purely intellectual way in order for his neurotic behavior to begin to lose its appeal.

The key difficulty here is that a noncircular criterion of 'deep knowledge' must be provided, one that does not depend upon behavior change. If this difficulty is surmounted, one wonders how plausible the doctrine would be. The development of therapies alternative to traditional analysis, e.g., behavior modification, arose in part out of the recognition that a gap between revelatory experiences of a presumably cathartic nature and significant behavioral changes persisted in patients who had been psychoanalyzed. Thus even if it can be shown that the link between ignorance and appeal ought to be viewed as responsibility absolving, it may either be difficult (1) to define or (2) if defined, to demonstrate its genuine applicability to many disturbed persons.

To summarize. As yet we have been unable to discover a condition beyond a vague requirement of rationality which permits a prima facie responsible agent to be excused from genuine moral responsibility.

Although a paranoid may be characterized as autonomous for reasons adumbrated above, the feeling that he is not fully responsible may be based, not so much on his irrationality, but rather on the extraordinary rigidity of his personality. Although we do associate maturity and mental health with flexibility, resilience, openness, and an ability to learn from experience and adjust to changing conditions, the relation between such traits and responsibility is not straightforward. If we are inclined to excuse highly rigid persons, it may again be that we perceive their rigidity as a sign of some sort of incapacity, perhaps of a sort our conception of freedom has already taken into account. This example may also remind us of an elementary, but important, point which has not recently been highlighted. Since we have distinguished responsibility for actions from responsibility for wills, we must distinguish within the class of autonomous agents those we are exonerating for their actions from those we are exonerating for their wills. Some inflexible persons are responsible for failing to rise above their characters when the occasion requires it. Similarly, a prima facie responsible agent who is heteronomous is not on that ground released from liability. It may be perfectly reasonable to insist that the agent desist from acting on the externally induced desire, just as it may be reasonable to expect a person to rise above his limitations whatever the etiology of those limitations. (To be sure, the frequency of occurrence and strength of the desire might constitute mitigating circumstances – it is a pity to be cursed with such bad luck.)

Nonetheless, we are supposed now to be bracketing this consideration in order to see if any disability vis-à-vis the will is relevant, even if, as we have just reiterated, it never constitutes a sufficient excuse when the focus is on action.

EFFORT REVISITED

Clarification may be effected by applying results earlier achieved on the level of action. Effort may be crucial in a similar way on the level of will or character. When we earlier noted that moral responsibility and autonomy diverge for wills, we did not pursue the independently interesting question concerning the conditions of moral responsibility for will. In fact, by focusing on effort, we can see more clearly the bearing of autonomy on moral responsibility.

For example, one fact that is disturbing about heteronomous desires is the loss of control that typically accompanies them. If an OD-like source induces them in me, my efforts to prevent future instances may be inefficacious. Of course, if clever advertising techniques induce them, my efforts to restore control over the development of my tastes and desires may be more successful and I would consequently have less of an excuse if I knowingly permitted myself to be manipulated.

Conversely, autonomous desires can be disturbing, as in the case of the schizophrenic, because efforts to change – if, contrary to usual fact, such are possible – would be inefficacious. Of course, such efforts, whether undertaken by a sick or healthy person, express conflict and, therefore, the absence of total endorsement of the trait singled out for extinction. But we must remember that these considerations play no significant role. Per se, they neither render the trait external to the self nor absolve the agent of moral responsibility for possessing it. Reinforcement, passive acquiescence, bona fide efforts at change – these are the morally decisive factors.

We have thus provided, in passing, the obvious answer to the question: If a paranoid schizophrenic is autonomous, why is he not also morally responsible for his condition? Why, in our terms, is he not morally demoted for his state? The answer must be based on the absence of conditions which would be sufficient for rendering efforts to change successful.

Just as an agent who expends maximal effort to desist from doing A succeeds at least in absolving himself of moral responsibility for A, so a person who in fact has the wherewithal (in spite of his mental condition) to take all steps in his power to change his character guarantees at least that he is free of liability arising from the persistence of the unwanted traits. And, although the conditions of the ability to exercise this effort have never been stated, we can all agree that the lack of said conditions is equally sufficient for complete exoneration, so long as the agent would undertake the effort were the conditions present.

Just as we were earlier able to exempt from responsibility a person who fails to attempt to change only because initiation in this direction would be blocked by a counterfactual intervener (yet assign responsibility to one who would fail to attempt to change because he does not want to), so we are able to exempt our current subject whose impairment is based on his own cognitive malfunctioning or lack of minimal rationality.

But what gives us the right to treat cognitive impairment, an internal condition, like a counterfactual intervener, an external agent, and unlike desire, another internal condition? The possession of minimal cognitive skills, or rationality, is treated as a necessary condition of the assignment of moral responsibility for the familiar reason that a person lacking such skills cannot be a member of the moral community, i.e., engage in moral reasoning, have knowledge of right and wrong, apprehend distinctions necessary to apply moral rules, etc. Animals may have moral rights in that others may be under an obligation to treat them with a certain respect. But unless a being is rational, his behavior cannot be grounds for a revision of the community's perception of his moral worth, i.e., its views of his moral responsibility. How can his moral worth change unless he *knowingly* behaves better (or worse) or tries harder (or less) to *apply moral rules more carefully*? Nonculpable moral ignorance excuses in a way hatred does not because we determine moral worth by predicting what an agent would do were he omniscient, capable, and fully rational, *not* what he would do were he omnibenevolent. This brings us back to the centrality of intention to moral worth, to the all-importance of the *directing* of our behavior under ideal conditions.

Although a person lacking minimal rationality is not a member of the moral community insofar as his failures do not negatively affect his moral worth, a person whose failures are due to a paucity of benevolence does not for this reason alone enjoy the same privileges. For his failings do not ground his expulsion from the moral community, but rather require that he remain within, as one of the inferior members.

These conclusions suffice for our purposes even if there are extreme cases of malevolence, perhaps those resulting from a special psychological condition such as psychopathy or a deep philosophical commitment to relativism or nihilism, which require us to treat such individuals as if they, like those deficient in rationality, are entitled to ostracism rather than castigation.

PSYCHOPATHOLOGY

It is a relatively straightforward matter to apply these results to the schizophrenic or paranoid personality. Although theoretical dispute is rife in this area, and we are consequently enjoined from describing any results as having received widespread acceptance, our limited philosophical motivation may not require uniformity or stability on a scale greater than we actually find.

A recent, fairly prevalent outlook on this issue embodies an information processing model in which a sharp distinction is made between the paranoid and the schizophrenic.[20] Each processes information very differently from one another and from normals. For the schizophrenic, the stimulus will typically be recorded and identified accurately at the very early stages of information processing. The automatic, pre-attentive process will provide the schizophrenic with a percept. His short-term memory may be adequate to permit him to form a discrete representation activated by the external stimuli. The problem arises at the conceptual level, the level at which focal attention and controlled processing occur to achieve a higher level of organization and complexity. The assemblies, or configurations of information units, exhibit low associational strength in the schizophrenic, resulting in inconsistent or poorly developed conceptual schemes. The schizophrenic may actually have an advantage over normals in the special examples of stimulus recognition in which it is important to rely as much as possible on the perceptual qualities of the signal rather than the contextual constraints usually required for specification and disambiguation. But tasks which rely upon association and long-term memory will display the schizophrenic's deficit.

The paranoid's problem is just the opposite. His difficulties arise at the initial encoding because he distorts the icon by his (idiosyncratic) schemata. Without a categorical set, he will be deficient in recognition of figural characteristics. With one, therefore, he can more readily process information in a highly biased way. Moreover, the configural assemblies, unlike the schizophrenic's, are strong and, unlike the normal, few in number, resulting in the typical obsessiveness of his delusion and the rigidity of his personality. This latter trait, rigidity, appears as well in the paranoid's inability to shift assemblies appropriately, e.g., when his set leads to a misinterpretation of the situation. A related deficit occurs when conflicting assemblies are pitted against each other by the presentation of information in a context in which only some of the information is supposed to be incorporated by one of the assemblies.

We thus see distinct cognitive styles, each of which is appropriate for only a narrow range of situations. The normal adapts by integrating the two styles, thereby enabling himself to deal effectively with a much wider range of situations.

Even a detailed elaboration of the above would constitute at most a theoretical description of these psychotic types. Explanation is minimal although constraints on etiology are implicit and specific explanatory hypotheses are suggested by the account.[21] Nonetheless, the picture that emerges combines two notions we have touched upon as central to the deficiency of these groups: naturalness and integration. Both forms of schizophrenia involve deviation from a pattern which develops normally and which would permit the rule-governed integration of percept and concept.[22] Whereas the paranoid resolves this problem by the use of conceptual schemes unmodified by recalcitrant experiential data, the schizophrenic processes data automatically, without benefit of integration with conceptual structures or patterns evolving from earlier experiences.

Magaro hypothesizes that, in childhood, this abnormal development may be the consequence of excessive stimulation, where the excess is a function of the amount of incoming stimulation relative to the (individually variable) threshold level of the child. Thus, 'even if the child had extremely high thresholds and required intensive levels of stimulation to respond, a highly stimulative mother . . . would produce an optimal level of stimulus input'.[23] And, of course, other combinations can be described. The child becomes a paranoid or a schizophrenic depending on the manner of resolution in the face of overstimulation. The budding schizophrenic will be unable to form conceptual connections as the result of the perceptual onslaught, whereas the paranoid will defend his tenuous and precarious concepts against perceptual input.

I mention these details only to render plausible the notion of natural development, not in a general sense, but rather in an operational one. That is, in this context (and possibly similar ones pertaining to other pathologies), certain lines of development can be labelled 'abnormal' (*excessive* stimulation due perhaps to *abnormally* low thresholds), even if a general definition is wanting. Moreover, for those who feel more comfortable about naturalness when it is physiologically grounded, we may point to the 'abnormally' low receptor thresholds that account for some instances of the illness, if the above hypothesis is sound, and to the speculation that both groups have a major difficulty with transcallosal transfer (of information), possibly structurally based, resulting in the use of the hemisphere inappropriate to the task at hand.

The notion of naturalness by itself can bear little weight. We do not have a general notion and, therefore, lack a general explanation in these terms for withholding judgments of moral responsibility. If a neurotic can reject his moral demotion, as he is sometimes entitled to do, on the grounds that his personality has evolved unnaturally, I certainly would not want to try to explain in these terms what his development lacked.

The concept of integration is more promising in spite of earlier observations that an autonomous agent need not exhibit an integrated or even conflict-free personality structure. First of all, we were then thinking of autonomy in terms of independence, concluding that independence is different from integration. Now we are trying to characterize the conditions of moral responsibility in terms of mental health, whether or not we use the term 'autonomous' as a synonym of 'healthy'. Secondly, there is a significant difference between the presence of distinct, even conflicting desires or interests and the serious dysfunction constituted by the inability to integrate perceptual and conceptual processes. The latter deficit is pervasive and fundamental, touching upon the person's cognitive relation to the world and, therefore, upon *all* relations to the world, insofar as cognition is an element in all human activity. A failure to integrate all one's desires is a shortcoming of a far lesser magnitude, even when serious moral conflict is a corollary. One can get along reasonably well – we all do – without a unified moral theory or a decision-making *mechanism* to resolve or eliminate conflicts. One cannot get along well with the cognitive dysfunction of the schizophrenic, a condition, like severe retardation, which renders its victim deficient in minimal rationality, frequently cited here as a key component of moral responsibility.

The link between these thoughts and the hypothesis of the centrality of effort is that the deficiency of the schizophrenic explains his failure to be morally responsible for the development of his personality because it explains why he is unable to control effectively that development. It is clear that he cannot begin to take steps to change or that preliminary efforts, were they possible, cannot be guided rationally to completion.

Without the link to effort and intention, we would be unable to generalize the account to other instances of exemption from moral responsibility. A neurotic impulse which generates a self-destructive behavior pattern may persist for years and become the focal point of one's life. It is otiose to label each onset as heteronomous – the person can no longer count the desire as external unless he actually learns that he is being victimized by an OD-like source. Nor can he avail himself of the built-in excuse of the severely mentally ill – cognitive breakdown. As to integration in general, it is not clear the extent to which his life lacks integration (although as neurotic we suppose some conflict to be present) or the extent to which this is important (since some lack of integration is not serious disintegration).

What makes this person a neurotic is not identical with what absolves him from moral responsibility for his will. Assuming his neurotic impulse is an established part of his personality, the only relevant question concerns his power to change, either now by taking steps to reduce or eliminate future occurrences or in the past by having taken similar actions. Had he failed in the past to initiate a plan of action which might make him healthier, when he was in a position to do so, he may now have to reap what he has sown. He may, in other words, be derivatively responsible for past failures to inhibit the direction in which his life is going. In fact, as earlier noted, such omissions, if they can be counted as tacit identifications, play a causal role in the internalization of these desires and impulses, thereby contributing to their being eventually counted as autonomous.

What emerges is a blend of three outlooks: mine, libertarianism without either incompatibilism or a nonempirical metaphysic of the self (is there anything left?), and Frankfurt's identification without ownership. What we extract in other words is the centrality of reinforcement, the directed activity of endorsing certain directions at the expense of others. Where this is possible, failure to take advantage is a ground of blameworthiness. This is perhaps rarely possible for those judged to be psychotic and often not possible for certain neurotics. We differ from Frankfurt and the libertarians by refusing to embellish this description along metaphysical lines. We do not, as they both do, have a conception of the self which requires either the expulsion of the rejected desire from the self or a transcendental origin for the act of identification or reinforcement. We earlier provided the reasons for our refusal to accept Frankfurt's conception of identification. It should be equally clear that our defense of compatibilism constitutes the basis for our refusal to follow the libertarian out of the causal realm to secure freedom.

PRIMA FACIE AND FULL RESPONSIBILITY

Let us return to Wilton, our prima facie responsible agent, to see if our deliberations have uncovered any reason to withhold a straightforward charge of blameworthiness. We note for the last time that, in light of Wilton's ability to refrain from performing the act he knew to be heinous, any reduction of the moral responsibility for his will or character is at best mitigating in relation to his liability arising from the act and, depending on details, possibly very slightly so.

Yet let us suppose that Wilton has in the past taken decisive steps on many occasions and in a variety of ways to redirect his character along more acceptable lines. He has been ineffective, not only insofar as his objective did not come to pass, but also because he found himself becoming more and more tolerant of his own hostile, antisocial impulses. As these impulses grew stronger, his inclination to resist them grew weaker and his sense that he is embarked on a lifestyle it is imperative not to succumb to became dimmer and dimmer.

We must now identify a problem in our portrayal of Wilton for it appears from our earlier description that he must be an amoralist. In order to embody the hierarchical theorist's idea that freedom is incompatible with dissonance, we had Wilton not minding his motivation. In order not to absolve Wilton of moral responsibility on grounds of moral or factual ignorance, we had him aware that what he is doing is wrong. So Wilton does not mind being immoral, in which case he must be amoral, i.e., unmoved by moral considerations.

But we do not want an amoral Wilton, for there may be problems in thinking of him then as morally responsible. We must, therefore, suppose that he regards his motivation as at least somewhat unsettling. Although he is not, therefore, paradigmatically free for the hierarchical theorist, he is free enough even on that conception if we suppose that moral reasons do not weigh very heavily with him. Not only does he prefer the action he performs to the moral alternative, he also prefers being the sort of person he is in spite of his acknowledgement that moral concerns deserve some weighting.

Do we now have a coherent picture? It may be said that no one who acknowledges the force of moral reasons can fail to render them primary at least to the extent that he cannot ever have reason on balance to do what is wrong.[24] But this objection fails by conflating the ideal with the real. Even if Wilton's acknowledgement of the force moral reasons possess commits him to their supremacy, he just finds that his actual weighting is discrepant. If this objection were sound, only amoral people would act immorally and, unfortunately, that is not the way it is.

The qualification of Wilton's freedom is not troubling in the context. In order to explore potential limits on Wilton's freedom or autonomy arising from etiological matters, we wanted Wilton to be as free as possible in terms of the immediate context of action. We now see that if he is to do something immoral, yet in a wide sense be a moral agent, he cannot throw himself into his action with total abandon. So we imagine him experiencing mild regret at what he is doing. Moreover, if we wish to find grounds of exoneration by supposing past efforts to change, we are tacitly supposing that at least in the past the conflict and, therefore, the unfreedom had been deeper.

Given Wilton's efforts in the past, we may not regard him as responsible for his unfortunate nature, and given that it is now quite hard (but not impossible) to resist that nature, we may *to some extent* mitigate the liability arising from the act. Since we have stipulated that the strength of motivation (combined with other matters such as the degree of heinousness of the act) do not make it unreasonable to expect him to expend the effort required to refrain from the act, the mitigation would perforce be slight.

Conversely, a failure during that period of his psychological history when it was at least to some extent within his power to set things right to make any attempt to do so may be grounds for charges over and above those arising from the act itself. He has made his bed and now must lie in it. But the elaboration of the converse is not our primary concern. The thrust of this chapter is the delineation of conditions under which a charge of blameworthiness may rightly be *dismissed*. No doubt a lot more can be said to clarify the conditions which are *sufficient* for moral responsibility.

If effort or directed activity is the key again, how are these conclusions affected by bizarre hypotheses regarding the origin of such undertakings? Should Wilton's blameworthiness be reduced or eliminated if an OD or a hypnotist caused him to initiate efforts he would not have initiated on his own?

To answer this, we need only apply lessons hopefully learned from earlier chapters. If an agent tries as hard as can reasonably be expected of him to prevent A, he is not morally responsible for A, although the explanation of his undertaking may reveal that, at *some* level, he is not a very nice fellow.[25] We prefer a person whose efforts are autonomous, i.e., generated from within the structure of the personality, to one whose undertakings come about fortuitously by being the object of an OD's capricious act. But where responsibility for A is the issue, we can ask no more of an agent than that he do what he can to prevent A, whether A be an action or personality trait.

While mentioning relevant issues not addressed in this book adequately or at all, we should again place in a position of prominence a statement of the conditions of power or ability.

Although some people are absolved of responsibility because their efforts are undertaken, others, like the schizophrenic, are absolved as the result of an inability even to undertake a relevant effort. To the extent that this issue has been addressed, we engaged in chapter 6 in a fair bit of hand waving. Corresponding to varying degrees of width in the concept of power are wider or narrower intrinsic states, i.e., states which issue in action when the appropriate desire is activated under specified conditions. The more narrowly the state is specified, the larger this set of conditions must be. (The sense in which John McEnroe cannot play tennis today because he is bound and gagged invokes a wider sense of 'can' insofar as the intrinsic state required for this sort of power is not present, although a proper part of it, which suffices for his having the power in a different sense, is.)

Ignoring details, we know that the schizophrenic lacks an appropriate intrinsic state. Were he to want to be different, no effort of any reasonably serious sort would be forthcoming. Of the various ways in which his intrinsic state may be deficient, we earlier emphasized malfunctioning at the cognitive level of information processing. Other pathological conditions may result in immobilization as the result of extreme emotional interference, so that a desire to undertake a course of therapy to eliminate the condition induces a powerful emotional response which inhibits any such rehabilitative efforts.

However these glosses are ultimately replaced by genuine information about the conditions of ability or power, I have argued that the distinction will be preserved in a deterministic context or world. What the schizophrenic lacks may be different from what an addict lacks. But if misery loves company, the discovery that the world is deterministic will not comfort those poor souls. We will not all automatically join them in their impotence.

11

Responsibility and psychological theory

BELIEF AND RESPONSIBILITY

The observation that the conception of ourselves as moral agents is bound up intimately with features of folk psychology is commonplace. We have in this work insisted that an agent is morally responsible for a state of affairs only if he is the sort of being who can generally direct his behavior towards (and away) from states of affairs. Thus, we need a psychological theory that permits effort directed to an end or action guided by an intention. This would certainly not be possible unless human beings have beliefs and behavior is a function of belief.

Thus, those radical versions of eliminative materialism which anticipate a displacement of psychological theory so complete that we must regard the concept of belief – as well, of course, as the other remnants of folk psychology – as being then discarded are committed to the disappearance of the moral evaluations of human beings resting upon those remnants.

The contemplation of this stage may be rendered more palatable by the conviction that the rejection of beliefs as useful theoretical concepts does not automatically require the elimination of belief-talk as outmoded. But can such an extreme divergence between science and commonsense persist indefinitely? Would we not anticipate an eventual erosion of the commonsense idioms now entrenched so deeply as to make it virtually impossible to imagine what it would be like in such a world?

Commonsense idioms coexist comfortably with scientific ones when scientific theories are applied to phenomena individuated by concepts in ordinary language. Davidson drew our attention to the fact that both singular causal judgments and the causal generalizations of commonsense may be underwritten by scientific theories formulated in a different, technical idiom.[1] To explain why grape stains are difficult to remove or why rhubarb leaves are poisonous is not to replace these generalizations in jeopardy.

This argument, however, would appear not to be available in the current context to the optimist, i.e., one who envisions a prevailing spirit of cooperation between science and commonsense. For the commonsense generalizations which survive theoretical explanation link terms embedded in ordinary, pretheoretical language. (Of course, this is a relative matter. Botanical discoveries might cast doubt on the viability of the category 'rhubarb plant'; but it will take a lot more to achieve this end than the discoveries which explain the poisonous character of the leaves of these plants.) Beliefs, on the other hand, are supposed to be the very states which explain behavior, i.e., the states of mind which, given their complex relation to others, intervene between stimulus and response and tell us why that stimulus led to that response. They are, therefore, competitive with alternative theories of behavior in a way the fact that this is a rhubarb leaf does not compete with alternative accounts of poisoning. To be sure, he may have been poisoned for other reasons and it may even be that rhubarb leaves are not (always) poisonous. But we have a well-confirmed empirical generalization linking rhubarb leaves and poisoning in contrast with a theory of behavior in which belief states are invoked as *theoretical* states of the system rather than noncontroversial input or stimulus conditions.

But is this clearly so? The thoughts which naturally induce philosophers to construe belief as an internal theoretical state, linked indirectly to belief-expressions, have a flip side. The more internal beliefs get, the less belief-like they become. Cognitive theories tend, for example, to treat them exclusively in terms of content. What gets processed or stored in the mechanism is information, whether it is treated sententially or in terms of more remote units, such as lists, problem spaces, or bytes. We look kindly on computer simulations of thought when we do not expect simulations of the other aspect of belief, mode. Belief is a different mode from desire, although they may be identical in content, e.g., that I will be alive tomorrow. Belief is one mode, desire another; within each mode, individuation is effected by content. If the simulation of belief is just the simulation of content, and if the states of a computer can represent sentences or propositions, computers can have beliefs. Many mental models concentrate on content, not mode, as if storage in the human mind is a phenomenon like storage in a memory bank. The question is whether or not it, the sentence or whatever, is there, not whether or not it is affirmed (or barely believed or under evaluation or . . . , where a variety of cognitive modes may be given). Some philosophers actually endorse this approach for cognitive psychology. Stalnaker, for example, goes even further, recommending that beliefs be identified with propositions, abstract entities related to, but identical to neither sentences nor neurological states.[2]

Perhaps modal distinctions, then, must be defined on the behavioral level, but in a way which permits us to retain the idea that beliefs are internal states. An internal sentence is a belief when, typically, it explains disposition to *assent* behavior, a desire when it typically explains disposition to *seek* behavior, etc. Of course, each such state can also explain a variety of types of behavior in addition to the type which is mode-determining for that group.

What is a disposition to assent? As Dennett has said, it is not a disposition to utter or say. I may be disposed to say many things I do not believe. He notes, 'sometimes we salt away a sentence because we like the sound of it, or because we will later be rewarded for producing it on demand, or just because it has a sort of staying power in our imagination'.[3] The key question then becomes the difference between saying and asserting (or assenting).

Assent does appear to have a characteristic we are looking for, privileged access, a feature (internal) beliefs lack. For if assent or acceptance is an action which represents some sort of commitment to the truth of the proposition accepted, we know that we have performed it, even if we are victims of self-deception vis-à-vis the internal state. But Dennett has cited a variety of circumstances in which we make a kind of commitment to a proposition, from deep conviction at the one end to the utterance of a sentence we enjoy the sound of and have no reason to disbelieve. In between is a context in which we are forced to put something down on the multiple choice test and choose the one which sounds the least dumb; and a case of muttering a platitude we have never bothered to expunge from the body of utterances we habitually bring forth in spite of the fact that it is inconsistent with other beliefs to which we now firmly adhere; and many others.[4]

Now, if assent just *is* the act of commitment, we divorce it *entirely* from belief for I can commit myself publicly to propositions I clearly disbelieve.

What is missing is a truly phenomenological account of belief, i.e., an acknowledgement that we perform these actions with a variety of degrees of *felt* confidence, not to be confused with the underlying degree of confidence or subjective probability, which is an inferred characteristic of a theoretical belief-state.

We are not required to resolve these controversies here. For the concept of belief that is implied in intentional or effortful action *is* an explanatory one – it construes belief as causally related to behavior. If, therefore, belief is rejected as an explanatory notion, what we will be left with, felt confidence or assent, will be too weak to sustain our current conception of a morally responsible agent. As Dennett notes, the states arising from acts of assent are a poor guide to prediction of behavior unless they coincide with (internal) belief.[5] If I am to be blamed for the way I *guide* my behavior, I am being blamed on the assumption that I am a creature with beliefs.

COGNITIVE PSYCHOLOGY

If cognitive psychology is to retain the intentionalist character of folk psychology, it must explain behavior and capacities by reference to states sufficiently similar to the paradigm intentional states, beliefs and desires. Since desires are individuated by reference to content and the content specifiable by a sentence ('that I acquire a Polo watch', 'that I become a great philosopher'), organisms must enter sentential states, i.e., certain neurological events or states must be identified in terms of or related to sentences, so that reference to those states will constitute a (partial) psychological explanation. We may call the view that there are these 'mental sentences' and that they play a crucial causal or explanatory role 'sententialism'.

Others see mental sentences as but one sort of representational vehicle, bound to the folk psychological starting point of the cognitive psychologist. The development of representational mechanisms not cast in a sentential mode is now commonplace. Characterizations of information or content within these wider frameworks invoke notions like problem spaces, lists, arrays, and (nonpropositional) mental models. They may embody conceptions of information processing based on the reduction of uncertainty or negative entropy. Psychologists need not be confined to representations of a sentential variety and the problems – for example, the difficulty of explaining language acquisition when your explanatory resources always presuppose a linguistic framework[6] – this limitation creates. In fact, there may be representations, e.g., images, which are not linguistic at all.

It is clear to all that cognitive psychology is too young to permit reliable predictions as to the eventual character of the representational structures which will eventually emerge as the dominant ones. Although it may, therefore, be premature to announce the death of sententialism, it is certainly premature to conclude that a far weaker doctrine, what I will call 'weak sententialism' is moribund. Weak sententialism demands only that sentential structures play some significant role in our mental architecture, but does not preclude the inclusion of other representational forms (like images or arrays). The significance of weak sententialism is that it is strong enough to sustain the picture of ourselves as responsible beings. To explain action by a mental machinery which invokes sentences does not preclude the incorporation of the rest of the cognitive psychologist's arsenal. If frames, arrays, lists, semantic nets, and images are important, why not sentences as well?

Philosophers, with their traditionally polemical temper, may fail to have noted the eclectic character of many cognitive psychologists who do not have the same axes to grind. The theories of Johnson-

Laird, Kosslyn, Anderson, Minsky, and Newell and Simon all invoke propositions at *some* level of processing.[7]

But I do not want at all to herald a victory even for weak sentientialism for the issue is so poorly defined. Let us begin with the familiar observation that, if we require psychological theories to be computable, they can be translated into Turing machine notation. Hence, regardless of the concepts used to describe the features of the models postulated by the psychological theory, we can replace these concepts with strings of symbols. Although the resulting form of representation involves discrete symbols, they are not per se sentences. Sentientialists would retort that, just as a computer can instantiate a variety of languages which differ in their level of abstractness, so a human being can truly be regarded as, among other things, an instantiation of a theory which postulates operations on sentences (and perhaps a host of other representational entities). In fact, the sentientialist can note that such considerations can be used on his behalf. Nonsentential representations are naturally described sentientially. When Johnson-Laird represents 'All the A are B' as:

a = b
a = b
  (b)
  (b)

he tells us that 'the use of parentheses is supposed to correspond to some mental tagging of the elements to indicate that the corresponding individuals may, or may not, exist'.[8]

The anti-sentientialist might object that the scientist's *report* of his theory of mental models must perforce be sentential. He reports sentientially – there is no other way – a structure whose elements are nonsentential. Granted. If there is an issue, then, it must be a broadly empirical one as to what human beings are 'actually' like, not how we may represent them in order to achieve successful predictions.

We have now replaced one unclear question by another, and in addition have assumed the burden of the realist-instrumentalist controversy along the way.

The burden is a heavy one. We may suppose, as suggested above, that the sentientialist will be undaunted by the fact that our functional organization at some subpersonal level will not reflect the familiar intentional distinctions we make at the personal level and that, therefore, individual beliefs cannot be identified as explanatory elements of the model. At this level, there is no relatively insolable entity, a particular belief, characterized sententially, invoked to explain some utterance. The structure of thought, which accounts for a variety of phenomena, including acts or recollection and other verbal behavior, will not incorporate units which can be paired with individual intentional units like beliefs. A third-party description of a person as acting from a certain belief will not be grounded in a psychological theory which pairs such descriptions with distinct functional states.[9] The sententialist will respond by arguing for the invocation of sentences and beliefs at a higher level. Yet how can we be sure, if they are invoked, that they are not merely 'idealized fictions' or constructs whose reality is exhausted by their calculative role?

On behalf of a pro-sententialist answer, Dennett notes the emergent character of belief ascriptions. A chess-playing program may be said by a designer to 'believe' it should get its queen out early, playing just like a person who has this belief, although 'nowhere is anything roughly synonymous with "I should get my queen out early" explicitly tokened. The level of analysis to which the designer's remark belongs describes features of the program that are, in an entirely innocent way, emergent properties of the computational processes that have "engineering reality"'.[10]

Now if we bracket Dennett's view that attributions of beliefs and desires are instrumentally justified in terms of their predictive utility, a position that 'shields ascriptions of belief and desire from most sorts of scientific falsification',[11] and extrapolate from the chess example an argument that such attributions, interpreted realistically, are shielded from falsification by dint of their emergent status, we must address Stich's objection to this move:

If we were to run across (what appeared to be) a person whose conversation, chess playing, and other behaviors were controlled by an enormous, preprogrammed branching list of what to do when, I think our intuition would rebel at saying that the 'person' believed that I was about to attack with my queen – or indeed that he believed anything else! Entities with innards like that don't have beliefs.[12]

Although it is true that this 'person' does not have beliefs, and that, therefore, there are constraints on the functional mechanism explaining the behavior that seems belief-inspired, the question at issue is whether *we* might turn out not to have beliefs. Unless we are totally ignorant of our underlying mechanisms, this is different from the question of the possibility of simulating our behavior by a mechanism not informed by beliefs. The point is that we can be reasonably confident that we are significantly dissimilar from Stich's 'person with apparent beliefs.' We can, in other words, disassociate ourselves from the clear cases of behavior-apparently-inspired-by-belief which turn out to be illusory. We know enough about the inner workings of our mind to conclude that a far more sophisticated demonstration, one clearly unavailable now, is required to establish that *we* are devoid of intentional states.

Stich's example does, however, point to the conclusion that, even if we treat belief as an emergent feature, since its postulation on the basis of appropriate behavior is not compatible with any internal account, no a priori considerations preclude the emergence of a successful non-modular theory which will clash with the assumption that there are beliefs. The retention of intentional states at a higher level of description may not be all that comforting if their role is not explanatory. So an a priori case either for weak sententialism or for the underwriting of moral agency by psychology cannot be made.

The issue is further complicated by unclarities pertaining to the concept of a sentence or a language. For we must be in a position to decide that a representational structure is or is not modular. Yet consider Churchland's speculation that 'any declarative sentence to which a speaker would give confident assent is merely a one-dimensional *projection* . . . of a four- or five-dimensional "solid" that is an elemental in his true kinematical state. . . . Being projections of that inner reality, such sentences do carry significant information regarding it and are thus fit to function as elements in a communication system'.[13] But they reflect only 'a narrow part of the reality projected'.[14]

. . . a form of language far more sophisticated than 'natural' language, though decidedly 'alien' in its syntactic and semantic structures, would also be learned and used by our innate systems. Such a novel system of communication . . . would enhance epistemic evaluation . . . since it would reflect the underlying structure of our cognitive activities in greater detail than does natural language.[15]

The latter portion of this quotation indicates, as do other

statements of Churchland, that the envisaged displacement of folk psychology will incorporate a new orientation towards human cognition, one which retains notions like communication, information, and epistemic evaluation. Whether or not 'belief' is associated with too many outmoded (to be) associations and theoretical excrescences to survive this journey, 'cognition' and 'epistemic evaluation' reappear unscathed. Since these states continue to play the causal roles expected of them, since, that is, we act on the basis of our epistemic evaluations, my intuitions tell me that we will also retain the idea that human beings are responsible agents. If this is a mistake, the reason will have to be drawn from more specific features of these theory sketches than have been provided. As it stands, it appears we will retain the idea of a bit of information and the proposition-like attitudes associated therewith.

Bracketing the issue of the reality of a representational structure used by psychologists to explain and predict behavior, and conceding that Churchland might be right, we would then be unable, in the absence of a sufficiently general theory of syntax, to provide a *general* definition of the modular-nonmodular distinction. The upshot of this and preceding reflections is that no compelling reasons to accept or reject weak sententialism have yet emerged.

Some current psychological research, however, leads Stich to believe that a different sort of challenge to belief may be mounted. He cites some tentative results which suggest the falsity of certain empirical presuppositions of belief-guided behavior. Data from the literature on dissonance and self-attribution support the speculation that the cognitive system which mediates nonverbal behavior is isolable from the system whose output is verbal expression and explanation. The processes which underlie behavioral responses are inaccessible to the subject whose description and account of the causally relevant processes and states are error laden, being grounded in (crude, inaccurate) socially shared theories about psychological explanation rather than insight into the actual intermediary between stimulus and response.

Stich's response to the above is as follows. 'It is a fundamental tenet of folk psychology that *the very same* state which underlies the sincere assertion of "*p*" may also lead to a variety of nonverbal behaviors'.[16] But if these findings can be generalized, then states similar to the one underlying our own ordinary utterance of '*p*' do *not* also participate in the production of our nonverbal behavior. . . . If we really do have separate verbal and nonverbal cognitive storage systems, then the functional economy of the mind postulated by folk theory is quite radically mistaken. And under those circumstances I am strongly inclined to think that the right thing to say is that *there are no such things as beliefs*.[17]

Thus, if the behavior controlling system diverges from the verbal explanatory system as described above, we should say that there are no beliefs and everything else that follows from this admission, including, if we are right, that no one ever acts intentionally or tries to do certain things or acts for a purpose or, consequently, is morally responsible for certain states of affairs.

Although the evidence currently available is meagre in relation to the dual systems hypothesis, the case against belief is significantly flimsier than we are led to believe. As far as I can see, the results, which by the way corroborate many earlier experiments, indicate that human beings can be very wrong in explaining their own behavior, are often unaware of the processes which *do* explain their behavior, and produce corrigible and, therefore, occasionally erroneous reports of their own mental states and processes. Each of these results has been advanced numerous times by philosophers and psychologists from various traditions and with different overall programs.[18] The collective weight of these conclusions is a far cry from the demise of the concept of belief. I have two reasons for saying this.

The weaker reason is that the explanation of the behavior of the subjects, including the very dissonance that grounds the radical inferences, is studded with the notion of belief. ' . . . If subjects are led to behave in ways they *find* uncomfortable or unappealing and if they do not have what they *take* to be an adequate reason for enduring the effects of this behavior, then they will come to *view* the behavior or its effects as more attractive (italics mine)'.[19] Thus, we are owed some recasting of all of this; but I have no objection to bootstrapping and am openminded, therefore, about the prospects of rewriting. Stich *suggests* a cheap way of doing it when he describes the hypothesis under consideration as the view 'that verbal and nonverbal behavior are subserved by different belief-like cognitive subsystems'.[20]

But my principal objection is that our *present* concept of belief has long been recognized to be linked only tenuously to behavior, both verbal and nonverbal. Numerous philosophers of mind during the last twenty years or so have pointed to the difficulty of characterizing belief in terms of a dispositional statement whose consequent describes behavior. Everyone knows that the antecedent would have to be indefinitely long or hedged in one way or another, that it might be advisable to shift to probabilistic or tendency judgments, that some antecedent clauses will refer to states, e.g., desire, as complex as belief. My point is that any discrepancy between verbal and nonverbal behavior can just as easily be explained in terms of these considerations, which do not force a rejection or bifurcation of the concept. If I want an apple, I will not do *anything* to get one. Believing that one is in the next room, I may or may not go to get it, depending on a variety of factors. Thus, some behavioral manifestations depend on very different conditions from others and the verbal expression of a belief may consequently depend on a distinctive set of considerations, e.g., perhaps awareness, not required for nonverbal manifestations. Just because the mechanisms underlying verbal production incorporate distinctive paths through the mental machinery does not in itself constitute a case that a univocal concept of belief is not at some node common to the pathway leading to nonverbal response.

The failure of dispositional analyses of belief *as* analyses of the 'ordinary' concept can explain our hesitancy to accept incorrigibility (if I believe that I believe that p, then I believe that p) or transparency (if I believe that p, then I know that I believe that p), the traits *re*rejected by dissonance theorists. Believing is one thing, recognizing or affirming the belief another, and there can be interferences which undermine the usual associations between the two. The acknowledgement of such matters – disputed, to be sure, by many philosophers – has never to my knowledge been advanced as a stipulation concerning a new concept of belief, but rather features, perhaps not evident ones, of our old concept.

I turn now to a challenge to belief regarded by many as the most disturbing of all.

A WORLD WITHOUT BELIEF

The threat to belief which has of late engaged the attention of many philosophers arises precisely in the context of our concern. As McGinn has noted, the concept of belief is strained by its double-duty use.[21] When we communicate our beliefs, we think of them as possessed of truth-conditions, and when we invoke them to explain behavior, as we must at least for the sake of moral agency, we treat them as intrinsic states of the agent, e.g., representations whose semantic properties, as relations to the world beyond the agent, are causally irrelevant to behavior.

These components and the concerns they reflect are distinct and independent – total content supervenes on both taken together. We get different and potentially conflicting standards of individuation – and hence different conceptions of what a belief essentially is – according as we concentrate on one or the other component or content.[22]

Fodor, Putnam, Burge, Stich, Kaplan, and others have advanced considerations on behalf of this conclusion. The basic idea is that ascription of content to a belief-utterance depends to a significant extent on facts independent of either the internal representation or the physical state of the person. Putnam's Twin-Earth cases show that persons can be intrinsically identical, physically and psycho-logically, yet their syntactically identical belief-utterances ('Water is wet') have different meanings.[23] Burge's arthritis case[24] and Stich's endive-chicory case[25] reveal the social dimension of meaning, i.e., the necessity to interpret an utterance in terms of features of the linguistic environment of the speaker which may have had no causal impact on the person. Again, we are provided with illustrations of identical speakers uttering identical sentences, yet meaning different things by those sentences just in virtue of their membership in different communities. (Putnam talks of the division of labor whereby both social agreements and the opinions of experts fix the extensions of terms used by *all* the standard speakers in the community.)

For Fodor, the moral of the above is that semantic features of representations can play no role in a science of behavior and cognitive psychology must, therefore, restrict itself to formal operations.[26] Stich adopts a principle, autonomy, similar to Fodor's methodological solipsism, according to which psychologists are restricted to states and processes which supervene on the internal physical state of the organism. Historical and environmental facts relevant to content ascription must be ignored unless they make a physical difference to the organism.

The project naturally generated by the above reflections is the bifurcation of belief into its two components. 'The explanatory force of the content ascription attaches only to the contribution the words in the content clause make in their capacity as specifiers of internal representations; their referential properties play no explanatory role.'[27] What may we expect is left over when we remove content or semantic representation? A natural answer, Stich's, is purely syntactic objects. Another, McGinn's, is cognitive role. This idea is explained in terms of Field's probabilistic semantics in which a sentence's cognitive role (Field uses 'conceptual role') is determined by the subjective conditional probability-function on that sentence.[28] The intuition is that these assignments are based not on the state of the world, but rather on the speaker's conception of that state, for example, on the description *he* assigns to the names he uses. A third idea, Dennett's, is notional attitude.[29] Rejecting a purely syntactic account such as Stich's, Dennett proposes that we retain semantic interpretation, but fix it by environments which may or may not be *real*. We can characterize the organismic contribution to the determination of propositional attitudes in terms of the individual's 'world,' regardless of the extent of its coincidence with the actual world. Others, like Burge, are skeptical of the strategy dictated by methodological solipsism and prefer to rethink its individualistic orientation.[30] It is preferable, he suggests, to reconstruct our conception of psychological explanation along social lines than to define the bifurcation which would, if it could be produced, permit us to retain the individualistic orientation some see as virtually a conceptual requirement for psychology.

What is the bearing of all this on our concern? The skeptical argument we must address is that beliefs cannot guide behavior (a condition of moral responsibility) because beliefs are essentially individuated by content and are, therefore, not individual psychological or physical states.

It is clear that if Robinson acts the way he does because he believes that water is wet or that aspirin relieves arthritis and is instantaneously and secretly whisked to Twin-Earth, where, not only is water XYZ rather than H_2O, and the speakers there use 'arthritis' to refer not only to what we do by it, but also to aches in the thigh, the change in belief-content necessitated by the switch will not change Robinson's behavior.[31] One unexciting consequence of this is that behavior guided by a belief would persist if the belief were replaced by a different one, so long as the replacement belief is related to the original in the right way. This conclusion does not require us to give up the position that beliefs are necessary conditions of actions. In the real world, Robinson would act differently if he were to surrender the belief that water is wet, because that belief will *not* be replaced by an equivalent one. The fire would not have ensued if the match had not been struck because there was no other combustible material present. And even if a fire would have occurred in some other way, a way preempted by the match striking, we still pick out the match striking as the cause. Similarly, Robinson is watering his plants because he believes that water H_2O is wet, even if God dictates that the only way Robinson can surrender this belief is by replacing it with the belief that water XYZ is wet.

Notice also that we can be confident that the striking of the match caused the fire even if we cannot produce a precise definition of the replacement class, i.e., the class of event-types tokens of whose members invariably lead to fire in the presence of oxygen and 'sufficient' heat. The characterization of the replacement class depends, of course, on one's stand on the best way to extract 'speaker's meaning' from the truth-theoretic component of meaning.

On Stich's syntactic theory of the mind, Robinson is an easy case. Since the switch changes neither the sentence-type he 'believes' nor the behavior it partially explains, no changes in his psychological state have taken place. A theory like Stich's must build its psychological generalizations from local generalizations, ones applying to an individual at a time. For two individuals related in the same way to one syntactic type may behave very differently (because they assign different meanings to the sentence) and one individual related over times to one syntactic type may behave very differently at different times (because he changes his meaning assignments).

It is difficult to see how these local generalizations could be organized into a general theory rather than just collected together. For how do we relate the similar behavior of a Frenchman who assents to 'Il pleut maintenant' and an Englishman who assents to 'It is now raining' or the similar behavior at t_1 and t_2 of that Englishman who assents to 'It is now raining' at t_1 and 'Rain is falling now' at t_2?

Stich's response might well be 'Put up or shut up' and, as we shall see, he is entitled to this response *even if* something like Field's definition of conceptual role is adequate. For Field, the conceptual role of 'Water is wet' will not have changed for Robinson because the sentence prior to the switch is equipollent to the sentence after the switch, i.e., he continues to assign the same (subjective) probability values to the sentence conditionally on other sentences. (How can these epistemic facts change in light of a change – H_2O to XYZ – having no effect on Robinson?)

If equipollence defines the replacement class, we may retain the idea that a belief guides action in that the action would be different were the agent to surrender the belief or any other equipollent to it.

Field's view perhaps enables us to define identity of cognitive role for a speaker at a time and permits us then to understand why Robinson grabs his umbrella whether he assents to 'It is now raining' or 'Rain is now falling'. But Field concedes for familiar Quinian reasons that he cannot extend his definition across speakers and suggests we surrender the idea of interpersonal identity of conceptual role (as well as the idea of intrapersonal synonymy over time). So the problems of comparison apply across speakers (at one time) and times (for one speaker).

That is the reason Stich may object to the charge earlier levelled at him. Even with an account of conceptual role, we have no natural way of relating different linguistic contexts.

As far as our project is concerned, however, we have made some progress insofar as the causal relation between belief and behavior is a little less unintelligible. We might imagine that psychological theory will identify cognitive role as the property of beliefs in virtue of which they have causal efficacy. In other words, relative to other facts such as the *other* beliefs of the agent, belief b_1 causes some behavior in part because it has cognitive role R_1. For example, b_1's being R_1, together with other facts, including the agent's other beliefs, might determine that the probability of b_1 is .9. It may be that predictions of behavior are more reliable when they take into account these probability assignments or the degrees of belief of the agent than when they are restricted to an either-or judgment as to whether the agent believes b_1 or not.

And if Stich insists that the causal role of beliefs is grounded in the formal relations between the syntactic objects to which psychological states are mapped, rather than the cognitive role of those objects, even if they have such roles, why may we not, in a conciliatory spirit, suggest that the causal efficacy of Robinson's current neurological state is based upon its status as a token of the sentence 'the conditional probability-function, restricted to E, is P_{re}', where E is a sentence Robinson also believes? That is, why not combine the accounts by identifying as crucial the very sentence specifying the cognitive role of a 'believed' sentence?

Yet Field himself notes that the determination of a conditional probability-function is not only a highly complex affair, but one which represents an idealization. The verbal and nonverbal data constituting the evidence, no matter how massive, would not permit a unique assignment without a variety of conventions, including assumptions of rationality. Conventions are crucial even if we decide to permit indeterminate probabilities or substitute upper and lower probabilities for completely determinate assignments.

Idealizations, the need for conventions in empirical inquiry, the gap between theory and evidence are all familiar features of scientific investigations into both the natural and the human realm. There is one element, however, which Davidson and Putnam regard as sufficiently special as to preclude the satisfaction of Stich's autonomy principle by beliefs in general or beliefs assigning conditional probability-functions in particular. Beliefs of the latter sort in fact display this feature most dramatically. For, as suggested above, they cannot be ascribed without an extensive range of interpretations of other verbal and nonverbal behaviors, incorporating meaning assignments and belief attributions, which permit even the most irrational person to be counted as a member of the community of believers. The situation is *radically* different from one in which many empirical assumptions are required before an inner state can be postulated. The assumptions Davidson and Putnam have in mind are not a posteriori at all, but rather posits permitting us to construe the entities with which we interact as rational beings.

For Putnam the elaboration of these conventions is not a part of psychology at all.[32] There are many ways of doing it. We were naive to think that scientific psychology could in principle replace the casual, occasionally insightful observations of the humanist, or that the interpretations of humans would become more 'objective' than the interpretation of texts.

Yet whereas Putnam seems to conclude that beliefs, since they are imputed rather than discovered, cannot be thought of as literally in the head, Davidson disagrees.[33] The familiar way of individuating beliefs (context), Davidson notes, is not the only way. The description under which beliefs will be caught by the scientific net is physical. Not wishing to challenge the assumption that beliefs exist and that they cause behavior, Davidson bypasses the observations of Putnam (and Burge) simply by rejecting content individuation. Believing, like other events, can be described in an indefinite number of ways. Thus, for Davidson, our efforts to individuate beliefs in terms of narrow content (e.g., Field's conceptual role) are not required to provide an ontological foothold for them – they exist anyway – nor will they provide a theoretical underpinning for cognitive psychologists in their search for psychological laws covering behavior, for such a project is doomed anyway. Psychological and physical categories are not nomically compatible.

It may well be that, in light of everything else Davidson believes, he should give up beliefs as explanations of behavior and adopt Putnam's position or an explicitly eliminativist strategy like McGinn's:

There is however the question . . . as to whether the genuinely explanatory states are themselves beliefs of some sort, i.e., whether we can ascribe those purely explanatory states by way of a content specification. To claim that the explanatory states are beliefs would be to claim that underlying any nonsolipsistic ascription of belief there is a purely solipsistic belief . . . I doubt that we have any such beliefs and I do not know what their ascription would look like. . . . It is just that we ascribe such nonpropositional causally explanatory states *by* ascribing genuinely propositional attitudes.[34]

Although Davidson might object in principle to one of McGinn's premises, to wit, that beliefs are *essentially* individuated by content as given by truth-conditions (on the general ground that events have no essential properties), perhaps his retention of the assumption that beliefs are causally efficacious is unmotivated. There are brain states which cause behavior because of their physical properties and there are no laws dictating that the possession of physical property P_1 gives rise to the possession of any particular psychological property. Moreover, the whole nature of the enterprise of 'belief-desire psychology' (interpretation theory: Putnam) with its own set of commitments and criteria is radically different from scientific ascription. Why continue to call these physical states 'beliefs'?

But if McGinn and Stich are right, the rejection of belief by itself may not undermine moral agency. For I would think that the important question is the truth of belief-ascriptions and the related possibility of causal implication relations between belief-sentences and behavior-sentences. So perhaps we can even hedge on the earlier claim that moral responsibility requires *beliefs* and behavior guided by beliefs and substitute a weaker argument.

This strategy is plagued, however, by the fear that we are retaining the truth of 'My belief that p is _____' in spite of the fact that the subject term does not refer to a belief only because we are not quite psychologically (?) ready to capitulate completely to a radical eliminativist position. We are not as comfortable here as in an intersubjective context in which referential success is achieved in spite of misdescription. I get to tell you that the man standing in the corner is angry because you know to whom I am referring when I say 'The man drinking the martini is angry' for, although the man in the corner only looks as if he is drinking a martini, it is evident I am referring to him.

If we eschew the above option, we are left with two responses to the concerns of Davidson and Putnam. I said above that these thoughts are grist for Stich's mill. For the syntactic theory is designed explicitly to bypass all these worries about the attribution of beliefs to another. The cognitive states of a subject are characterized in terms appropriate to that subject. If he assents honestly to a sentence, he believes it and we may then seek generalizations linking this state with others, as well as with stimuli and responses. Putnam and Davidson's high faluting worries become irrelevant. If these two are right, a subjective conditional probability-function, embodying in its application the community's constitutive ideals of rationality, fails miserably to pick out an intrinsic characteristic of the believer, one insulated from causally independent factors such as the community of which the believer is a part. (Of course, as an account of cognitive role, offered with a different agenda in mind, Field's may be right on target.)

An alternative to the syntactic theory would then require a rejection of the Davidson-Putnam line, or at least that aspect of it which threatens the idea that a belief is an internal state of the believer. The threat derives from the view that belief-attribution represents in part a feature of the attributor, based on an unavoidable commitment on his part to interpret behavioral data as products of a rational agent (even if he is acting *very* irrationally). Interpretation here is not empirical in character, but represents rather a kind of social Kantianism, one intrinsic to a community a priori committed to treat its members as persons or agents.

Austin once said, 'In philosophy it is *can* in particular that we seem so often to uncover, just when we had thought some problem settled, grinning residually up at us like the frog at the bottom of the beer mug'.[35] When philosophers abandon 'untenable dualisms,' they often just replace one for another. I wonder if Putnam's distinction between functionalist psychology and interpretation theory is one of these. It goes without saying that an ascription of personhood or rationality runs very deep and is presupposed in all our dealings with other members of our comunity. But, to seek an analogy in the physical domain, so is the belief in gravity. Does this mean that there are postulates of physical theory that deserve to be separated out as a priori? (I presume that Putnam is not making a general Kantian point that all experience involves a contribution of the subject because that would surely be an illicit way of denying that beliefs are intrinsic states of the believer – *no* states are intrinsic in that sweeping sense.)

As to Davidson's contrast argument, to wit, that I do not understand an ascription of irrationality unless it is advanced against a background assumption of basic rationality, it does not follow that I must assume that *that* irrational agent is basically rational. I can imagine degrees of irrationality leading to the loss of personhood. We tend to be sympathetic with Davidson's argument because we realize that even the most extreme sorts of mental breakdown leave systems of verbal and nonverbal patterns of rationality reasonably intact. This is to be expected considering that, as a species, we are hard wired for linguistic competence. But it is easy to *imagine* a breakdown so severe that we can place no plausible interpretation on behavior. And if I can imagine this for one 'person,' I can imagine it for my 'community' – a real nightmare.

To be sure, I am imagining this from the perspective of my rationality. And I could not discover this or anything else were I not rational and were there not a host of other conditions present – but one of these is not the rationality of the object of investigation.

But even if we can deny that the being before us is in any way rational, is not the constitutive ideal implicated as soon as we impute some belief?

First of all, we have addressed the point that belief ascriptions are holistic by noting that an adequate account of cognitive role permits holism without surrendering the idea that beliefs are intrinsic. We noted that the cognitive role of a sentence is not sufficient for behavior. Any behavioral prediction depends as well on information concerning a variety of beliefs. More importantly, the beliefs which are implicated, directly or indirectly, by a given belief will be related in appropriate ways by the probability assignments. (In the simplest case, if Jones believes Q and R is a logical consequence of Q, then for any S, $P(Q/S \leq P(R/S))$.)

Second, suppose we have finally found a way to link individual belief states with individual brain states. Suppose then we discover that the very beliefs presupposed or implicated when a belief state is attributed are associated with brain states which are themselves nomically related. So holism is reflected in the physical domain by nomic connections. I think materialists would be rightly more impressed with these results than with the objection that the nomic relation in the physical sphere is weaker than the conceptual relation in the psychological sphere in that the sense in which one belief presupposes another is stronger than the sense in which one state nomically implies another. If these results confirm physicalism, holism is compatible with the material and, therefore, intrinsic character of beliefs.

More significant than holism is what I shall call communality. When we impute a belief, Davidson notes, we presuppose not just a network of beliefs, but that we, the interpreters, share the bulk of these beliefs.[36] We cannot place an adequate interpretation on an utterance unless we share the vast majority of beliefs implicit in the concepts and logical operations we invoke in the interpretive act.[37]

Communality would appear to threaten the individual nature of belief by positing as necessary to a belief the extraindividual fact of sharing. Moreover, equipollence, which earlier permitted us to nullify the changes on belief content wrought by social and physical environmental variations, is of no use here. I should like to argue that this threat can be dismissed in a way which will demystify this most recent effort to erect an impassable gulf between Naturwissenschaft and the Geisteswissenschaften.

It is commonplace to note that the application of a concept which is a part of a scientific theory carries with it a variety of lawlike assumptions. To classify behavior as mammalian is to place this behavior in a context which presupposes that the object is an animal who has evolved in a certain way and shares a variety of structural and behavioral traits with other animals similarly classified. It would take just as enormous a breakdown of familiar, background assumptions for me to withdraw the conclusion that I an observing mammalian behavior when I see what I would normally describe as a chimpanzee suckling her young as it would to withdraw the conclusion that Jones has expressed the belief that it is raining when he utters the words 'It is raining'.

There are differences, to be sure. An imputation of rationality, not mammalhood, brings with it an infinite or at least indefinite number of other states. But this is an issue separate from communality (although the potential infinity of beliefs does create a separate, but, I believe, surmountable, problem for the view that beliefs are intrinsic). The most interesting difference, which is responsible for the inscrutability of communality, is that the interpreter is himself a member of the very class he is imputing to his subject, i.e., a believer. That is precisely the reason he must have so much in common with his subject.

Of course, I am a mammal too. But the imputation of

mammalian status is not ipso facto a mammalian act (although only mammals do it). Imputation of anything *is*, however, ipso facto, an act of belief. So it is a part of the logic of investigation that the study of belief presupposes a social context in which the sharing by scientist and subject of a variety of intentionalistic assumptions must be taken for granted. This no more justifies the cryptic conclusion that beliefs are social[38] than the fact that all mammals share a great deal in common justifies the conclusion that mammalian states are social. Communality derives from the sharing of intrinsic states implicit in membership in the same class.

But if two beings are believers, why must they share the bulk of their *specific* beliefs? This admittedly more dramatic similarity derives from biological and psychological similarities, possession of a common language (or universal grammar), similar individual histories and, possibly, social relationships. The fact that vast similarities are presupposed in belief attribution is not an argument that the similar states are not intrinsic ones.

The rationality posit is, to be sure, rooted in biology *and* practical necessity. We will not be easily convinced that we are in the nightmare earlier described. So the posit is deeply entrenched. But as Putnam says when reconstructing Davidson's argument, there may be *no* level at which we are as rational as we often think we are. This is true and reflects not the bifurcation of two enterprises, functionalist psychology and interpretation theory, but rather the naivete of available theories in functionalist psychology. Many theories make us far more rational than we are. There are reasons for this, e.g., it is methodologically simpler to formulate rational decision theory a priori, then adjust it for the realities. But we must remember to adjust!

With respect to our concerns, these adjustments (e.g., the rejection of simple transitivity of preference) do not necessarily imply the abandonment of belief. This is a bald claim, one I am not making good on here. But it seems to me that one can go a long way in acknowledging the irrationality of people without surrendering the belief in belief.

I will not decide here between the syntactic theory and one based on cognitive role. I hope I have shorn up the latter a bit, thereby strengthening a fundamental tenet of folk psychology that happens also to be a condition of moral agency, namely, that we do the things we do because of the beliefs we have.

CONCLUSION

If cognitive psychology retains enough of the intentional structure of folk psychology to permit the core notion of action directed by an agent in virtue of that agent's beliefs, then the deepest threat of scientific psychology to moral responsibility will have been repelled. Although theories differ significantly in terms of the extent they permit human beings to regard themselves as masters of their destiny, the sweeping denial of any human control can only be based upon the total rejection of that conception. The most radical version of psychoanalytic theory permits its clinical practitioners to view their activity as occasionally destined to achieve desirable results as they work with patients who, for whatever unconscious reasons motivate them, are *trying* to get better. And, to glance at a different part of the field, we may expect a dramatic increase in neurological explanation of facets of human behavior. Yet these very advances, even if they are accompanied by a greater emphasis on genetic components of human development – assuming, of course, we fall short of the eliminative materialist's goal of the total elimination of language other than neurological or physiological, with the resultant abandonment of behavior directed by belief – will not require us to acquiesce in the character and personality we happen to have. The developments in the neurosciences are likely to go hand in hand with technological advances, pharmacological and otherwise, which will provide the basis for deeper changes than we are now able to envisage.

These issues themselves raise enormous moral questions. But if it is obvious that they concern, not the existence of extraordinarily improved methods of human control, but rather the morality of their use, we may at least rest *our* case. Moral responsibility will not vanish – in fact its range, the class of states of affairs agents will be morally responsible for, will increase dramatically – and we will, therefore, have to continue to judge human beings along this dimension. Although we have been unkind to those who would sweep away the notion altogether, we have made it only slightly easier to apply the idea in the untidy, context-bound, and value-laden arena in which such judgments are made and assessed.

Notes

1 *Introduction*

1 R. Nozick, *Philosophical Explanations*, Cambridge, Mass., Belknap, 1981, p.291.
2 F.H. Bradley, 'The Vulgar Notion of Responsibility in Connection with the Theories of Free-Will and Necessity', *Ethical Studies*, Oxford, Clarendon Press, 1927, pp.1–57.
3 For a detailed critique of determinism, see P. Suppes, *Probabilistic Metaphysics*, Oxford, Basil Blackwell, 1984.

2 *The concept of moral responsibility*

1 Joes Feinberg, 'Action and Responsibility', *Doing and Deserving*, Princeton, Princeton University Press,1970, p.136.
2 H.L.A. Hart, 'The Ascription of Responsibility and Rights', *Proceedings of the Aristotelian Society*, vol.49, 1948/49, p.175.
3 Feinberg, op. cit., pp.124–9.
4 D. Hume, *An Enquiry Concerning Human Understanding*, L.A. Selby-Bigge (ed.), Oxford, Clarendon Press, 1902, 2nd ed., pp.98–9.
5 R.B. Brandt, 'Blameworthiness and Obligation', in A.I. Melden (ed.), *Essays in Moral Philosophy*, Seattle, University of Washington Press, 1958, pp.3–39.
6 N.O. Dahl, '"Ought" and Blameworthiness', *Journal of Philosophy*, vol.64, no.13, 1967, pp.418–28.
7 This statement is an oversimplication of Brandt's position. But it is not a distortion and my argument does not depend upon the details of that position.
8 This position is also taken by R.L. Franklin, *Freewill and Determinism*, New York, Humanities Press, 1968, p.206.

9   Feinberg's distinction between having a fault and being at fault is helpful here. See J. Feinberg, 'Sua Culpa', *Doing and Deserving*, Princeton, Princeton University Press, pp.187–221.

10 I shall adopt in this book a view of intentional action defended earlier in 'Purposive Action', *American Philosophical Quarterly*, vol.7, no.4, 1970, pp.311–20.

11 L.A. Blum, *Friendship, Altruism, and Morality*, London, Routledge & Kegan Paul, 1980, p.150.

12 Discussions of moral luck and related issues may be found in R.M. Adams, 'Involuntary Sins', *The Philosophical Review*, vol.94, no.1, 1985, pp.3–31; B. Williams, 'Moral Luck', *Moral Luck*, Cambridge, Cambridge University Press, 1981, pp.20–39; Blum, op. cit.; T. Nagel, 'Moral Luck', *Mortal Questions*, Cambridge, Cambridge University Press, 1979, pp.24–38. Earlier discussions of relevance are C.D. Broad, 'Determinism, Indeterminism, and Libertarianism', *Ethics and the History of Philosophy*, London, Routledge & Kegan Paul, 1952, pp.195–217; R.E. Hobart, 'Free Will as Involving Determination and Inconceivable Without it', *Mind*, vol.43, no.169, 1934, pp.1–27.

13 Blum, op. cit., pp.188–9.

14 Ibid., p.190.

15 Adams, op. cit., p.23.

16 I. Murdoch, 'Vision and Choice in Morality', *Proceedings of the Aristotelian Society*, suppl. vol.30, 1956, pp.32–58.

17 G. Watson, 'Free Agency', in G. Watson (ed.), *Free Will*, Oxford, Oxford University Press, 1982, pp.96–110.

18 H. Frankfurt, 'Freedom of the Will and the Concept of a Person', *Journal of Philosophy*, vol.68, no.1, 1971, pp.5–20.

19 J. Feinberg, 'Problematic Responsibility in Law and Morals', *Doing and Deserving*, op. cit., pp.25–37.

20 See, for example, R.J. Richman, 'Responsibility and the Causation of Actions', *American Philosophical Quarterly*, vol.6, no.3, 1969, pp.186–97.

21 This may presuppose a non-Prichardian conception of action, i.e., one according to which we do more than simply will something to happen.

22 See, for example, B. Williams, 'Persons, Character and Morality', in A. Rorty (ed.), *The Identities of Persons*, Berkeley, University of California, 1976, pp.197–216; M. Stocker, 'The Schizophrenia of Modern Ethical Theories', *Journal of Philosophy*, vol.63, no.14, 1976, pp.453–66; S. Wolf, 'Moral Saints', *Journal of Philosophy*, vol.79, no.8, 1982, pp.419–39; R.W. Adams, 'Saints', *Journal of Philosophy*, vol.81, no.7, 1984, pp.392–401.

23 Ibid.
24 I again presuppose my analysis of purposive action in 'Purposive Action', *American Philosophical Quarterly*, vol.7, no.4, 1970, pp.311–20.
25 Stocker, op. cit., p.463.
26 The expression is taken from D.C. Dennett, *Elbow Room: The Varieties of Free Will Worth Wanting*, Cambridge, Mass., Bradford, 1984.
27 H.L.A. Hart, *Punishment and Responsibility*, New York and Oxford, Oxford University Press, 1968, p.225.
28 Here we again allude to (voluntary) control to placate the incompatibilist, but preclude neither an ultimately deterministic account of control nor even an eventual reduction of its significance.
29 Not really, as we shall learn in chapter 7.
30 A well-known defense, for those events which are acts, is provided by A. Goldman, *A Theory of Human Action*, Englewood Cliffs, Prentice-Hall, 1970, chap. 1.
31 H. Frankfurt, 'Alternate Possibilities and Moral Responsibility', *Journal of Philosophy*, vol.66, no.23, 1969, pp.829–39; J. Fischer, 'Responsibility and Control', *Journal of Philosophy*, vol.79, no.1, 1982, pp.24–40.
32 P. van Inwagen, 'Ability and Responsibility', *Philosophical Review*, vol.87, no.2, pp.201–24.
33 J.L. Mackie, *The Cement of the Universe*, London, Oxford University Press, 1974, p.62.

3 *Causal and moral responsibility*

1 One may, of course, challenge the modal character of some on this list.
2 J. Fischer, 'Responsibility and Control', *Journal of Philosophy*, vol.79, no.1, 1982, pp.39–40.
3 Ibid., p.34.
4 R. Taylor, *Metaphysics*, Englewood Cliffs, Prentice-Hall, 1983, 3rd ed., pp.48–50.
5 Fischer presents an account of compulsion with which a libertarian might be content. Any one of three conditions suffices for compulsion or unfreedom, one of these being causal determination. I am here raising a question about the inclusion of this condition.
6 Fischer, op. cit., p.35.
7 Even then, since both have instituted separate sufficient conditions, Frankfurt would say that both are fully morally responsible for the action.

8   See chapter 5.

9   In 'Three Concepts of Free Action' (*Proceedings of the Aristotelian Society*, suppl. vol.49, 1975, p.118) Frankfurt exonerates the unwilling addict on the grounds that he takes the drug only because he is addicted *rather than* because he likes to. Are we to suppose that his enjoyment or satisfaction is causally irrelevant to his behavior?

10 'Autonomy', in L. Cauman, I. Levi, C. Parsons, R. Schwartz (eds), *How Many Questions? Essays in Honor of Sidney Morgenbesser*, Indianapolis, Hackett, 1983, pp.301–21.

11 This point will later have to be modified.

12 A special case we shall later examine will require us to qualify this judgment.

13 'Autonomy', *How Many Questions? Essays in Honor of Sidney Morgenbesser*, op. cit., pp.302–6.

14 This may not be true of certain unusual personality types.

4 *Intention and moral responsibility*

1   D. Hume, *An Enquiry Concerning Human Understanding*, L.A. Selby-Bigge (ed.), Oxford, Clarendon Press, 1902, 2nd ed., pp.98–9; R.B. Brandt, 'Blameworthiness and Obligation', in A.I. Melden (ed.), *Essays in Moral Philosophy*, Seattle, University of Washington Press, 1958, pp.3–39; N.O. Dahl, '"Ought" and Blameworthiness', *Journal of Philosophy*, vol.64, no.13, 1967, pp.418–28.

2   This point was made in the previous chapter.

3   We might also demand that agents acquire or attempt to acquire relevant knowledge, including knowledge of one's abilities and limitations.

4   Chapter 3, pp.41–2.

5   See discussion of chapter 3, pp.42–4.

6   The conception of intentional action at the basis of this account is developed in my 'Purposive Action', *American Philosophical Quarterly*, vol.7, no.4, 1970, pp.311–20.

5 *Addiction*

1   I say 'virtually' because of the unorthodox views of T. Szasz, *Ceremonial Chemistry*, Garden City, Doubleday, 1974.

2   We shall, later in the chapter, discuss 'phenomenological irresistibility' and compare it with other varieties.

3   For my account of intentional action, see 'Purposive Action', *American Philosophical Quarterly*, vol.7, no.4, 1970, pp.311–20.

4 J. Fischer, 'Responsibility and Control', *The Journal of Philosophy*, vol.79, no.1, 1982, p.27.

5 These three labels are somewhat arbitrary. Clearly, I am adopting them for these specialized uses.

6 Op. cit. In this work, Szasz applies his general views on mental illness to the specific area of addiction, concluding that these labels represent the negative judgments of power structures, e.g., the psychiatric community, on a group of persons who may then be easier to control and whose autonomy will then be easier to destroy.

6 *Power*

1 See the earlier discussion of this matter, pp.49–50.

2 R. Chisholm, 'J.L. Austin's *Philosophical Papers*', *Mind*, vol.68, no.289, 1964, pp.24–5.

3 D. Davidson, 'Actions, Reasons, and Causes', *Journal of Philosophy*, vol.60, no.23, 1963, p.688.

4 Defense will be provided later in the chapter.

5 'Purposive Action', *American Philosophical Quarterly*, vol.7, no.4, 1970, pp.311–20.

6 Davidson has criticized various attempts to link intention with belief, but none affects this claim. He notes, for example, that an intention to do A does not imply a belief one will do A, and that one can do A intentionally without knowing (or even believing with any confidence) that one is doing A. (See 'Intending', *Essays on Actions and Events*, Oxford, Clarendon Press, 1980, pp.91–6.) My claim, distinct from these, is that B cannot be a person's intention in doing A unless he believes A has *some* chance of eventuating in B. If B is important and A is the only possible means to B, a person may do A with B as his intention, even if, due to the unlikelihood of success, he does not believe he will do B.

7 J.-P. Sartre, 'Existentialism and Humanism', P. Mairet (tr.), London, Methuen & Co., 1948, pp.41–2.

8 I would interpret the remarks of A.E. Falk, 'Some Modal Confusions in Compatibilism' (*American Philosophical Quarterly*, vol.18, no.2, 1981, pp.143–4) along these lines.

9 Berofsky, op. cit.

10 I deem this result a partial response to incompatibilist observations as expressed by Falk. 'Now either this impossibility of the agent's willing otherwise implies that the agent lacks the power to do otherwise or it doesn't. The strong intuition which Chisholm's paradox elicits so vividly is that it does. This intuition is the incompatibilist's bedrock' (Falk, op. cit., p.146).

11 See, for example, D. Hume, *An Enquiry Concerning Human Understanding*, L.A. Selby-Bigge (ed.), Oxford, Clarendon Press, 1902, 2nd ed., pp.98–9; R.E. Hobart, 'Free Will as Involving Determination and Inconceivable Without It', *Mind*, vol.43, no.169, 1934, pp.1–27; M. Schlick, 'When Is a Man Responsible?' *Problems of Ethics*, D. Rynin (tr.), New York, Prentice-Hall, 1939, pp.156–8; and P.H. Nowell-Smith, *Ethics*, Harmondsworth, Middlesex, Penguin, 1954, pp.278–85.

12 M.R. Ayres, *The Refutation of Determinism*, London, Methuen & Co., 1968, chap. 7.

13 A.S. Kaufman, 'Moral Responsibility and the Use of "Could Have"', *Philosophical Quarterly*, vol.12, no.47, 1962, pp.120–8.

14 'The Irrelevance of Morality to Freedom', in the Faculty of the Department of Philosophy, Bowling Green State University (eds), *Action and Responsibility*, Bowling Green, Department of Philosophy, Bowling Green State University, 1980, pp.42–5.

7 *Contingent necessity*

1 See, for example, G.H. von Wright, 'The Concept of Entailment', *Logical Studies*, London, Routledge & Kegan Paul, 1957, pp.166–91; A.R. Anderson and N.D. Belnap, Jr., 'The Pure Calculus of Entailment', *Journal of Symbolic Logic*, vol.27, no.1, 1962, pp.19–52; and A.R. Anderson, N.D. Belnap, Jr., with contributions by M. Dunn et al., *Entailment: the Logic of Relevance and Necessity*, Princeton, Princeton University Press, 1975.

2 This is, of course, strictly inaccurate. A deterministic account may entail that there exists an event of a certain type at a certain location and time. If A is the only candidate fulfilling this description, we may wish to say that it is determined. But the issue will be taken up explicitly later in the chapter.

3 In subsequent chapters, principally 9, the notion of a deterministic account will be rendered more precise.

4 See, for example, B. Aune, 'Abilities, Modalities, and Free Will', *Philosophy and Phenomenological Research*, vol.23, no.3, 1963, pp.406–10; and J.T. Saunders, 'The Temptations of "Powerlessness"', *American Philosophical Quarterly*, vol.5, no.2, 1968, pp.100–1.

5 P. van Inwagen, *An Essay on Free Will*, Oxford, Clarendon Press, 1983, pp.68–78, 93–105.

6 M. Slote, 'Selective Necessity and the Free-Will Problem', *Journal of Philosophy*, vol.79, no.1, 1982, pp.5–24.

7 Ibid., p.8.

8 Van Inwagen, op. cit., p.123.

9   Ibid.

10 Aune, op. cit., pp.406–10.

11 T. Guleserian, 'Factual Necessity and the Libertarian', *Philosophy and Phenomenological Research*, vol.32, no.2, 1971, pp.188–204.

12 For a refreshing display of this resistance, see F. Mondadori and A. Morton, 'Modal Realism: The Poisoned Pawn', in M. Loux (ed.), *The Possible and the Actual*, Ithaca, Cornell University Press, 1979, pp.235–52.

13 We reserve for chapter 9 discussion of details concerning deterministic accounts which would not be relevant now.

14 The work of D. Davidson, for example, 'The Individuation of Events', N. Rescher et al. (ed.), *Essays in Honor of Carl G. Hempel*, Dordrecht-Holland, D. Reidel, 1969, pp.216–34, has brought such problems to the attention of philosophers.

15 We would have to extend this to unchanged and, possibly, instantaneous events as well. Deterministic accounts apply to these just as plausibly as to events.

16 R. Taylor, *Metaphysics*, Englewood Cliffs, Prentice-Hall, 1983, 3rd ed., pp.33–4.

17 *Determinism*, Princeton, Princeton University Press, 1971, especially chap. 5.

18 Ibid., especially chap. 5.

19 B. Chellas, *Modal Logic*, Cambridge, Cambridge University Press, 1980, pp.197–8.

8 *Laws as necessary truths*

1   N. Rescher, 'Lawfulness as Mind-Dependent', N. Rescher et al. (eds), *Essays in Honor of Carl G. Hempel*, Dordrecht-Holland, D. Reidel, 1969, p.182.

2   'Laws of Science and Lawlike Statements', P. Edwards (ed.), *Encyclopedia of Philosophy*, New York, Macmillan & Co., 1967, vol.4, pp.411–12.

3   Although we occasionally mention propositions for the sake of convenience, I should like to think that a commitment to their existence can be avoided. But this would have to be demonstrated and I wish to concentrate in this book on other matters.

4   See, for example, G.H. von Wright, 'The Concept of Entailment', *Logical Studies*, London, Routledge & Kegan Paul, 1957, pp.166–91; A.R. Anderson, and N.D. Belnap, Jr., 'The Pure Calculus of Entailment', *Journal of Symbolic Logic*, vol.27, no.1, 1962, pp.19–52; and A.R. Anderson, N.D. Belnap, Jr., with contributions by M. Dunn

et al., *Entailments: the Logic of Relevance and Necessity*, Princeton, Princeton University Press, 1975.

5   A semantics formulated in terms of model sets is, of course, only one possible approach.

6   The point is conceded by the incompatibilist P. van Inwagen, *An Essay on Free Will*, Oxford, Clarendon Press, 1983, p.64.

7   For details of the system of contingent necessity, see chap. 7.

8   Chap. 7, pp. 107–8.

9   R. Clark, 'Concerning the Logic of Predicate Modifiers', *Nous*, vol.4, no.4, 1979, pp.311–35.

10 Ibid., pp.330–5.

11 B. van Fraassen, 'Meaning Relations among Predicates', *Nous*, vol.1, 1967, pp.161–79.

12 A. Morton, 'The Possible in the Actual', *Nous*, vol.7, no.4, 1973, pp.394–407.

13 One of the many complexities the discussion ignores concerns the need to expand the set SL to accommodate sentences whose antecedent or consequent is compounded out of atomic sentences.

14 T.R. Miles and E. Miles (tr.), London, Methuen & Co., 1963. Michotte reports (p.262) that the subjects 'say that they see no *necessity* that object *A* should drive away or carry off object *B*, and that it could quite well stop after reaching *B*'. But he concludes that the question should have been put differently to them. 'The experiments can be described, as we have seen, by saying that the blow dealt by object *A drives away* or *carries off* object *B*; it is *A* which does everything, and *B* which is completely inert. This amounts to saying that *A exercises a constraint* on *B*. The change of position of *B* is certainly not "free"; it is something "forced" or "imposed" by *A*. In this sense, then, there is clearly a "necessity" for the change of position of *B* – a necessity which arises as a result of the blow which it received from *A*'. Since Michotte does not say that this description is provided by the subjects, I think we are entitled to conclude that Michotte is advancing an hypothesis as to the way in which the subjects might have (should have?) described what they saw. If so, it would be difficult to provide a better example of a theoretical construction being imposed upon experience. Notice the sequence of inferences that must be drawn before the idea of necessity is reached. Moreover, we are not even taking the subject's report to show that *he* is really constructing, rather than just reporting. It is Michotte who is placing words in the mouths of his subjects.

15 *Determinism*, Princeton, Princeton University Press, 1971, pp.231–41.

16 Detailed argument for this conclusion may be found in *Determinism*,

op. cit., pp.224–31. This account allows for perceptual knowledge in both ordinary cases of perception and ones that require specialized training, e.g., X-ray reading and wine tasting. In a case of the latter sort, facts about the perceived situation are sufficient for both the belief in question and its truth, given standard conditions of perception and the appropriate training.

17 W. Kneale, *Probability and Induction*, London, Oxford University Press, 1949, pp.223–59; H. Reichenbach, *The Theory of Probability*, Berkeley, Univesity of California Press, 1949, pp.427–82; and H. Feigl, 'De Principiis non Disputandum . . . ?' M. Black (ed.), *Philosophical Analysis*, Ithaca, Cornell University Press, 1950, pp. 119–56.

18 See M. Black, 'The Inductive Support of Inductive Rules', *Problems of Analysis: Philosophical Essays*, Ithaca, Cornell University Press, 1954, pp.191–208.

19 See P.F. Strawson, *Introduction to Logical Theory*, London, Methuen & Co., 1952, pp.248–63.

20 See P. Edwards, 'Bertrand Russell's Doubts About Induction', in A. Flew (ed.), *Logic and Language: First Series*, Oxford, Basil Blackwell, 1952, pp.55–79.

9 *The regularity theory of laws*

1 J. Pollock, *Subjunctive Reasoning*, Dordrecht-Holland, D. Reidel, 1976, p.21.

2 D. Lewis, *Counterfactuals*, Cambridge, Harvard University Press, 1973, pp.71–2.

3 I am grateful to Michael Slote for helpful comments on an earlier draft pertaining to counterfactuals.

4 *Determinism*, Princeton, Princeton University Press, 1971, chap. 6.

5 Van Inwagen offered the following criticism of my earlier account (*Philosophical Review*, vol.82, no.3, 1973, p.403). Suppose that T_1 and T_2 are true, independent, and explanatorily complete theories. T_1 implies that if P were the case, Q would be the case, whereas T_2 implies the conflicting counterfactual that if P were the case, $-Q$ would be the case. (Consistency is oberved by supposing that P happens to be false.) Since one of these counterfactuals is not true, there must be a non-law in either T_1 or T_2. But on my account every generalization of T_1 and T_2 is a law because it is part of a theory relative to which there is no theory more comprehensive.

There are failings in my earlier account. But I tried to impose constraints on theories so that, in my sense of 'theory', the claim that there are two theories with the properties of T_1 and T_2 is a powerful claim. I regard van Inwagen's assumption that there can be a situation of this sort virtually question begging. Since he offers no examples, I regard myself as under the same obligation to address it as would someone who advances the view that all x is y, when presented in its entirety with the response, 'Well, some x might not be y'.

6 For details regarding my views about the sentences which should be included in R, see Berofsky, op. cit., chap. 5.

Kim has advanced an argument to show that the converse of this sentence is not true. (See his review of *Determinism* in *Journal of Philosophy*, vol.70, no.20, 1973, pp.770.) There can be 'discontinuous points' such that every relevant state has a deterministic account; but the state of the world at t_1 might not be determined by its state at t_0 if one of these points lies between t_0 and t_1. One can, of course, strengthen the definition of 'determines' to rule out such points. A more recalcitrant problem concerns the discrepancy between the denumerably infinite number of sentences in the language and the larger number of states (of continuous qualities) assumable by entities. If there is a deterministic account for each R-sentence, determinism might still be false for it seems to be intuitively possible that, in some sense, a state described by no sentence in the language (and the discrepancy guarantees the existence of such a state) might not be determined. First of all, this discrepancy creates a problem concerning quantification and related matters that is far more general than one concerning the formulation of the thesis of determinism. Secondly, I proposed a solution in *Determinism* (pp.149–51). (Van Inwagen cites the problem – p.402 – but fails to mention that I attempted to solve it.) What I proposed briefly is that, since we have the problem of understanding quantification over real numbers anyway, where we want to count some sentences with such quantifiers as true (e.g., laws), we need only remind ourselves that such sentences are required in deterministic accounts. For suppose that, in language L_2, 'S_2' describes state S_2 and there is no deterministic account of 'S_2'. That is, no state description sentence plus theory entails 'S_2'. Now, L_1 is a poorer language than L_2 for, although it contains all the laws and theories L_2 contains, it cannot express state S_2. We now have the worry that an omniscient speaker of L_1 cannot discover the falsity of determinism. Of course, the issue before us is not confirmation or disconfirmation. As in the case of any general theory, the evidence may all point in the wrong direction. The point is that if there is a deterministic account for all R-sentences in L_1, and L_2 contains the same body of laws and theories, determinism will not be 'false in L_2' so long as S_2 is a type of state other types of which are subsumed under those laws and theories. For if T_1 is true, its generalizations, some of whose variables range over the real numbers, 'cover' instances which may not be expressed in L_1, the language of T_1. The discovery that T_2 is false, where T_2 is in L_2 the equivalent of T_1 in L_1, is a discovery that T_1 is false even though 'S_2', the sentence for which T_2 fails, is not expressible in L_1. This does, to be sure, presuppose an arguable interpretation of quantification. And there are other problems concerning the relation between laws and instances which arise in virtue of the denumerably infinite character of the languages.

7   Kim, op. cit., p.771.

8   One example of such an approach is that of R. Sharvy, 'Truth-Functionality and Referential Opacity', *Philosophical Studies*, vol.21, nos.1/2, 1970, pp.5–9.

9   N. Cartwright, 'Do the Laws of Physics State the Facts?' 'For Phenomenological Laws', *How the Laws of Physics Lie*, Oxford, Clarendon Press, 1983, pp.54–73, 100–27.

10   I say this in spite of J.L. Mackie's attempt to combine identity with necessity in *The Cement of the Universe*, Oxford, Clarendon Press, 1974, primarily chap. 8. My objections may be found in my review of the book in *Journal of Philosophy*, vol.74, no.2, 1977, p.103–18.

11   In the third edition of *Metaphysics*, Englewood Cliffs, Prentice-Hall, 1983, chap. 9. R. Taylor appears to have revised his views so that this description no longer is applicable.

12   Berofsky, op. cit., chap. 4.

13   This remark does not itself preclude the possibility that singular causal judgments do not (always) imply that cause determines effect. See G.E.M. Anscombe, 'Causality and Determination', *Causation and Conditionals*, London, Oxford University Press, 1975, pp.63–81.

14   Such is the view of A.C. Ewing, *Idealism*, London, Methuen & Co., 1934, p.172.

15   Berofsky, op. cit., pp.242–50.

16   We shall shortly address the question as to whether this characteristic resides in the generalization or the process itself.

17   See M. Steiner, 'Events and Causality', *Journal of Philosophy*, vol.83, no.5, 1986, pp.358–62.

18   M. Bunge, *Causality*, Cambridge, Harvard University Press, 1959, p.80.

19   The notion of an account is formal, characterized in terms of derivability. It is thus different from an explanation, at least according to those who view explanation as requiring additional, pragmatic conditions.

20   Mackie, op. cit., p.207.

21 Ibid., p.208.

22 Above, p.138.

23 We are using Goodman's terms differently from the way he used them.

10 *Autonomy*

1   Since Wilton is free, he does not mind performing this terrible act he could have prevented. Is he utterly amoral then? This problem will be taken up shortly.

2   H. Frankfurt, 'Three Concepts of Free Action: II', *Proceedings of the Aristotelian Society*, suppl. vol.49, 1975, pp.121–2.

3   One may talk of degrees of independence and, correspondingly, degrees of autonomy. A slave may be prepared to reject his status if he comes to believe that the master cannot or will not secure his happiness. So his desire for happiness remains autonomous. Or he may even be prepared to accept any degree of misery or degradation so long as he believes the master has the right to treat him any way the master wishes. An even more extreme case would be a slave whose subordination is contingent only on his identification of the master as the master, not an imposter.

4   For an elaboration of the case, see my 'Autonomy', in L. Cauman, I. Levi, C. Parsons, R. Schwartz (eds), *How Many Questions? Essays in Honor of Sidney Morgenbesser*, Indianapolis, Hackett, 1983, pp.301–20.

5   Frankfurt would agree. See his 'Coercion and Moral Responsibility', in T. Honderich (ed.), *Essays on Freedom of Action*, London, Routledge & Kegan Paul, 1973, p.83.

6   Of course, Wilton, as free, is harmonious. As we shall soon see, neither autonomy nor moral responsibility requires this.

7   For a more detailed critique, see my 'The Irrelevance of Morality to Freedom,' in the Faculty of the Department of Philosophy, Bowling Green State University (eds), *Action and Responsibility*, Bowling Green, Department of Philosophy, Bowling Green State University, 1980, pp.42–5.

8   I. Thalberg, *Misconceptions of Mind and Freedom*, Lanham, University Press of America, 1983, p.119.

9   Ibid., chap. 5.

10 Ibid., p.124.

11 Ibid.

12 Ibid., p.125.

13 Ibid., pp.112–14; D. Shatz, 'Free Will and the Structure of Motivation', *Midwest Studies in Philosophy*, P.A. French, T.E. Uehling Jr,

H.K. Wettstein (eds), vol.10, Minneapolis, University of Minesota, 1986, pp.451–82.

14 Thalberg, op. cit., p.113.

15 See chapter 5 for the elaboration of such possibilities.

16 Shatz notes, as a complication, that the discovery of F_1 ought not to make the person weak-willed.

17 Since a failure of rationality is typically a general condition affecting all or most behavior, the tendency is to regard this requirement as a condition of a responsible agent rather than just an agent's being responsible for a specific action. But I shall not here pursue this distinction.

18 'Review: Jonathan Glover, *Responsibility*', *Journal of Philosophy*, vol.70, no.11, 1973, p.333.

19 J. Feinberg, 'What Is So Special About Mental Illness?' *Doing and Deserving*, Princeton, Princeton University Press, 1970, pp.288–9.

20 Such a case is made by P.A. Magaro, *Cognition in Schizophrenia and Paranoia: The Integration of Cognitive Processes*, Hillsdale, Lawrence Erlbaum Associates, 1980, placing his results within the theoretical framework of U. Neisser, *Cognitive Psychology*, New York, Appleton-Century-Crofts, 1967, and *Cognition and Reality*, San Francisco, Freeman, 1976.

21 I am aware that this remark invites the request for an explication of the distinction between explanation and description, a request that will remain unsatisfied.

22 Magaro, op. cit., p.212.

23 Ibid., p.234.

24 Michael Slote was helpful in clarifying this point for me.

25 Recall one of the morals drawn in chaps. 3 and 4.

11 *Responsibility and psychological theory*

1 D. Davidson, 'Causal Relations', *Essays on Actions and Events*, Oxford, Clarendon Press, 1980, pp.91–6.

2 R. Stalnaker, 'Propositions', in A. MacKay and D. Merrill (eds), *Issues in the Philosophy of Language*, New Haven, Yale University Press, 1976, pp.79–81.

3 D. Dennett, 'Brain Writing and Mind Reading', *Brainstorms*, Montgomery, Bradford, 1978, p.47.

4 Ibid., p.48.

5 D. Dennett, 'How to Change Your Mind', *Brainstorms*, op. cit., pp.306–7.

6 I am alluding, of course, to the problem presented to recent

philosophers by J. Fodor, *The Language of Thought*, New York, Crowell, 1975.

7   P.N. Johnson-Laird, *Mental Models*, Cambridge, Harvard University Press, 1980; J.R. Anderson, *Cognitive Psychology and Its Implications*, New York, W.H. Freeman, 1985, p.133; M. Minsky, 'A Framework for Representing Knowledge', in J. Haugeland (ed.), *Mind Design*, Montgomery, Bradford, 1981, p.124; A. Newell and H.A. Simon, 'Computer Science as Empirical Inquiry', *Mind Design*, op. cit., p.65.

8   Johnson-Laird, op. cit., pp.163–4.

9   For a discussion of these issues, see S. Stich, *From Folk Psychology to Cognitive Science: The Case Against Belief*, Cambridge, MIT, 1983, pp.237–42.

10 'A Cure for the Common Code?' *Brainstorms*, op. cit., p.107.

11 Stich, op. cit., p.243.

12 Ibid., pp.244–5.

13 P. Churchland, 'Eliminative Materialism and Propositional Attitudes', *Journal of Philosophy*, vol.78, no.2, 1981, p.85.

14 Ibid.

15 Ibid., p.86.

16 Stich, op. cit., p.231.

17 Ibid.

18 In defense of the corrigibility of causal judgments in psychology, I defended these claims, citing psychological literature outside the Freudian framework, in *Determinism*, Princeton, Princeton University Press, 1971, pp.133–4; see also D. Dennett, 'Toward a Cognitive Theory of Consciousness', *Brainstorms*, op. cit., pp.164–73.

19 Stich, op. cit., p.232.

20 Ibid., p.233.

21 C. McGinn, 'The Structure of Content', in A. Woodfield (ed.), *Thought and Object*, Oxford, Clarendon Press, 1982, pp.207–58.

22 Ibid., p.211.

23 H. Putnam, 'The Meaning of "Meaning"', *Mind, Language and Reality: Philosophical Papers*, vol.2, Cambridge, Cambridge University Press, 1975, pp.215–71.

24 T. Burge, 'Individualism and the Mental', *Midwest Studies in Philosophy*, P.A. French, T.E. Uehling Jr, H.K. Wettstein (eds), vol.4, Minneapolis, University of Minnesota, 1979, pp.73–121.

25 Stich, op. cit., pp.63–4.

26 J. Fodor, 'Methodological Solipsism Considered as a Research Strategy in Cognitive Psychology', *The Behavioral and Brain Sciences*, vol.3, no.1, 1980, pp.63–109.

27 McGinn, op. cit., p.215.

28 H. Field, 'Logic, Meaning, and Conceptual Role', *Journal of Philosophy*, vol.74, no.7, 1977, pp.379–409.

29 D. Dennett, 'Beyond Belief', in Woodfield, op. cit., pp.38–52.

30 T. Burge, 'Other Bodies', in Woodfield, op. cit., pp.116–18.

31 This is true on the assumption that descriptions of behavior are not intentional so that they are not infected by the same problems. One must describe Robinson's behavior not as the seeking of relief from arthritis. For a discussion of the nature and importance of this requirement, see Stich, op. cit., pp.165–70, 194–8.

32 H. Putnam, 'Computational Psychology and Interpretation Theory', *Realism and Reason: Philosophical Papers*, vol.3, Cambridge, Harvard University press, 1983, pp.139–54.

33 D. Davidson, 'Mental Events', *Essays on Actions and Events*, Oxford, Clarendon Press, 1980, pp.207–27.

34 McGinn, op. cit.

35 J.L. Austin, 'Ifs and Cans', *Proceedings of the British Academy*, London, Oxford University Press, 1956, pp.130–31.

36 D. Davidson, 'Judging Interpersonal Interests', in J. Elster and A. Hylland (eds), *Foundations of Social Choice Theory*, Cambridge, Cambridge University Press, 1986, pp.195–211.

37 Perhaps it follows that I must also suppose most of your beliefs are true. But talk of truth complicates matters unnecessarily. It certainly does not follow from these considerations that most of your beliefs are true. There might be – or I might believe there is – a Cartesian demon who deceives you and me about most matters. (To be sure, Putnam has raised issues that bear upon such skepticism. See H. Putnam, *Reason, Truth, and History*, New York, Cambridge University Press, 1981, pp.1–21.) Anyway, communality is the relevant trait in this context.

38 Elster and Hylland, op. cit., p.206.

Index

ability, 59, 68, 70, 74–9 87–8,
   93–5, 177–8, 186–7
accidental generalizations, 147–57
accountability, 19–21
actions, 64, 81–2, 100, 103, 164,
   167; and character, 45–6, 51,
   177; in Effort-Thesis, 50, 69; as
   free, 67, 162–3, 165; as free
   according to compatibilists,
   70–1, 73, 75, 78, 80; as
   intentional, 76–7, 188, 191,
   210; as irresistible, 61–2; as
   necessary, 84–5, 99, 126, 160;
   and power, 65–6; versus states
   of affairs, 24–7, 30; as
   unalterable, 86; as unavoidable,
   53–4
Adams, R.M., 10–11, 13–14
addict, 37–40, 48, 56–60, 81, 161,
   163, 174–5, 187; as unwilling,
   38, 40, 47, 49; as willing, 38;
   see also addiction
addiction, 3, 5, 47, 55, 56–60,
   63–4
agent causation, 32, 143–4, 168;
   see also causation
agent worth, 11–19, 21, 23, 45
Anderson, J.R., 193
Anscombe, G.E.M., 129
associationism, 26, 28–30
Aune, B., 105–6
Austin, J.L., 206
autonomy, 5, 160–2; 165–78,
   182–3, 185–6; principle, 200,
   203
axiom economy requirement, 146,
   150, 152, 157–9

belief, 188–210
blameworthiness, 2, 8, 21, 27–8,
   44, 47–50, 53, 63, 160, 184 186
Blum, L.A., 9–11, 13, 19
Bradley, F.H., 1
Brandt, R.B., 8, 46
Burge, T., 199–200, 204

Campbell, C.A., 32–3, 129
Cartwright, N., 141
causal connectedness feature,
   142–5, 153–4
causal necessity, *see* necessity,
   factual
causal priority feature, 142–5,
   153–4
causal responsibility, 22, 31, 37,
   44–5, 50–1, 53
causation, 29, 32, 34, 41, 143–4;
   actual sequence, 35, 53;
   alternate sequence, 35; direction
   of, 117, 137, 142–5; idealist
   theory of, 143 character, 3, 5,
   9–13, 17, 23, 37, 41, 44–6, 48,
   50–2, 161–4, 167, 177–8, 184
Chellas, B., 119
Chisholm, R., 71–3, 129
choice, 86, 89–90, 93–5, 164, 172
Churchland, P., 195–6
Clark, R., 125–6
coercion, 5, 44, 79, 161–6, 175
cognitive role, 200, 203, 206–7,
   209
communality, 208–9
compatibilism, 32, 36, 73, 184; *see
   also* compatibilist

227

Index

holism, 207–8
Hume, D., 8, 18, 46, 90

identification, 38–40, 162–6, 169–72, 183–4
impotence, 3–5, 57, 62–3, 66–7, 71, 79–80, 87, 162–3, 175, 187
incompatibilism, 4, 18, 36–7, 41, 73, 86, 88, 165, 183; *see also* incompatibilist
incompatibilist, 1–14, 17–36, 45, 51–5, 63–70, 75, 78–90, 95, 100–3, 108, 110, 112, 120–31, 160–1
independence, 171–3, 182
indeterminism, 13, 70–1, 81, 86
inevitability, 4, 31, 123–4
instrumentalist, 141
integration, 171, 181–3
intension, 60, 73, 124, 126
intention, 12–13, 161; in action, 76; and agent worth, 16–18, 21, 179; causal account of, 72–3; and desire, 74; and effort, 14, 183; ethic of, 3, 51; and freedom, 175; and responsibility, 9, 22, 35, 45, 188; states, 194–5; theories, 78
inus condition, 29
irresistibility, 36–44, 46, 48, 55–64

Johnson–Laird, P.N., 192–3

Kant, I., 10, 15–7
Kaplan, D., 199
Kaufman, A.S., 82
Kim, J., 138
Kosslyn, S., 193

law (of nature), 84–90, 93–5, 98, 112, 120–59, modal status of, 4, 122–3, 128, 133, 153, 159
Lehrer, K., 74, 79
Lewis, D., 136
libertarians, 7, 26, 33, 39, 99, 106, 140–1, 164–7, 183–4

liberty of indifference, 81

McGinn, C., 199–200, 204–5
Mackie, J.L., 29, 148–9
manipulation, 165–6, 172, 178
mental health, 68, 161, 171–2, 175–7, 182–3
mental model, 190, 192–3
methodological solipsism, 200
Michottee, A., 130
Minsky, M., 193
modal collapse, 106, 113, 115, 117
modal fallacy, 86
modal notion in incompatibilist argument, 33
modal status of initial conditions, 85, 95–6
modal systems, 112, 118–19, 122
modality: irreducibility of, 63, 121, 127, 129; meaning of, 126; number of interpretations of, 100–1
moral luck, 10, 13
moral responsibility: account of, 1–10; as accountability, 20–1; and addiction, 56, 63; and agent worth, 21–3; and autonomy, 162–3, 166–73; and causal responsibility, 31–44; for character or will, 164–5; and compatibilism, 129; and contingent necessity, 99–100, 102–3; and control, 13; derivative, 34–5, 43, 46, 103, 183, 186; and effort, 160–1, 177–8, 183, 186–7; and freedom, 161; and ignorance, 175–6; and inevitability, 123–4; and intention, 45–55; as mental health, 182; for moral agents, 185; and necessity, 82, 122; object of, 24–30, 111; and power, 69–70, 80; and psychological theory, 188, 196–7, 205, 210; as rationality, 175–6, 179; as reason sensitivity, 174; and